The Essence
of the
Garden

The Essence
of the
Garden

HANNAH WILLETTS

F

FRANCES LINCOLN LIMITED
PUBLISHERS

This book is dedicated to the memory of my father, who showed me how to take my first cuttings, and to my mother, who continued to water them.

Frances Lincoln Limited
4 Torriano Mews
Torriano Avenue
London NW5 2RZ
www.franceslincoln.com

The Essence of the Garden
Copyright © Frances Lincoln Limited 2006
Text copyright © Hannah Willetts 2006
Frontispiece copyright © Hannah Willetts

First Frances Lincoln edition: 2006

British Library Cataloguing in Publication data
A catalogue record for this book is available from the British Library.

ISBN 10: 0-7112-2587-7
ISBN 13: 978-0-7112-2587-9

Printed and bound in Singapore
by Kyodo Printing Co. (S'pore) Pte Ltd

2 4 6 8 9 7 5 3 1

CONTENTS

Preface

These snipe flights over the garden are launched from notes made over a period of twenty years. So, although arranged seasonally, they do not follow the progress of a single year, but do amount to a typical year.

Traditional Imperial measurements have been written throughout. Normal usage for me, they have a kinder rhythm within an English sentence, unhampered by the interruption of often ludicrous conversions in parentheses, which irritate more than they inform. This is not intended to be a textbook. The garden does not enjoy average growing conditions, so any measurement given may be viewed through either end of a telescope.

Much of England's wealth, architecture and way of life from the early Middle Ages until the early twentieth century was founded upon wool. The words for measurements developed from this trade: a yard was the length of cloth held between turned-away nose-tip and outstretched opposite finger-tip; a foot was the span between wrist and elbow; an inch was the width of a thumb. Weights, likewise, were based upon the bulk of a fleece, of a sack of wool, of a bolt of woven cloth. Arable agriculture also played its part, not only with land measurements, but also with weights of grains and seeds; even the carat-weight of a jewel is based upon that of a seed. Such a rich heritage of tradition and etymology should not be lost, particularly when much of the practical meaning is still of use, unlike the hundredth part of a poilu's pace.

I would take this opportunity to offer my thanks to my sister for the discreet brushwood of support she has tendered throughout the writing of this book; to the unknown friend who sowed the initial seed; to Ann Arnold for allowing me to use her painting of my garden on the cover; and to the wasp of Twickenham, Alexander Pope, whose words remind me to keep on with the endless weeding.

> Another age shall see the golden ear
> Imbrown the slope, and nod on the parterre,
> Deep harvests bury all his pride had plann'd,
> And laughing Ceres reassume the land.

Hannah Willetts, 2005

WINTER

IT IS THE DEAD OF WINTER. That oxymoronic season of quickstep rhythm, when the quick is merely sluggish, and the slow, one hopes, is just playing possum. In deathly life the garden sits as tight as a broody hen while the weather hurls itself into its habitually destructive frenzy. There is always too much of it at this time of year: too much ice, too much wind, too much rain. But then, as Marion Cran explained, England is just sent to try us.

The last ten days have seen the full gamut of winter weather, most of it happening, holus-bolus, within the same twenty-four hours: mordant gales, deluging rain, hail, a wall of blizzarding snow, bitter black ice, inspissated gloom of Johnsonian dimensions, more sluicing rain, more gales, amber-warning floods, temperatures of 17°F, temperatures of 48°F, brilliant sunshine, a rainbow, and yet more gales and rain: a fairly typical ten-day period in a normal English winter, in fact. Never mind why do we garden; *how* do we garden?

The soil looks like melted milk chocolate, smooth and greasy, after being pounded and poached by all the rain, viewed through a scumbled layer of torn and scattered twigs and branches – mostly alder; they shed sprays of crimson catkin-buds as a balloonist sheds ballast. But it is no great matter for the alders. There are plenty more; the leafless trees are aswirl with smoky-carmine from a distance, so prolific are the budded bunches. I gather armfuls of this brash to pack the nervous stream banks and confuse the grabbing torrent, as the rain, mixed with snow-melt, swells the 4-foot, churning lava flow of mud that was once the 4-inch, chuckling stream. The noise of its brawling is tremendous, as thick branches and large rocks are drubbed about within the force of its rage. Standing close to the bank, I can feel the vibration of its magnitude shuddering through the ground, through my feet. It is deafening, dislocating; it is also very humbling, this brute power of Nature on the rampage.

First World mankind has become entirely divorced from Nature. We take offence when it dares to defy us, and feel slighted that it does not know its place: how dare Nature make our little lives uncomfortable, when it is meant to be there just for our pleasure? If we want to abuse it we will; it has no right to bite the hand that starves it. I hope that Nature survives to have the last laugh, but given our determination in what we see as adversity, I doubt it will.

Here, I aim to share the laughs: sometimes Nature nods, and I appear to have my way; but mostly it just waits (with a nudge, now and then, to guard against complacency), pressing the pause button, knowing it is only a matter of time before it can reclaim that which I have borrowed. I tread softly, meanwhile, as our dreams are the same, Nature's and mine.

But, being winter, the cloth is sombre, the embroidery is sparse. One must look for the detail, which may be small and gently coloured in the low light. The now leafless boundaries spread the garden out over the surrounding fields, and fling the eye wide to the horizon. All the enveloping greens of hill and meadow lend a verdancy to the scene that urban gardens cannot glean, even when densely packed with evergreens, as those will be vertical, enshrouding, hatched with deep shadows. Here, there are few shadows in the flat light of winter. There are some sparkling moments of scintillating sharpness, such as when a thick layer of royal-icing snow cloaks the rich fruitcake of the earth, and the stream gleams deeply like black obsidian; but rarely whole days of such glamour – there is usually too much wind, so a cloud will blow in and rub out the sun. Winter days are mostly mourn and drear.

Best of all are the mornings in early winter when hoarfrost encircles every leaf and stem with crystal-studded orphrey. The rosettes of geum, potentilla and polistychum ferns parade their silvery blanket-stitching of ice; the yellow satin stripes on *Carex oshimensis* 'Evergold' are further banded with white velvet; bruise-purple sage leaves are purfled with pewter. Once, I found early violet flowers encased in ice as though in aspic: clear enough to see their colours, strong enough to hold their stems aloft.

But as winter crawls onwards, and temperatures plummet to Ginnungagap, where the frost giants dwell among the roots of Yggdrasil, ice crystals will form beneath the crusted carapace of the frozen soil, which heaves and cracks to reveal the jewel-encrusted sculpture within, just as a broken quartz displays an amethyst. This frost-erupted soil can bring death to any newly planted shrub, and to primroses and cowslips, who seem to find it impossible to stay firmly tucked-up in bed. If there is no timely thaw to allow them to be persuaded back, I will heap bagged-up compost over the exposed shrub roots, or stones, if there is nothing else that is not frozen, and I shall have to pot up the primulas until the soil has softened once more.

More usefully, the frost will lift the weedy interstices between paving stones as much as an inch proud of the flags, looking as though a coarse fishing net has been spread out on the path to dry. When ice slackens the reins at last, it is a messy, finger-numbing, but easy task to lift the netted weeds, and the thick anti-macassars of moss that swathe every stone, leaving starkly delineated paths – for once stone-black, rather than furred emerald-green.

But such iron frosts can go on for weeks, with temperatures hovering around 0°F by day, and minus double figures each night. My first winter here was interminable, with no heat in the house but open fires, and outside temperatures plunging to −18°F. Indeed, inside temperatures were not much balmier: my bedroom was 10°F; my bedside glass of water froze solid. Next it began to snow, and went on until it was almost 3 feet deep. At least then it was warmer, as drifts sealed the doors and impeded the draughts. But then the rains came, which were almost as torrential as Louis Bromfield's Indian monsoon, and the stream flooded the garden (such as it was, in those early days). It was a dramatic baptism.

There will be snow every winter. 'We'll have a picture,' someone will say, as the sky begins to broadcast its intentions. The silence upon waking, on mornings when the world is wrapped in ermine, is matched by the intensity of reflected light. Bewildered birds rush for freshly scattered food, choosing high-octane bread for a fast fix before relishing seeds and peanuts. Only when there is snow lying do starlings come for food, thrushes too, when their usual insect breakfast lies buried fathoms deep. Desperation makes them timid, these normally confident birds; the snow disguising their aggression – whited sepulchres, indeed.

When Horatio's 'nipping and an eager air' brings a heavy snowfall at the turn of the year; when the trees are wreathed with serpents of snow, and each tiny twig has its own thin white snake; it will be safe, then, to take a broom to buffet the evergreens, to make them slough their loads before branches break. Later on, when fresh snow lies deeply in March or April, my wayward feet, snow-blind and astray, can wreak still more havoc on buried spring shoots. It is better, in this instance, to practise Christian Science by convincing myself that the groaning, snow-bent branches are not really suffering. If a frost-free night follows, all may be well. More likely, the snow will be further weighed down by leaden layers of ice, and the new spring growth, spread out on the ground like the spokes of a wheel, will be smashed at the heart – pressed to death as surely as a sultan's unfaithful concubine. Low-growing mounds are particularly vulnerable: lavender, still carrying last year's stems (to help it through the winter, ironically), will be unzipped by ice and split like kindling; an aged *Daphne mezereum*, in full flower, was uprooted and toppled by the density of driven snow; rosemaries and brooms have burst into splinters with such regularity that I have stopped growing them. Even a pyracantha, pilastered against the house, had inch-thick branches snapped, when four days of double minuses followed a 10-inch snowfall in March 1995.

Prolonged deep snow is not usual, however; more's the pity; its protectiveness would be welcome, instead of the penetrating frosts and half-hearted thaws that punish then cajole alternately. But when an inch or two of snow has fallen overnight, I like to check on the visitors to my garden, before melting has smutched their spoor. I would expect to see the tracks of fox, cat, badger, squirrel, field mouse, vole; and the neat prints of birds, varying in size from chaffinch (anything smaller would weigh too little to make an impression) to blackbird, who seem to overbalance easily, as their catamaran prints are accompanied by those of stabilizer wing-tips – shallow dabs, eyelash-soft, and brushed diagonally across the snow – and on up to pheasant, within whose profound arrow tracks the smallest birds could shelter. I recall with great joy the sight of a cock pheasant and a marsh tit sharing the same scattering of food. When the marsh tit spotted a particularly enticing seed, just out of reach, it calmy hopped on to the great central toe of the pheasant (as long as itself), as a springboard towards its chosen titbit. The pheasant, just as calmly, continued with its own breakfast. They are companionable birds, pheasants, who will potter around in the garden, keeping up a constant monologue of quietly fussy comment, even when I am busy there myself. Their footprints, one in front of the other like a well-schooled catwalk model, are bisected by a tramline in the snow as their stiff tail feathers trail over the previous prints. After a few hours scarcely an inch of the garden's snowy coverlet has been missed by the deeply incised stars and single stripe – no wonder the soil, once visible again, is so panned.

I shall hope not to see that rabbits or deer have visited the snowy garden. But it is exciting to trace the spoor of polecats, stoats and weasels, who dance through now and then, with their attention-seeking antics and hypnotic pirouettes; less so mink, escaped convicts who are said to be responsible for the disappearance of water voles, whom I now never see, alas. Brown rats come and go, as is inevitable with the stream – an eight-lane motorway of opportunity for such itinerants. No footprints in the snow, but a pervasive presence resounds throughout the garden, as, with a squealing cry and a gentian flash, a kingfisher darts above the stream. Its auburn breast and emerald wings seem fabulous in the austere English snow scene, like meeting a flamingo in Glencoe.

An early start to winter will slaughter countless slugs, when sharp frosts are recurrent in November and December. Snails should be safely suspended within a hibernaculum by then, their shells tightly sealed, to await the return of spring. When low walls collapse I find these dormant snails inside, stuck together in clusters as large as grapefruits. But slugs remain active throughout milder winters, so an early frost massacre will allow successful drifts of snowdrops later on. One mild winter I noticed that all my snowdrops were blind – not one flower in what should have been a snowy tablecloth of *Galanthus nivalis* spread beneath my boundary hedge. I could detect nothing, so sent some stems to Wisley. Under strong magnification, minute slug trails were visible – no doubt the flowers taste as sweet as they smell. Apparently *Leucojum vernum* flowers are tasty too, as not one was left to bloom. Thankfully, mild winters are not the norm – global warming notwithstanding – so my snowdrops and snowflakes make a fine show when we have the usual winter, described by Parson Woodforde as 'very cold, barren, growless weather'.

Snowflakes, *Leucojum vernum*, make the bolder show of the two, being bigger in every way, and having rich, shining green, strappy leaves, that catch the eye more readily than the gentle glaucousness of most snowdrop foliage. The green-gimped white lampshade flowers hang two to a stem on the form *L.v.* var. *vagneri*, and are edged with yellow on *L.v.* var. *carpathicum*. This has never settled down with me, although whether that is naughty temper, or simply that the yellow sickens its constitution, I know not; the other forms could not be more accommodating. Why, then, are they not seen more often? Many gardeners seem unaware of their existence, and confuse them with an English native, the so-called summer snowflake, *L. aestivum*. As this will flower in early April in warm gardens, confusion is excusable. But these, captivating as they are, clumped in wet meadows, are twice as tall, at 2 feet, but with smaller flowers than their earlier, continental cousin, so are less effective in the garden, particularly as they bloom at a time of plenty, rather than treading an almost empty stage as the spring snowflake does. Indeed, *L. vernum's* flowers make their entrance on stage like a pantomime genie through a trapdoor, rushing their cue by opening partially when still below ground, and then surging upwards, with arms outstretched, to shake out their lanterns fully under the winter-white spotlight.

There were large patches of snowdrops here when I arrived, seeded under the hedge, and sprinkled among the imbroglio of gooseberry and alder scrub along the stream wall. These were cleared out as soon as root removal made it possible, and added to the others; and I continue to extend this snowy chain along the hedge each spring by splitting a clump or two as the flowers fade. Other forms and species have been planted elsewhere in the garden over the years: I am no galanthophile, but admire them when the differences are evident to my untutored eye.

Galanthus ikariae shows a fundamental difference. It has bright green, glossy leaves, ransom-broad, and is easily confused with the wild garlic, excepting its smell. I have found that this snowdrop's flowering time is variable, sometimes appearing first of all in January, sometimes delaying, other years, until early April. There seems to be no climatic explanation for this, nor does either extreme occur only after they have been divided. It just happens, apparently at the whim of this characterful plant itself. My bulbs came from my parents' garden, where I believe they flowered later than *G. nivalis*, but not with such extreme unpunctuality as to be noteworthy. *G. ikariae* seems to have had many a surname change, with subspecies to distinguish the more widespread bulb found on the Levantine mainland, from the rarified (but otherwise identical) bulb seen only on the island closest to where Icarus fell into the sea. Less romantically, both are now subsumed by a group called Latifolius, and two further species, *G. platyphyllus* and *G. woronowii*; so only heaven and taxonomy know now what my bulbs are called. No matter, to me they remain as Icarus's snowy wings reduced to drops of wax.

Major differences can also be seen on *G. elwesii* and *G. caucasicus* (now reduced to a botanical variety of the former, and renamed *G. elwesii* var. *monostichus*). Both have wide, ultra-glaucous leaves – upright and enfolding on the first, with a reflexed tip at maturity; more lax and arching on *G. caucasicus*, which, again, is variable both in height and flowering time. Its flowers are long and rather narrow, the outer segments flaring backwards, in bright sunshine, like a pagoda roof. The flowers on *G. elwesii*, conversely, curve inwards firmly, like sugar tongs, modestly concealing the extra green splash on the inner segments. This, looking like a solid o above an x, gives the impression of a boiled egg sitting in an eggcup. *Galanthus elwesii* is a large snowdrop, but not such a giant as *G.* 'Brenda Troyle', which grows to 12 inches tall, and whose flowers are more than an inch long, with a substantial jade bridge thumbprint within. It is a strong, no-nonsense grower, too, and is usually the first to flower here, although its position is quite sheltered and sunny, encouraging an early alarm call, no doubt.

Some snowdrops like damp, dappled shade – our own native (if it is native) included; others prefer sun, with a good deal of baking in summer, and sharp drainage. *G. elwesii* is a sunbather, as is *G.* x *allenii*, which has broad, mat leaves in light yellowish-green, and a bad reputation for wilfulness. Another one (a sun worshipper, that is, although it is not unknown as a prima donna) is the autumn-flowering *G. reginae-olgae*, which will deign to flower here only after a burning summer, and even then only in December.

Many people claim that a double snowdrop, a double form of any plant indeed, is an aberration firmly to be discouraged. I think they miss a great deal of beauty and personality by being so censorious. *Galanthus nivalis* f. *pleniflorus* 'Flore Pleno' is mercurial in the design and amount of its doubling, from year to year. Often a clump will start the season single, and gradually increase the doubling, as more flowers open, like a tentative player of backgammon. Even more profoundly rosetted doubles, like the Greatorex 'Ophelia', as trim and engine-turned as a ceiling boss, once it gets into its stride, and brilliant malachite green, seem to need a run-up to perfection, like a coloratura-soprano beginning with scales.

The yellow-marked double, 'Lady Elphinstone', is said to resent *déménagement* to such an extent that she will turn green with apoplexy for the first season in her new home. Being aristocratically expensive, the one and only bulb that I planted had its flower bud nipped out by a *sans-culotte* slug before I could tell the colour of her blood. It seems that this treatment was even more *de trop* than the replanting, as there has been no flower scape at all this year.

Snowdrops, in general, can be temperamental residents in the garden. They seem to need several seasons to settle down; sometimes taking a year off when they don't appear above ground at all. This can be disconcerting when you attempt to plant something else in their space, only to find a perfectly healthy bulb sitting there. Am I failing so signally to find them a conducive billet, that best feet cannot be foremost, even though the spirit may be willing? Are they sulking because they are missing some element vital to their wellbeing? Or because they can't bear their neighbours? Or perhaps the taste and temperature of that inch of soil? Or is it simply pretty Fanny's way? Who knows? Sometimes they will go on the following year quite as normal – but is this stoicism in the face of severe adversity, or have they simply forgotten what all the fuss was about?

Fuss to the point of fussissimo has been my experience of *Galanthus nivalis* 'Viridapice', although, being a form of the native snowdrop, with green splashes on its wingtips, it should be relatively content with its surroundings here. Not a bit of it. Three times I have tried it, never to be seen again. Clearly I am not viridapice-fingered, when it comes to snowdrops, as I have failed with 'Pusey Green Tip' too (although, to be fair to myself, this one failed because a cat chose to powder its nose, rather too scratchily, just where the new shoot was about to emerge). And with the donkey-eared snowdrop of the Scharlockii Group, which has a faint green shadow to its outer segments too, as well as its greatly extended, split spathe. Perhaps I should have whispered 'King Midas has asses ears' into its planting hole, and buried it with the secret. I'll try that next time.

Other snowdrops will settle down readily and easily: well known for its perfect manners and steadfast growth is 'S. Arnott', which is similar to *G. nivalis* in every way, but more so. One of my favourites is 'Magnet', another dependable snowdrop. It has large flowers like heavy baroque pearls, dangling from elongated pedicels, so they tremble in the slightest breeze. *Galanthus* 'Straffan' is reliable too; its parent was sent home, like many another snowdrop, by a botanically minded officer on active service in the Crimea. Once established, it displayed its charms to a nearby native, and the resulting infant was named after the estate in Ireland where it appeared. It is noticeably different, producing two flowers from each bulb, one after the other, which, inevitably, prolong its season. It is said that the first flower is like its Crimean parent, the second like its Irish; but I confess I can see no difference between the Cossack and the colleen.

Perfect for picking to display with snowdrops are the fresh new leaves of *Arum italicum* subsp. *italicum* 'Marmoratum', with dashing white veins marbled on gleaming green. Their furled umbrellas have been thrusting through the soil for a few weeks before the snowdrops bloomed, so are just the right size to accompany them. The leaves grow ever larger (although the marbling blurs and fades), until the pea-green flowering spathes appear in late spring, then wither, together with the now redundant spathe, leaving the purple stems thick with steadily ripening berries. They grow easily from seed but take several years to show their stark white lacing. The variety *A.* 'Chameleon', though less conspicuously veined, has splashes of cream and swirls of grey. The native lords and ladies, *Arum maculatum*, is ravishing in early leaf too. Its polished fir-green arrows can be plain, or have smudges of black foxing. The flaring spathes are either creamish-green or a moody, greyed crimson, with Jack, the erect spadix, cassocked in a tone darker than his embracing pulpit. The autumn berries, displayed on green stems, are a clear orange, and a little smaller, perhaps, than the ample scarlet fruits of 'Marmoratum'. Here, the heavily berried stems crash down to the ground, and are devoured by slugs; but following dry summers they stand exalted, so I imagine that lighter soils would give them their best chance, although in such conditions they would require less sun than I can give them.

Often tricky to establish is the winter aconite, *Eranthis hyemalis*; its varnished doubloon flower centred on a prinked green ruff. Like snowdrops and bluebells, it is best planted 'in the green', so choose your friends from among those who are well-blessed enough to spare you a growing clump. Dorothy L. Sayers claimed it would succeed only where Roman blood has been spilt. I interpret this rather more democratically than 'where some buried Caesar bled', and it may encourage you to invite your Italian friends to stay in time for rose pruning. Winter aconites appear reluctant to flower even when they are established, having the endearing habit of backing out of the ground, as though unwilling to face the world, by pushing out bald pink knees and elbows first, before dragging out their bashful flowerheads. Pheasants find these knees irresistible, tweaking out the premature flowers and scattering all the shreds of bullion petals. Given the chance, the green ruffs should expand as the flowers fade, and the bent pink knees will become long green stems – long enough to cast seed beyond its own clump, and make your garden Croesus-rich in time.

Cyclamen coum is as startling in its vibrant pink as the winter aconite's polished gold when surrounding colours are winter-muted. Easy to establish, colonies can be decimated by vine weevil grubs, unless you have a visiting pest controller in the shape of a badger. Of course, the tubers will be tossed out in its zeal to reach every last grub, but, as they can be replanted elsewhere, that is surely the lesser of the two weevils. I salvaged several dozen seedlings from this kind of adventure, and replanted them on either side of the front door, around the feet of two large peonies. This works well, as the peony stems have been cut to the ground before the cyclamen's debut; then the peonies' splendour takes place after the cyclamen have retreated to summer dormancy. Interspersed among them are *Crocus tommasinianus*, in silvery, wood-pidgeon lilac, and *C.t.* 'Ruby Giant', which is neither ruby nor a giant, being only a whisker larger in flower than the species, and bright purple. These overlap with the latter stages of the cyclamen flowers, and are a heartening sight on days of cheerful sunshine, awash with venturesome bees.

Varieties of *Crocus chrysanthus*, early to flower, are massed in snowdrifts of samite ('Snow Bunting' and 'Ard Schenk') and cloth of gold ('Romance' and 'E.P. Bowles'). Further colour is gained by the coromandel stripes of 'Gipsy Girl' and *C.c. fuscotinctus*, clotted 'Cream Beauty' and the ultraviolet sheen of 'Blue Pearl'. I love them dearly, but so do birds, so the start of flowering is somewhat fraught. When sheets of colour take over from isolated incidents, the birds lose interest, and the flowers remain whole, rather than in ragged-robin-tatters.

Other flowers who attempt to wake up early must run this avian gauntlet too. Pheasants are the major culprits: nipping off buds of the Christmas-flowering *Narcissus* 'Cedric Morris' and shattering every flower of *Iris* 'Katharine Hodgkin'. I noticed it first several years ago, when each arching, cobra-head bud of *Fritillaria meleagris* was picked and dropped. Was some atavistic defence instinct being enacted by the pheasant at the sight of all those rearing snakes' heads, I wondered? Or a territorial rite at the recognition of usurping, checkered guinea fowl? Now, several hundred ruined flowers later, I suspect he only does it to annoy, because he knows it teases.

More engagingly, a jackdaw once picked flowers, but only blue ones, at nesting time. Later, when the chimney the pair had used was rebuilt, a veritable Wallace Collection of blue was discovered: broken bits of ceramic tiles, plastic, nylon twine, wire, pottery and glass shards — but all blue. I should have enjoyed seeing the nest still further garlanded with his bouquets of pulmonarias and grape hyacinths. What a spoony old romantic — Mr Jackdaw: 'They match your eyes, darling', (and they do, too). But was it a jackdaw, or was it perhaps a bower bird?

Hamamelis

ON STILL, DAMP DAYS IN WINTER, scents will hang in the air. Some shrubs hug their scent closely, others will fling it out towards my approach. Less enticingly, the fervid reek of fox will permeate the air with the evanescence of Mrs Gradgrind's pain: it is somewhere about, but I'm not sure where.

I grow two winter-scented honeysuckles that combine toughness and delicacy in equal measures. Each displays a constitutional bravura that brooks the leanest quarters, whereas their flowers, a dainty froth of creaminess from December to May, give a suite-at-Claridges impression of coddled care. Not so: some will be browned by frost, but the conveyor-belt of buds ensures replacements. *Lonicera fragrantissima* is an angular, gaunt shrub, so should not be planted to row stroke in the border, but further down the boat, where its winter style will be trenchant, but its summertime humdrum a tepid timpano rather than a booming bass. I planted mine, first of all, near a frequented gate, to reap the benison of the swooningly sweet scent each time I took the kitchen peelings to the compost bin. Perhaps it made better compost, as the bucket would have been emptied with a lighter hand, after a mood-lifting snort of the honeysuckle. But it began to lean outwards over the path, yearning for more light, and in trimming it I was losing flowers. So I moved it to the Wilderness, with bluebells and periwinkle around its feet. Here it has more light and space to spread, and its dark background throws the ivory-white flowers into bold relief. But having more air around it means that its scent is held close to its chest like a nervous card player, so I must sniff the flowers, now, rather than absorb the scented air.

This access to the prevailing winds also means that it has dropped all its leaves by winter, which is a great help to the onlooker, as one can see the flowers more easily. Its partial evergreen habit was held against it for this reason, and relegated it to the gentle obscurity of old gardens since the arrival on the scene of *Lonicera* x *purpusii*. This natural hybrid between *L. fragrantissima* and *L. standishii*, is meant to cast its foliage before flowering, again, throughout the winter. Perversely, mine keeps most of its leaves, which, being large, olivine-dark, and shiny (*L. fragrantissima*'s are larger, but are a lighter green, and mat), look perished with purple all winter. The variety 'Winter Beauty' has purple stems, which are striking in summer but less obvious in winter, when one could do with an eyecatcher. I have contrived a dark background for it, by 'borrowing' the huge alder bole beyond the stream, but the white flowers do not stand out as distinctly as those of its parent *L. fragrantissima*. *L.* x *purpusii*'s flowers are smaller individually, although the clusters are more numerous, and they are a sharper white, with the same contrast of lemon-velvet stamens. The scent is the same too (if, perhaps, a trifle dimmer on *L.* x *purpusii*) – fresh and delicious, like lily-of-the-valley frappé, with none of the heady, cloying richness of summer-flowering honeysuckles. 'Winter Beauty' is a first-class shrub, then, but, to me, it is the beautiful daughter of a still more beautiful mother, to twist Horace widdershins.

Hailing from the acidic, leaf-mouldy forests of Japan and North America, hamamelis should not be the first choice for gardens on the limey side of neutral. But I do confess to a mulish determination to succeed with it. I am not the type of gardener who insists upon growing an awkward squad of aliens that demand raised beds lined with polythene, special soil, and personalized water butts. But then neither am I the kind who plays the hand she is dealt, unquestioningly. A challenge is always a useful discipline, provided it remains a challenge and does not devolve into the realms of obsession. One can try a couple of times, but not keep on trying – especially with plants as expensive as hamamelis. Part of the challenge is the mental elbow grease necessary before any purchase takes place: researching the conditions, geology and aspect of the plant's original home (by which I do not mean the inevitable Dutch polytunnel where it grew its first roots; although even that must be borne in mind in the hardening-off process prior to planting). What it needs in the way of quartermastering, its *bêtes noires*, its quirks and fancies: all of these are paramount. Next in consideration are its height, girth and shape, and colour last of all. Hamamelis hybrids seem to tolerate less acidic conditions than the species, and smile with equanimity upon a little lime if the soil never dries out and you can provide potash in the form of vintage bonfire ashes, at planting time and each spring after flowering. This will help to open clay soil, as will manure (which also helps to keep the pH reading down) although the hamamelis is not fanatically greedy for muck. The border where mine is planted was alluvial silt that could be sliced with a butter knife, but has been improving steadily in texture each year with a seasoning of garden compost. The hamamelis seems content, anyway, having quadrupled in size in nine years.

In fact, this is the second attempt: the first, *H.* x *intermedia* 'Pallida', was bought in flower and planted with due reverence and plenty of potash but it fell foul of their one weakness by failing to break its dormancy after the flowers faded. Instead of leafing out and growing on, it simply faded with the flowers. Young plants have this tendency – indeed I still pass a *mauvais quart d'heure* each year as the flowers dwindle on my replacement shrub, *H.* x *i.* 'Arnold Promise', but so far, so good.

While 'Pallida' has a cool citron sizzle to its flowers, 'Arnold Promise' has a warm glow, which I like better. Its exuberance sits more comfortably with the piquant scent, and it beams through ice more stoically. The petals of 'Pallida' have a transparency, when frozen, which encourages sympathetic shivering. 'Arnold Promise' is so joyous in its fortitude, it makes you smile rather than shiver. The flowers, like the be-ribboned rosette on the red-heeled shoes of a Jacobean dandy, toss their spicy scent into the air for yards around them. Such generosity is astounding, and I walk towards it purposely each day to drink my fill. Nor is winter the only season of interest: the flowers mutate into curious seed pods, antler-hard and covered in a downy velvet. They are puckered into jowly, pug-dog faces, still sitting tight when next year's flowers unfurl. Then the hazel-like foliage is bewitched by late summer into a ravishing display of fiery colour.

H. 'Arnold Promise' is underplanted with a delightful, easy woodlander from the Caucasus, *Pachyphragma macrophyllum*, whose chalk-white umbels, flowering from January to May, look like miniature lace-cap hydrangea heads, above evergreen leaves that are large, heart-shaped and bottle-green. The flowers are said to be malodorous, but I can detect nothing of this, perhaps because the hamamelis' scent is so expansive.

A gentler, more flowery scent wafts in the air around *Abeliophyllum distichum*, an enchanting small shrub that comes from Korea. It is sometimes described as the white forsythia. This is misleading, as the only thing they seem to have in common is that they are both of the olive family. But then, so are lilac and privet, which do not owe their popularity simply to their affinity with forsythia, so I fail to see why the beauty of the family, the abeliophyllum, should be so humbugged. I could garden very happily without forsythia – why bother to bark yourself, when everyone else has a dog. I could also do without lilac, whose scent is droolingly divine, but whose two bad habits discourage me: suckering roots, and flowers that turn brown in the first (of many, in May) frost or downpour of rain. Privet can be a dull dog, but has its uses, which makes it sound like a handleless saucepan, sitting around waiting to be used, but invariably overlooked.

From November onwards, it would be difficult to overlook the abeliophyllum, as its naked, rather corky stems sprinkle their tips with quantities of nubbly, blackish bud-cases, which, as they grow, look as though the shrub has been dabbling sticky fingers in a potful of angular buckwheat seeds. By mid-February, these will be splitting to reveal white flower-buds, streaked with rosy-purple, opening to fringed bells that look like a cross between soldanella and deutzia. Although the shrub is perfectly hardy, it appreciates a warm spot to ripen its wood sufficiently in summer, to help it flower abundantly in the dog-watch of the year. Mine is wainscotted against the south wall of the house, where *Iris unguicularis* makes a tight skirting-board, corniced by clematis – a jackmanna, as Virginia Woolf called it, to keep the worst of the autumn rains from the iris's susceptible crowns. Even so, *Iris unguicularis* (*née stylosa*) cannot manage to flower every winter (and even then, not until March at the earliest, here), but is worth the wait, and the risk of rot, and the occasional replacement, for the sake of the exquisite flowers of lavender or violet tissue-paper, and the sublime scent. The abeliophyllum appreciates the same warmth, but does not require the lime-kiln conditions of crumbled mortar and drought-dust in which the iris should revel – if this were only Algeria. The little shrub's habit of painting its foliage briefly in August, then dropping it almost immediately, must help to ripen the bare wood in the warm autumn sunshine. It helps the iris too, by drawing back the curtains for its own St Luke's baking. I hope that the iris will catch the abeliophyllum's dependability of flower by its proximity, so that I may be bowled over by a tandem of scents.

There is a hint of aniseed hidden in the sweetness of *Daphne mezereum*'s scent. Having lost my previous plant (old age succumbing to hypothermia one very cold winter), I missed the heavenly perfume that reached out to tug my sleeve as I passed even more than the look of the shrub – it was not at the front of the queue when poise was handed out, being an ungainly shuttlecock in shape, with flowers of a rather petulant pink. But looks, as we were told as children, are not everything; it is character that counts. *Daphne mezereum*, that Cornish thriller-writer, overflows with character as much as scent, with an unexpected little twist of sharpness to both, just to keep our interest to the end.

Mayfield

THE SNOWDROPS SPILLED OUT on to the verge through the arabesques of the old wrought-iron gate. Such sheets of white, it was the massive sandstone wall that looked as though it had been planted among them, rather than the other way round. Perhaps it had. Wall, bulbs, and gate were older than time; no one could remember them not being there.

From the gate, the hoggin path snaked around the hollow ash tree. Someone had once said that, about snaking, and I remembered it later when the adder was seen, curled slumbrously inside the tree. They all looked, but not me – I was too young, they said; I was always too young to see or hear or understand. So my memories are disjointed episodes, just fleeting pictures pausing for a second in front of my eyes, then blurring. And I will say to my sister, 'Was it really like that, at Mayfield?' and she will reply, 'Not quite, don't you remember?' Do I? Or do I just recall what I have been told since, like remembering the old photographs in the big red album, but not the taking of them?

I remember the kitchen garden, the windrows of vegetables as distinct as words on a page, and the scarecrow my cousins had made, which I thought was real; I remember being scared. I remember the gigantic compost heap, like a haystack, with a little wooden ladder leaning against it. We would climb up and jump off. And the pear tree with the remains of an old swing – just a knotted rope now – that we used to hang on to and twizzle until Jimmy, the fox terrier, would snap at our ankles. There were huge stone gateposts at the start of the kitchen garden, with neither gate nor wall attached – just menhirs of stone, weathered and rounded, soft to the touch. And row upon row of raspberries. 'Just pick me another punnet of raspberries,' my grandmother would say, and we knew that a family conclave was happening and we were unwanted inside. So we would pick and eat and scratch our hands against the pale stems and fill the little chip-straw baskets; but it would be the same the next day – 'Just pick me another punnet.'

There was a stream that flowed across the garden through the leaning orchard, where the long grass was spangled with lady's smock and primroses, little wild daffodils and solomon's seal. It came in under the wall, a sight which I found fascinating, believing that it sprang from below ground exactly beneath the fern-hollowed tunnel, the water making a conscious decision to flow this way rather than that. It was tea-peaty from off the moors. My sister missed her jump and had to wear my cousin's thick grey stockings with her silver shoes for my grandmother's birthday party. I remember that, but nothing about the party.

Nearer the house was a vast lawn with herbaceous borders to one side against a high wall. There must have been the classic border plants of lupins, pyrethrums, Japanese anemones and phlox, but I see none of them as I try to picture it. Beyond the lawn was a formal rose garden with a swoopy pergola, whose overhead timbers had warped into swags, echoed by the looping ramblers, and a tiny pool with wax-white water lilies and goldfish, where I dropped a ring, on purpose, for my own fishy fairy story. By the kitchen door there was a mound – was it an old ice-house, I wonder? – topped by an underpinned yew tree with sinuous surface roots interlarded with St John's wort, which I loathed. My aunt tripped there, and broke a rib, and I have remained convinced that it was the odious hypericum that was the cause. Never shall I grow it.

The old stone house was L-shaped at the back, holding a flagged courtyard within the crook, further enclosed by a stable block, where we played in the loft up the breakneck stairs on rainy days. I remember the courtyard as a mass of flowers, but I can't recall any detail, sadly. We had big bushes of the common fuchsia at home, grown from Mayfield cuttings, so they must have been there, jasmine too, and my mother remembers a passionflower, entwined with roses, growing around the garden door. Probably I was more interested in the donkey in the meadow or the cows being called for milking at the farm across the lane. I remember roses at the front of the house, in the small garden between the railings and the elegant Georgian sash windows. One of the more satirical of the Romantic poets had lived there in the early nineteenth century. Perhaps it was he who planted the fig tree, or the fuchsia that I now grow, or, more likely, the passionflower.

Inside, I remember that the drawing-room felt as though it were under water, being low-ceiling-dim, and cool and pale green; and that the breakfast room was panelled with church pews and had a well in the centre of the floor. A little staircase led up from a cupboard to my aunt's room and the sun-drenched white landing held the scent of her potpourri in a pierced Derby pot, whereas the boot room, festooned with rods and baskets, always smelt of river weed and fish scales.

These gap-toothed memories are a little like the feeling of bewilderment one has during the first months of living in a city, before all the disparate areas that one knows quite well begin to knit together on the map of one's mind. But with my flickering mind-pictures of Mayfield, the knitting barely grows beyond the casting-on of stitches. And as time goes on, even those unravel.

Mermaid

THE 'MERMAID' ROSE IS DEAD, after all. The whole of its vast top growth was killed to the ground by two very hard and long spells of minus temperatures on the trot. By the following summer it was shooting again from the stump, so I revised my idea for replacing it with 'Alister Stella Gray' just in time not to order one. Now it is winter again, I can see the newly grown shoots properly, with all the herbaceous plants in front of them gone to earth, and I realize that they are, of course, suckers from below the scion. This makes them sound like nobodies below the salt, which is exactly what they are, in rosarian society: briar rose roots, used solely for their peasant vigour, to support the aristocratic stem grafted upon them. So I have pulled them off (always better than cutting them off, as that will simply stimulate further shooting, as does pruning), and must now dig out the root before they sprout from somewhere else.

After all the will ye, nill ye, I am glad to have it settled at last. I missed the 'Mermaid''s enormous, single, lemon-mousse blooms in the summer. It is a beautiful rose, and I have been fortunate that it has lasted so long and done so well, in what must have been disagreeably cold surroundings – it is not as hardy as most. But even as those shoots began growing, and I was saying 'How wonderful', most of me was thinking 'Oh no!' as my heart sank at the thought of having to resume bloody battle with it yet again. Pruning time was a nightmare; just tying in new stems was often worse. Any other mermaid with such weapons would be a danger to shipping. 'Mermaid' = vicious thorns, and I shall never grow it again.

Blood, sweat, tears and temper, swearing and apoplexy – these would be accurate if not attractive names for many rambler roses. If ever I were able to afford to employ a gardener (no, it would have to be two, on the one-to-wash, one-to-wear principle of one-to-work, one-to-recover in hospital), it would be in order to enjoy the rapture of all those ramblers in bloom, when butter wouldn't melt in their mouths, and the subsequent relief of being able to say 'And just give those ramblers a prune, Ted,' and walk away. Blue moons being about as likely as blue roses, I shall continue to eschew new ramblers, and suffer those I have already.

And 'suffering' is by no means an exaggeration. After a day's pruning, I look and feel like one of the more gruesome illustrations from *Foxe's Book of Martyrs*. It is rarely possible to get at the wretches immediately after flowering, as the borders are crammed at that time, and there are clematis or lathyrus entwined within the roses' embrace. I aim to reach them by October; often it is November, occasionally later still. The absolute deadline for all rose pruning is set by me at 20 January: appropriately, the celebration day of St Sebastian, who, by the look of him, has clearly been tussling with a 'Mermaid' or 'American Pillar'. Unlike the scantily clad saint, I am cuirassed and cuissed, *cap à pié* for the *joust à outrance*. It makes little difference; indeed, pruning *tutta nuda* would give fewer opportunities for the rose to reach out and grab me by the cuffs, trouser legs or tightly tied headscarf, or to wind in and truss me up like a cod fish in an inexorable trawler net. But as it is usually a bone-chilling day in midwinter, the tormented saint's fashion tips are not enticing.

And rarely can I finish it all in one freezing, finger-smarting, scratchy day – the rain will become just too icy and horizontal to bear, or the blood will be dripping just a little too freely down the secateurs, or the wind will whip a springy stem into my eye, and I swear once more and go inside to bind the wounds and growl at everyone. So the agony can be prolonged over days or weeks when the weather dips beyond endurance and I think, I'm too late, they'll never flower; but they always do – forgiving and, by that time, forgiven. Come a June morning of pristine sparkle, scent hanging on the air and gently swaying wands of blush and opal, clotted cream and parma violet, all thoughts of slashing thorns, whipping winds and ice rain are forgotten.

And therein lies the danger, as the catalogues arrive to order more during the Hoppy, Croppy, Droppy period of summer heedlessness rather than the Breezy, Sneezy, Freezy months of winter laceration. It is easy, then, to let one's mind idle over thoughts of the heavenly rambler

'Albertine', whose lingerie-pink blooms and warm scent of green tea are the essence of romance. Was 'Albertine' named after the Proustian character, I wonder? Or was she a *grande horizontale* of *fin-de-siècle* Paris, along with fellow roses 'Madame de Sancy de Parabère', 'Ghislaine de Féligonde' and 'Zéphirine Drouhin'? None matches my timing, two being too late and the others much too early; all were doubtless highly respectable bourgeois ladies, whose reputations should be enhanced by their named roses, rather than damned by my scurrilous supposition. I apologize wholeheartedly for any offence, then fall unrepentently from pan to fire by wondering if Mme Albertine herself was just as spiteful as her glorious rose.

I had, for many years, the dubious pleasure of pruning the 'Albertine' rose in my parents' garden. As bonfires were discouraged, every yard of shark-toothed stem had to be snipped up and bagged up to take to the garden waste tip. A needle-studded hydra could not have been more unwilling to be subdued. I did not hurry down the alphabet of imprecation. The savage beauty succumbed to honey fungus, some years ago. Was it something I said?

Rosa rubiginosa is better known by its older name of *R. eglanteria*, the sweet briar, or eglantine: much lauded by poets through the centuries, and beloved by those of a romantic disposition for its delicious scent. This emanates from the leaves, particularly after rain – a gentle shower carried on a warm zephyr of summer breeze (one can't help that sort of thing, when contemplating the eglantine). It reminds me of warm, roasted apples, well stuffed with raisins and spices. Perhaps it comes from reading too much Shakespeare and Spenser but, to me, there is a strong essence of the Age of Gloriana about this rose; there are definitely sackbuts playing in the background. The brilliant pink flowers may bring to mind the rouge on the leaden cheeks of the Faerie Queene; the thorns certainly recall her temper – this is another rancorous rose. It is also extremely vigorous, so needs careful placing if you are not to be on too close acquaintance with its armature. When this necessitates rear-stalls planting, there ceases to be any point to it, as you are then too far away to catch the wafting scent. It used to be planted as a hedge on the railings around tombs, with its fragrant leaves pressed within the family Bible for remembrance. This hedging habit could well be adapted to a more prosaic use, as a ferocious anti-burglar, -

stray dog, -wandering bullock device, planted along your most frequented boundary. It wouldn't stop hungry deer, though; they are very fond of stuffed roasted apples.

Rosa canina, the wild dog rose, does the same job of stopping musets and fills every hedgerow around here in equal proportion to the wild honeysuckle, so the lanes all hum with bees. There is no more glorious sight, scent and sound – the epitome of an English summer. But I don't want a dog rose on my side of the boundary hedge. It is a fairy tale, indeed, that brings the prince to the bedside of the Sleeping Beauty in such an unsullied, bloodless condition of wholesome cleanliness, after his battle through the encircling briars. I have been reading the aptly named Mrs Gore writing about a natural hybrid of *R. canina* x *R. spinosissima*, in *The Rose Fancier's Manual* of 1838. It was found near Belfast by a Mr Templeton, who was awarded fifty guineas for its discovery, which may have been just enough, I suppose, to pay his hospital bill.

I am flirting with the idea of *Rosa moyesii* 'Geranium'. I have the perfect place, where it can grow to its full cascading glory, and where the evening sun will turn its pendulous, but prickly, ketchup-bottle hips to melting cabochon rubies. The flowers, though small, are a rich scarlet and very numerous. So, alas, are its thorns – raked along every twig and branch, clashing and flexing themselves and scratching the calendar to mark off each month until pruning day occurs and battle commences. Could I bear it? No, on the whole, I think not. But don't let me put you off. If you grow all of these cross-patch roses, I should be delighted to see them – but don't ask me before St Sebastian's Day.

Hellebores

I'VE ALWAYS BEEN SOMETHING of a helle-bore, as many friends will testify – the ease of culture, the ravishing colours, even the scent – I could, and frequently do, go on and on and, yawningly, on. They are now so accessible that there can be scarcely a gardener who does not know and grow them. But their popularity is a fairly recent phenomenon; it was not always so marked. Not so long ago, they were disparaged as dull and dreary, and scorned as native and green, so not proper flowers at all. It makes a change for me to smile benignly upon progress and to agree that some things really do get better, with time.

Christmas roses, *Helleborus niger*, were approved, being white and non-native – they, like most hellebores, come from Balkan woodlands. They were known, always and universally, as Christmas roses; hellebore as a name, came into use later with the vogue for *H. orientalis*, rarely if ever referred to as Lenten roses. But despite the esteem in which Christmas roses were held, not many gardeners seemed to grow them. They were more likely to be seen in gilded baskets in a Berkeley Square florist's than in gardens. So not everything helleborean does change for the better, as they are most often encountered, now, as plastic decorations (sometimes, regrettably, coloured purple) stuck on wreaths to hang on front doors at Christmas. I remember staying with an aunt one Christmas, whose splendid turkey and plum pudding paled into insignificance beside the silver bowl of Christmas roses on the table. Later she showed me how the plants had been swaddled in straw, to encourage the stems to grow longer, and covered with panes of glass suspended on wire stilts, to prevent rain from besmirching their pristine complexions. This explains their absence from most gardens: too much trouble.

There was a straggly clump here when I arrived, growing exactly where the builders were most likely to put their feet, so I moved half to safety and potted the other half just in case. Both halves died. No hellebore likes travelling, once past the back-packing stage of extreme youth, *H. niger* least of all. Having tried several more since then, with minimal success, I must conclude that they seem determined on recusancy to the bitter end; neither fine words nor buttered parsnips will avail. I have to admit to being beaten, for the time being at least.

Fortunately, there are easier hellebores, even easy white-flowered ones that will bloom in time for Christmas, something that no Christmas rose has ever managed for me. The various forms and hybrids of *H. orientalis*, which the tabloid-style catalogues persist in describing as 'the pink Christmas rose' but which are now most often found sheltering beneath the umbrella of *H.* x *hybridus*, can be effective in flower from November until June, with weed-smothering foliage for even longer. Longevity, for foliage, depends upon the gardener: you can leave it for ever, until it rots on the plant (and may possibly rot the whole plant too) or you can cut it off as soon as the flower buds begin colouring. This bit of fussing will tidy up the tawdry old leaves; it will save all the disease spores spreading from these spent leaves to the bran-new flower stems; it will clear the stage, to allow a weed and feed session; best of all, it will enable you to see the flowers in all their splendour.

The colour range, which began as shades of pink and white, has been extended so dramatically that it would be quicker to name the colours not yet available, although by the time you read this, they may be. Brown, I think, is still absent from the palette, but, given the deep crimsons and apricot-buffs that exist, it can be only a matter of time. Shape of flower is varied, too, with rounded petals or twisted, frilled and pointed, or double the amount. Flowers can be stargazing, face outwards or still hang their traditional heads with *la nostalgie de la boue*. Certainly the upwardly mobile flowers allow time-challenged gardeners to glimpse, on the run, all the internal spottles and spatters with which many of these hellebores are decorated. But I wonder if these saucers have the staying power of the more modest blooms, when they are so exposed to the worst of the weather. For those of us who still prefer to chuck the flowers under the chin to encourage them to reveal their charms, rather than have them presented to us, like John the Baptist, on a plate, there are still nodding hellebores available that guard 'their golden thrummes' – as Parkinson described the fluffle of creamy stamens within – as well as the dots and dashes that line the shimmering petals, from the inevitable severity of seasonal weather.

Primus inter pares, here, is a sumptuous black form, which is an Ashwood Garden hybrid. The contrast between the blackcurrant-jam petals and the clotted-cream swirl of stamens and nectaries (or honey-leaves, to use the charming medieval description), is magical close to, though I have to admit that this colour does not shout from a distance unless you place yours in front of some winter-golden evergreen or conifer. But gardening need not be obvious, despite what the television claims, so I prefer a quieter, if myopic, scheme, in which this superlative black is folded into a curdle of crimson and pink hellebores, all set out in front of a gleam of holly, with *Cotinus coggygria* 'Royal Purple' for later leafing to one side and *Viburnum* x *bodnantense* 'Charles Lamont' for simultaneous flowering to the other. This in a position facing fully south with no shade until late afternoon and reasonably alert drainage, although the soil is never parched. Half-shade, here, means that they would be held within the grip of frost for too much of the day, resulting in black leg rot more surely than black flowers. Almost as dynamic in colour as the Ashwood black hellebore, and even more vigorous in habit, is a papal-crimson form that I grew from seed. As with the black beauty, the colour of the blooms is echoed in the flower stems and newly emergent leaves. The crimson, therefore, is not so invisible against the soil as the black but comely Ashwood form.

Yellows have been around for a while, but are often nearer in tone to their other hybrid parent, *H. cyclophyllus*, in their ripe-gooseberry, golden-green colour. I bought an unflowered seedling (from the named form 'Primrose'), which is almost banana-yellow. Plain last year, it is sporting minute purple flecks this year, so perhaps this new fashion statement will become more pronounced as the hellebore hits its stride: these are long-lived plants, so must be given time to develop their performance. Somewhere in my seedling's ancestry must be *H. orientalis* subsp. *guttatus*, whose rash of purple spots on a white ground ranges from a slight measle to a full-throated pox. Here, these are always the first to flower, often as early as November, growing in full sun.

H. cyclophyllus itself is not far behind that, its fresh peridot-green an unseasonal hue to brighten dull winter days. Of the *famille-verte* hellebores, it is the closest to *H. orientalis* in looks and habit, so mixes well in a massed planting, and may introduce some extra-marital colours to the resulting seedlings that should appear around each clump. The other species with green flowers show more variety in their stance and flowering time. The next one to flower for me, in mid-February, is *H. odorus* subsp. *laxus*, which is a more timid version of *H. cyclophyllus*, being smaller in height and flower, and with demurely hanging bells of a sour apple-green. Now and then I have to nip off individual flowers that have gone black – some form of botrytis, I imagine, from which the whole family are apt to suffer. This seems not to trouble the plant (though maybe it would, if I failed to remove the infected flowers), but it does mean that I should not recommend it, nor choose, necessarily, to grow it again. Despite its specific name, I am not aware of any scent on my plant, but have heard it likened to hawthorn. To my nose, this equates to old fish markets, which could be another reason not to grow it.

A hellebore I shall want always to grow, is *H. foetidus*. It has laboured for too long under the 'stinking' epithet, undetectable unless you crush the leaves, so I am told; I fail to see the need. There are several forms, so my first choice would not be the English native of deciduous woodland and ephemeral lifespan, which is arthritically stiff and bent in habit. More upright and free-standing to 4 feet, although still short-lived, are the forms known as Italian, Miss Jekyll's and Bowles's, the main differences being that Miss Jekyll's form has no garnet edging to the small, but plentiful chrysoprase-green bells, which are said to be sweetly scented, and that Mr Bowles's form has a reddish flush to the stems. This redness is taken still further by the Wester Flisk Group, but with the disadvantage of the native style of growth – reclining on its elbows like a relaxed Roman consul. All of these tall-form characteristics seemed to be combined in one plant, which I grew from Ray Brown's seed called 'scented form'. It was quite 4 feet square, had olive-green, finely fingered foliage, topped by unripe tomato-red stems *and* flowers, with no ruby lipstick-edging but a crisp, earthy scent of freshly dug lemons that hung in the air around it. Its litter mates had the stance, one or two had the scent, but no other had the rufous colouring. Nor did any of them, not excluding the reddle, have any dynastic ambition, which was mortifying, as I had promised seedlings to many a friend: a sure case of swallowing my gudgeons ere th'are catch'd.

My plant of *Helleborus corsicus*, now known as *H. argutifolius*, cost me 15p from a garage in Gloucestershire where I stopped to buy petrol in 1984. I planted it (*faute de mieux*, in the only space then cleared in those early weeks of residence) opposite my kitchen window in some miserably sour soil. This became worse with time, as it was beneath the stone wall where I fed the birds and was blanketed, between sweepings, with sunflower-seed husks. Subsequently, I read that these contain an inhibitor to prevent the growth of any plant other than sunflowers. At the time, neither I nor the hellebore knew this fact, so its vigour, if anything, was enhanced rather than inhibited, although that could have been due to the broken earth pipe, which earlier had perfumed that patch of soil. It grew so enormous, with twenty-eight flower stems one year: they stood strongly without the need of staking (unlike their usual spreadeagle tendency) and, when spent, were too thick to cut with secateurs. The flower trusses were so vast that a friend enquired the name of my green rhododendron. Interestingly, the dank hole where it was planted had sun only for half an hour at dawn and a scant hour at sunset: not exactly a sun-drenched Corsican hillside. Indeed, the little corporal became so imperial in size that the steps to the stream could no longer be negotiated and a neighbour's cat could hide in tragically successful ambush to catch the feeding birds. So exile became inevitable; the other side of the path a convenient St Helena. In those early salad days of *corsicus*-acquaintance, I did not realize that, to a hellebore, it is no better hopefully to travel, than to arrive. *L'Empereur est mort.* Sadly, there was no Second Empire as, once again, there were no seedlings – it is often too cold, even in late March, when this hellebore flowered, for bees to be on the wing (despite their Napoleonic associations), so pollination cannot be guaranteed for any early blooming plant.

In less *farouche* and intractable conditions, hellebores will set quantities of seed and, provided these are sown fresh, they germinate readily. Hybrids between species have been discovered in the wild as well as in the laboratory, *H. corsicus* being a compliant parent. Crossed with *H. lividus* to produce *H.* x *sternii* and with *H. niger* to result in *H.* x *nigercors*, strains are

available showing greater or lesser amounts of each prototype. The plant of
H. x sternii that I acquired is almost entirely *H. corsicus*: all to the good,
perhaps, given the frost-tender status of *H. lividus*. Conversely, my form of
H. x nigercors appears to be almost pure *H. niger*, except for a glazed film on
the leaves, like a crust of beeswing on old port. The next generation, using
H. x sternii as a parent, introduces varieties known as pewter form
and 'Boughton Beauty', which are worryingly high (for my cold garden) in
H. lividus genes, showing its pinkish grey-green colouration in their flowers,
and its beaten-metalwork foliage. After an easy-ish winter, both still look
as though it will be never glad, confident morning again.

Of all these glorious plants, my favourite is another English native
woodlander, *Helleborus viridis*. It is a springtime dawdler, being completely
deciduous, and later in flower than most – as late as May, here – so awakens
and stretches its first fingers above the 10-tog mulch duvet weeks after its
kissing cousins have been flowering. For all its tardiness, it can easily be
overlooked, and full many a green hellebore is born to blush unseen, as its
emerald flowers, the richest green of all, are identical in tone to its foliage.
You must stop, and bend – genuflect in obeisance, indeed – and peer; not
just glance as you rush past, thinking 'Don't the hellebores look nice?' *H.
viridis* is not nice; it is sensational. It is small, modest and green *de haut en
bas*. Envy-green but untouched by any other deadly sin, unlike visitors who
covet with cupidity.

Mongolia

THE ETIQUETTE TO FOLLOW when speaking to non-gardeners can be ticklish. Someone commented the other day on 'daffodils showing already' in my front garden. As this was just before Christmas I was a little surprised, but wondered to myself if October's planting of new narcissus bulbs were pushing through early, as new bulbs sometimes will. Only later did I realize he had been pointing to the emerging leaves of *Nerine bowdenii*, whose sparkling fondant-pink flowers had recently finished, so, although it looks bizarre, and frequently all ends in tears when the iron frosts enter their souls, it is regular timing for these entrancing South African bulbs. Thankfully, the need to disabuse him did not arise in this instance, as he did not persist in pointing out his 'daffodils'. But what does one do? If I say 'In fact those are nerines,' it sounds like pedantic showing off, particularly when a non-gardener may not know a nerine from a nectarine.

Those who know a little garden-lore are almost more difficult to accommodate as, quite naturally, they like to air their knowledge – and who does not? – but often with too sagacious an air, which leaves no room for amendment without wounding pride. 'Your forget-me-nots are being swamped by that hosta,' (pointing to *Brunnera macrophylla* 'Dawson's White'); 'Your pink wisteria will get too big there,' (*Robinia hispida*); 'Isn't your lilac late?' (*Ceanothus* × *delileanus* 'Gloire de Versailles'); 'That camellia is growing well,' (*Prunus lusitanica*). Manners maketh friends more than perfect gardeners, certainly and, as most friends are looking round my garden simply out of courtesy to me, rather than in desperation to learn anything, I can't see that such mistakes matter.

The mispronouncers can make life interesting, as keeping the conversation going about a particular plant without once saying its name is good for the vocabulary, if trying, from the angle of the laugh lurking in one's throat. Once I managed over twenty minutes chat about Mongolia stellata, mongolias in general indeed, without once pronouncing it either mongolia or magnolia. But isn't that being patronizing? Letting the poor sap go on forever thinking that mongolia is right. Am I respecting their sensitivity or my own, by not correcting them? But there are always people who ask for correction, wanting to learn, and others who prefer being wrong to being – as they see it – criticized.

Equally, does one blaze away with both botanical barrels of genus and species to everyone, always? Or does one hold fire with common names? This begs the question of what to do about all those wonderful plants with no common names, but labyrinthine botanical titles that present no problems if you are used to polysyllables – *Dicranostigma lactucoides, Lindelofia anchusoides* – but which might as well be dyslexic Polish if you are not.

Some plants are inscribed upon our minds only by their common names: bluebell, primrose, snowdrop, daisy, buttercup, bracken, harebell, oak, hazel and so on. It seems pretentious to refer to them by their botanical names: lupinus, antirrhinum, cheiranthus, lilium, except, I feel, where species are concerned. It seems equally foolish to use half-and-half names – the glossier seed catalogues are guilty of this – whereby the common name is used for the genus, and the specific epithet as if it were a cultivar, frequently with a capital letter, often in inverted commas. Recently I have seen Daisy 'Serotinum', and Snapdragon 'Brown Blanket', whose pidgin translation beats flat-pack self-assembly instructions for the inapposite presumption that *Leucanthemella serotina* and *Antirrhinum braun-blanquetii* would be so far beyond uneducated punters to pronounce that they would leave the seeds unbought. Doubtless Ruskin would approve, as he too favoured making up common names where traditional ones did not exist. But it is a moot point whether the crass names might deter the educated punter, thereby equalizing the numbers of non-buyers. Some seed companies side-step this by including all the names, under both A for *Antirrhinum* and S for snapdragon, which is as good a form of market research as any other.

Someone wondered recently why I had planted rhubarb on my streambank. I explained to a disbelieving face that it wasn't an edible one. I then gilded the lily by adding that it had pink flowers. As yet, still an infant, my seed grown *Rheum palmatum rubrum* has not flowered. It will be just my luck if it proves to be cream-flowered, instead of pink. Its leaves are not pronouncedly raspberry-flushed, even underneath, so I should not be surprised, or unduly disappointed, except that my non-gardening friend will remember, and crow.

Tools

A POOR WORKMAN BLAMES HIS TOOLS. Good tools, however, do help to make better gardeners. Happily, it is not inevitable that good should mean expensive. Many of my most successful and workmanlike pieces have been acquired for very little from house sales and secondhand shops. Best of all are those that are inherited: well-worn and polished by long usage, moulded to the palm and the boot, tempered steel and close-grained ash. Perhaps they give guidance by association, imparting a little of their hard-gained wisdom to the novice.

It takes some experience to recognize which is the most suitable tool for a particular job. The choice is not always as obvious as one might suppose. I used to claim that I could look after the whole garden with a hand fork and a pair of secateurs: my back was younger then. Now I would say a spade, but I still agree with the secateurs. I never walk round the garden without them. They are the first tool I reach from the shed. My hands are small, so I prefer the ratchet type. They are lightweight, and not so strong as to tempt me to try too bold a cut, although their action gives an extra fillip of help when needed.

Large pockets are vital: secateurs in the right, non-compostible rubbish in the left. This is picked up and dug up everywhere, and comprises the jetsam of previous lives: china shards, glass, plastic, baler twine and quantities of crumbling chicken wire. To these are added bits of bindweed, dandelion clocks and other horrors of an explosive nature, destined for the dustbin. As a result, both pockets are eternally filthy. I can never hope to emulate those immaculate lady gardeners who can potter in dry-cleanable corduroy, tweed and cashmere. I am covered, head to foot, with dirt on the driest day, quicker than you can say *Abutilon megapotamicum*. I get burrs in my hair, thorns rip my coat, mud-laden boots brush my trousers at every step, my nose runs, my fingers bleed . . .

The second tool for which I reach is my trusty builders' black bucket. Just one if I am deadheading or cutting back kecksies; at least three if I am planting. I need one to hold dried chicken manure, which is stirred into each planting hole, one for the inevitable dug out rubbish – stones, roots, perennial weeds and so on – and one for compostible treasure. I have recently been given a Tubtrug, and already I delight in its integral handles. The one real failing of the builders' bucket is that its handle will always catch in anything whippy or stiffly branching just as you are trying to empty it into the compost bin. Naturally there will be a gale blowing, so you will need one hand to hold back the bin lid; something catches in the loops of the bucket, the contents end up on the ground and the handle, now free, clonks you hard on the knuckles.

My next choice is a spade, if either planting or weeding. Weeds come in two categories – pulled by hand or dug out, usually, by spade. My spade is a much valued inheritance, which has been smoothed and softened over years of prudent use. It is a Lady's Border spade, so *parva sed apta mihi*. It has a D handle, which I favour, giving greater leverage for less effort. It feels part of me as I dig, and will I hope, last as long as I do.

Planting may also need a trowel. Mine is stainless steel with an elegant swan's neck. I prefer to plant with a spade, as in my soil, which is tenacious and stony, digging any hole is tough work. Frequently however, there is room for only a trowel. Bulb planting is purgatorial – agony, but ultimately worthwhile – at least, that is ever the hope. Finding a temporary berth for all the excavated spoil can be puzzling, especially when planting daffodils, as the borders are still quite full at that time, so there is little room to stand a bucket close enough to receive the excess with any convenience. Tulips, buried later, are less taxing. Even so, standing between clumps of plants, avoiding low-slung shrubs, digging the hole, reaching for both bulbs and soil to replace: the Quangle-Wangle with his head in his slipper has nothing on my contortions.

Digging virgin territory (of which there is plenty – the bottom third of the garden is still Terra Incognita) is done with a fork, for the simple reason that, until it has been winkled in between the stones and broken up the clay, nothing else would penetrate short of mattocks and crowbars. Indeed, both of these murderous instruments have had their fifteen minutes of fame before the court, but the jury is still out on whether or not they are as effective as a well-wielded fork.

I broke my Lady's Border fork – irritatingly one of the centre tines. With damaged outer ones cut off, the remaining tines make a useful two-pronged carving fork, just right for de-dockulating or prising other recalcitrants. My present digging fork is no lady, but is a sturdy beast of burden, a good and faithful servant.

By over-abuse, my little hand fork has been bent into a straight line, if I make myself clear. Now it is all but redundant, as the strain on one's wrist is too great, in compensating for the reduced ergonomics. Having lost the habit of using it, I have yet to remember to employ its replacement, a stainless steel pigeon pair with the trowel.

I do not use a hoe. I find it backbreaking for me and guillotining for too many serviceable seedlings and bulb noses. Hoes are perfect for kitchen garden weeding between rows of annual vegetables, although even there you might find worthwhile bits and bobs if you have mulched the beds with garden compost. Outside the kitchen garden, the borders are teazled with a sort of bent trident or overgrown toasting fork. A most helpful tool, but I covet the one my father used, which had a 2-foot handle instead of the 6 inches of mine.

And that concludes my most frequently employed *batterie de jardin*. Various loppers and saws, hammers and rakes, half-moons and besoms, kitchen knives and dibbers see use every year, to a varying degree; but those are not in the best friend class.

More accoutrement than tool, gloves have intermittent use, but never with a happy smile or a song in my heart. I endure them for dry-stone walling and for reclamation work, where the ground seems to comprise only nettles, rusty metal and broken glass, and also for hedge cutting and rose pruning. At least, I use the left hand glove for that; my right hand remains gloveless, because I could not even pick up secateurs wearing a glove, still less manipulate them. Gardening gloves and small hands are as incompatible as an ant in clogs. Their manufacturers persist, it seems, in the belief that only men need really tough gloves, as tough jobs are men's jobs. The gloves made for women are skimpy in comparison – being designed, I imagine, to prevent scratching one's nail polish as one picks sweet peas. And skimpy or otherwise, they are still too big. I buy the smallest available, but still there is at least an inch to spare above each finger and thumb. This can only worsen as the glove stretches with use, so that picking up anything becomes impossible, as all I am grasping is excess glove. It is frustrating, and means that mostly I don't bother — they are more trouble than they are worth, especially as, like over-large shoes, they rub blisters with all the free movement. When will glove manufacturers realize that many small women have to do their own rough work? Still more of us choose to do it. Please will someone make some strong but small gloves for strong but small women?

Lilies

TODAY I HAVE BEEN REPOTTING LILIES. All of my lilies are grown in pots: they are not clubbable plants. Some have such an aura of solipsism that they need the exclusivity of a pot as a hypothetical pedestal. Besides, I have to consider my heavy soil, which they loathe, and the voraciousness of slugs in the garden, that will chew the new spring shoots as they emerge or, indeed, prevent any emergence by squirming into the soil and gnawing at the bulbs themselves. This nuisance is not abated entirely by using pots, as scaling the side merely sharpens the slug's appetite, and all pots have 'Maternity Ward' scrawled on them in snail-trail writing – a luminous signpost for every expectant snail-mama. But by keeping the pots in the shed over winter, and by vigilance once the shoots begin showing, the worst depredations can be averted. I used to return all the pots to the shed each night throughout their growing season: the lilies were perfect as a result and I could have won the All-England Arm-Wrestling Championship. But my biceps rebelled, and the lilies now are grouped around the front door, which is meant to give a watchful eye more opportunity. Sometimes it works.

But lately, with an explosion in the vine weevil population, my lilies are declining in number and quality. The grubs will eat all the new roots, forcing the bulb to make more before it can produce a shoot, which may then be eaten again, or will so weaken the bulb that it gives up altogether, sitting there with neither root nor shoot. Keeping the pots inside over winter probably helps the grubs remain active. So you pay your money, and the pests take their choice. Lifting the pot to tease out the old, bone-dry compost in late winter, I can tell immediately whether I shall find weevil grubs. If the pot is clean there will be tightly woven, dry brown roots (all last year's, so useless to the lily) to be scratched away from the plump bulbs, whose vital roots, for this year, cream and fresh, are just beginning to thread through the compost below. If there are vine weevil grubs in the pot, there will be no roots at all, dry or fresh, and the bulbs will tumble out with the loose compost. Every grub must be dispatched – there is no point tipping the old pot-soil on to the garden or compost heap until you are certain it is clean, unless you want to diversify into weevil farming rather than gardening.

But now a third problem has arisen: a field mouse has discovered the dry compost and has delved down to the bottom of the pots to make a larder for stored peanuts. Each nut has been collected from the stone where I feed the birds, which is 30 feet away over arduous terrain, and carried through a hole chewed in the door (here's one I prepared earlier), and then into the pot. A dozen 10-inch-diameter pots were filled with peanuts to an average depth of 3 inches, which must represent several thousand nuts, with a corresponding doubling of journeys to and fro. Poor mouse: all that effort for nothing, as the nuts were cemented together by mould, to be scraped out with a knife.

I presume that in its excavations, the mouse would have eaten some of the bulbs, particularly the small stem bulbils, which I imagine would be sweeter than the big scaly monsters. Certainly a mouse burrowed into the pot containing my one bulb of *Nomocharis pardanthina*, the enchanting lily relative with liberal leopard spots of purple inside the pendent shell-pink flowers. Now it is no longer a bulb, but merely a basal plate with one minute root. I cannot imagine it will have the fortitude to grow again. Wretched mouse!

All in all, there were few pots that had escaped the attention of both pests. One that did holds *Lilium pyrenaicum*, the zest-yellow Turk's cap, or turn-around gentleman, as it is known here in the Marches. The bulb has a pungent smell – clearly the mouse liked it as little as I do. Another escapee is the *L. speciosum* hybrid 'Black Beauty', whose flowers, blackberry-juice pink and richly scented, have a curious undertone of unpleasantness that attracts bluebottles in squadrons, so perhaps, again, the bulbs were unattractive to the mouse. Certainly these are vigorous bulbs; each one made two or three more within a couple of years, so now I have two large potfuls, instead of the three bulbs with which I began four years ago. This largesse is unprecedented, as *L. speciosum* itself won't have me at any price.

I'm not aware that it is meant to be particularly tricky, although it is intolerant of lime, like many another good lily, so finds even the rainwater here unpalatable, and after a couple of years will ebb and disappear. The huge white-flowered hybrid 'Casa Blanca' has *speciosum* blood too, and I can't keep that one either. Nor, sadly, can I please L. *regale* for more than a few years. Tolerant of lime, it is more likely a virus problem (to which they are liable), which causes them to sicken. Their puissantly powerful scent and Biedermeier curves make them the perfect lily, but, alas, not for me; or at least, not for long.

Asiatic hybrids do better: nameless yellows, oranges and reds, which I've had for more than twenty years; some early flowering, some late; some well below the Plimsoll line of tasteful colour; some scented, most not. They are pleasant enough, and worth growing, especially a late-flowering citrus-yellow form, but they'll not make anyone gasp in wonder. 'Casa Rosa' also misses the indrawn breath of admiration: its colour is a delectable strawberry ice-cream pink; its scent has an element of its L. *longiflorum* ancestors, weakened with each intervening generation; but its deportment is a disgrace – each slovenly petal cannot quite be bothered to align itself with its neighbour or hold its own shoulders back, so there are gaps at the base of each trumpet and an air of dishevelment.

More salutary is *Lilium lancifolium*, the tiger lily, in burning-bright burnt-orange, parded with black, whose generous temperament is betrayed by Lewis Carroll's spiteful character. Even its propagation is effortless, as it has the courtesy to produce little brown bulbils along the stem, sitting in every leaf axil, waiting to be rubbed off and planted. What could be more accommodating? But in front of every silver lining there must always be a dark cloud: *Lilium lancifolium* carries a virus, which it will transmit to all other lilies within aphid-calling distance. So confine your tigers to an isolated lair, and keep them firmly labelled. Like princesses carrying haemophilia, tiger lilies themselves show no symptoms of the disease they spread.

To grow anything in pots implies the added task of washing those pots from time to time. It can be a great chore, enough to make one think enviously of the pot boys of old, who, for a shilling a week, would spend long winter days with their chapped hands in freezing water scrubbing all the heavy terracotta pots: so easy to stain, so laborious to clean. But provided you wash those you have just emptied, rather than let them hide in a corner and breed, their number will be controllable (I nearly wrote containable, which would have been a Pooterish pun too far). It is just one more small discipline that helps run a tight ship and ceases to be a chore once it becomes a habit.

The pots I use for lilies are old terracotta ones, hand-thrown, so the rippled clay rope, from which the pot was raised, is still evident on the inside. I like that, as it means more water will be held in the undulations. Most of them are made from a rough, rather gritty clay, with a narrow, rolled lip on the edge, and simple drainage holes poked through the base with the potter's fingers. Having thrown and smoothed his pot, the potter has lifted each one from his wheel, ready for firing. His handprints mark the sides, the gripping thumb slightly deeper than the fingers; the pressure has squeezed the circle out of true. This slight peccadillo has given a wobbly unconventionality to their shape, which makes stacking them difficult, but lends an added charm to anything grown in them: not just lilies, but agapanthus, eucomis, galtonia, cistus, chocolate cosmos. Anything, indeed, that will benefit from the extra drainage and evaporation, or needs the greater weight to stabilize tall top-growth, or, on a purely aesthetic note, whatever looks best in faded old terracotta – and most things do.

With the years the number is reducing: frost shales the edges, sometimes just the rim, more often shattering the pot to half its depth. These now shallow pans are still useful for sempervivums, sedums or for small bulbs. A pair of these flat billycock pans are planted with small-flowered violas for winter bedding on either side of the front door. If a wedge is broken from the top of a pot, it can pass its pensionable years in a quiet corner of the garden, upturned and stuffed with moss, as a snug shelter for toads. Those pots too badly smashed to be serviceable, can be press-ganged into a second career as drainage crocks in the base of their still-working colleagues.

These crocks must be washed too, as bacteria, vine weevil grubs, snail eggs and associated horrors will dwell happily in the cracks and crevices. Scrubbed and stored, ready for use, they will last forever. Plastic labels can never be immortal, but will live longer if they are pushed down below the rim of large pots – it is light that causes them to become brittle. In any case, all plants look better with their labels out of sight. I make mine from plastic washing-up liquid bottles. (Memo to the manufacturers of environmentally friendly liquids: opaque, straight-sided bottles are more practical for secondary use than clear plastic, curved and waisted bottles.) Indelible laundry-markers or freezer pens will write clearly on the bottle plastic; pencil will not show at all. I never put labels in the garden, so all of those that arrive with bought plants are recycled into further service to identify seedlings or cuttings. Both sides, top and bottom, can be used, and re-used if your writing is small, or the ink can be scrubbed off with a pan scourer. Wooden lollypop sticks are excellent too, and, being biodegradable, can be employed with rather more extravagance: twice is their limit; the soil stains them black below compost level, and they rot at the neck. This can be irritating if your pots of seeds have not yet germinated, and adjacent lollystick labels have collapsed together: whose was which?

Equally annoying, again with long-dormant seeds, is ink that fades or washes off before germination. No doubt more viable but slow seeds have been discarded due to a faded label than for any other reason. At risk of sounding like an instruction manual: tip out the compost from ungerminated pots (whether faded or unfaded) and use it as top-dressing for potted shrubs or lilies. Often the seeds will germinate, given this second chance. The really well organized gardener would add the still-legible seed labels to the top-dressed pot too, as a belt-and-braces measure of identification.

How?

I WAS NOT BORN INTO THE horticultural purple, nor with a silver trowel in my mouth. My father was a good gardener because he was a man of infinite patience, with the gentle quietness that is appreciated by all living things, whether animal or vegetable. He always found time to stand and stare, and learnt much from such observance. A dedicated solitary potterer, he taught me that effective gardening is not just hard work followed by crossing-off achievements on an endless list of jobs to be jobbed. It must have periods of this-ing and that-ing, as you think, and settle things, and make decisions: digging a fork into your personal subsoil, to discover the why of your own garden philosophy and not just the how.

As a young man he had learnt how to care for the vines growing in a glasshouse in his parents' garden, enjoying the pruning, spurring and thinning precision of their nurture, as much as the courtly presentation to friends of the perfectly spaced bunch of sweet dessert grapes, nestling in a basket on a bed of its own leaves. The vines were planted outside and trained through the wall into the glasshouse, as was the buttery-yellow Tea rose 'Maréchal Niel'. This was the best rose of all in his estimation; it had been bred in 1864, but became the quintessential Edwardian rose, grown in this way.

An Edwardian himself, he had the experimental mind of the gentleman-amateur. Testing the one-way-streets of xylem and phloem was a favourite garden pastime: inserting cuttings upside down, to see which shrubs would be vigorous enough to root, despite their sudden cul-de-sac existence. Hydrangeas frequently would manage it, as would hardy fuchsias, which he always pronounced 'futures', and both my sister and I grow upside-down jasmines that he rooted.

One February morning, despite his firm belief in self-dependence, he bore my juvenile offer to help in the garden with characteristic fortitude. So I learnt about the 'future' that day in both senses. Firstly, I learnt that one should cut back the previous year's wood to allow new growth from the base but that one should not disturb the accumulation of leafy litter over the crown until later in the season when the shoots were growing fast, and frosts were lessening. And then, when inevitably I found a cut stem that was shooting already, he showed me how to take a hardwood cutting, pushing it deep into the soil in a sheltered corner of the garden, where it grows still. The magic worked, for me and for the cutting. Those roots took hold of me, binding me to the earth with such a will, that, like Antaeus, I regain spent strength only by its touch.

My mother taught us, from a very early age, to recognize wild flowers. I have a little pocket flora with her annotations in faded azure ink — centaury, Braunton Burrows, 1962; brooklime, River Dove, 1959; toadflax, Guest hospital, Dudley, 1963; primroses, Tan-y-bryn, 1960. Her interest was the foundation of my interest, and I am eternally grateful for such fascinating early guidance. Once encouraged to see a native plant as not just a pretty flower but as the result of its successful growth in a suitable location, it becomes second nature to associate plant with habitat and vice versa. It is an important concept to grasp when selecting plants: those that grow naturally in similar habitats, even though they may hail from different continents, will look right when planted together in the garden.

So when people say to me, 'How do you begin?' I am aware that I have never had to make a conscious decision to begin gardening, as it is simply something I have done all my life; as necessary to my wellbeing as blinking and breathing. Indeed, my own phototropism requires feet in the soil, face to the light, fingers in the green, for at least some portion of each day, else I feel pot-bound, choked with liverwort. It strikes me as the most appalling deprivation that a person can reach full-blown adulthood without ever having planted anything.

How then does one start? A house has been bought, garden attached and, for the sake of your blood pressure, we will pretend that no builders were necessary, so your topsoil is in the right place. The standard shibboleth is to wait a whole year to see what comes up. For reluctant gardeners, the year would fly all too fast; for normal people it would be impossible to wait so long. But in most cases this is not necessary, particularly if you buy your house in spring. At that time of year the early spring bulb leaves will still be in evidence, showing you where not to dig; herbaceous plants will be on the move, ditto. Even if the intelligent vendors had planted sheets of autumn crocuses, the foliage will be there, in spring, to guide you. Collect plenty of canes, and mark what to avoid when you start your own planting.

Then begin your watching brief, and learn to look with judgment on what grows in your garden. If you like it, keep it; if you don't much care for it, identify it at least before you dispose of it – preferably to a friend, in case you change your mind or, more importantly, if it is rare. But above all, keep looking. We rarely look; we glance with the brevity of a lens-shutter action and prefer to do our viewing safely outlined by television and computer screens, or the pages of a magazine, fostering the belief in our two-second attention span that requires constant fast-forward stimulation. Trees have a two-millennia attention span, all from the same spot; we have much to learn from them.

Watching light intensity is vital: noting how the available light throughout the seasons affects colours, shadows, corners of the garden, the soil. Mediterranean light, whether at Portofino or Polperro, vivifies strong colours to jewel-like glory; it sharpens the shadows, intensifies the depths of corners, parches the soil. In the soft, wet light of gardens in the English North West, these heavy colours are fogged on overcast days, dimmed by damp; whereas, fresher shades stay clear, even when mist seals a cataract growth over the visual garden. Colour exists only through the amount of light it absorbs and reflects, which is why all-white plantings work well in the stuffy gloom of some town gardens, but would be unbearably snow-blinding on a Greek island.

Look, then, at your own plants and light, and visit other gardens to do the same. Much can be learnt from other gardens: most importantly, what not to do in your own. Slavish copying of plant groupings or colours will never be as satisfying as marching to your own drum. As your plant knowledge increases you will realize that fashionable plants and colours are not necessarily the best. Reading will widen your plant horizons still more, not just those books that display calendar gardens shot through filters and vaseline, but those that fertilize one's mental garden. Only connect, as E.M. Forster advised about life; gardening requires a holistic approach too.

Inevitably there will be areas of your new garden that you would like to redesign to your own taste or needs. I am a great believer in consulting the genius of the place rather than a designer. However good the designer may be, and very few are very good, it will then be their garden, not yours. This may suit your requirements exactly, but don't belittle your own talents by thinking it is the only option, particularly if the re-jigged area is to be merely a matter of replanting. You may prefer to design your planting scheme on paper, marking out swathes or blocks and counting the number of plants you need to buy. Or you might like to make a list of the plants you want to include, acquire them, and then make your design on the border itself by moving the pots around until the sequence pleases you. I prefer the latter approach. Borders designed on paper remind me of plans for dinner parties, showing the table with spaces for names. The most brilliant mix of people might be assembled on paper, but not even an experienced hostess can make them perform together in reality if each individual is feeling dull, or ill, or just plain rude. Similarly, in the garden (rather than at the drawing board), you can lead a plant to the border but you cannot make it prink.

As you learn more about your garden's capabilities and restrictions, your reading and research will save you precious years of wasted growth as well as the expense of unsuited plants. Planting rhododendrons in strongly alkaline soil, or tender salvias in a cold, shady border, is like planting your own hopes and ambitions against the north wall of life: you are simply adding to your difficulties. You may be desperate for height to block out some neighbouring horror, or to mitigate a draught. It is not necessary to spend a week's salary on mature shrubs – they will probably die from shock anyway. Plant fast-track shrubs, like buddleia, malva or ceanothus, that believe in one crowded hour of glorious life. Living hard and dying young, they can be used as catch crops to fill spaces quickly between more leisurely plants or to nurse a shrub that might be tender in youth without a little shelter.

Charles II wanted everyone to be able to live under their own vine and fig tree. Doubtless his Medici background encouraged southern gardening tastes; for much of the country raspberries and plums might have inspired easier husbandry. My Bill of Gardening Rights would decree that every man is entitled to his own compost heap. It is fundamental to the how of gardening, and must be embraced (literally) by those who wish to become gardeners. Turning the compost is not one of the pretty jobs, but gardening is not just playing with the soft pedal down. Besides, like weeding, it gives you something to think about while you talk.

Looking and reading; that's all there is to it really. Except time, energy, patience, opportunity, money, flair, hard work, a cast-iron spine and a friable mind.

Evergreens

IN GARDENS AS COLD AS THIS there is indeed a cruel law agin the wearin' o' the Green: these are not benign conditions for evergreens. With frosts so stark, and gales so bleak, they stand little chance of processing any nourishment at all when their leaves look as though they have been swiped by a flamethrower. But dropping all the redundant foliage incites further risk, as the usually protected wood is then exposed to the full blast of the weather. Tender bark will split, just above the soil in most cases, and ice will spread to the heart of the defenceless shrub. It is a lingering death, working slowly from the ground up, leaving green tips and stems to give false hope that it can and will recover. Last year, after a relatively easy winter, I lost a *Viburnum* x *burkwoodii* in this way. Only a few years old, it had grown lustily from a 6-inch cutting to a robust 4-foot dome, and was covered with flower buds for the coming spring even as it died. It had dropped every leaf in previous, harder winters, but those had been more consistently cold, rather than the phony-war style start to winter last year.

V. x *burkwoodii*'s smallish leaves should have coped — it is the large-leaved evergreens that are most vulnerable to both wind and frost — but they are mat in texture, which means that they will not shrug off moisture like the wax-coated conifers or shiny hollies. This absorbency affects grey- and silver-leaved shrubs too: their woolly coats are designed to deflect hot sunshine and to hold on to the scant moisture that comes their way in their native haunts. The Marches not being the maquis, the design spells disaster: rosemary and lavender, santolina, helichrysum, artemisia and cistus all hunch their thin shoulders against the damp and ice, and cringe at the cold, heavy soil. As wan and pallid as consumptives, they wheeze their way to an early death.

Nor can senecios tolerate the conditions for long (if I call them brachyglottis no one will know what I mean, even if it is now correct). The

great silvery salvers of *B.* (Dunedin Group) 'Sunshine' always struggled to
emulate a dirty pewter charger here, hating the rheumy winters and shrill
springs, which continued to knock back adventurous new growth until May
or June, so that the increasingly gnarled basal branches were all too evident
for most of the year. Cuttings root with gratifying ease, so one is urged to
renew 'Sunshine' as one would lavender. If the cuttings grew on into the
cobby little bushlets that warmer, drier gardens enjoy, I should continue to
renew them both with enthusiasm, but as they are wizen from birth, here,
the habit soon palls. There are better plants on which to waste one's time.

Such as the oddly neglected *Brachyglottis* (*née Senecio*) *monroi*, which is a more
distinguished, ladylike plant than the ubiquitous 'Sunshine'. It is said to be
somewhat less hardy, but perversely, I found it tougher, as, by giving it the
best drainage possible on the edge of a dry wall, it was exposed to every gasp
of wind and weather. It shrugged off everything for fifteen years, until two
long winters of persistently biting temperatures (with daytime lows of 14°F,
nights even lower, and a couple of nights plummeting to a numbing −18°F)
killed the stalwart old trooper in the end, as well as a self-layered shoot, and,
to my chagrin, the safety-net cuttings I had taken. It had been a plant of
great presence, sitting atop its wall. Compact but never prim, relaxed but not
untidy, it rarely needed pruning as such, merely the pinching-out of any
frosted tips. It flowered only once, in the summer following the first of the
two mortally-wounding winters, when it tried to hedge its bets on unlikely
survival with a seed or two that, sadly, came to nothing.

Perhaps in warmer surroundings it would loll with the gangling
gaucheness of its sister 'Sunshine' and flower with the same profusion of
rough ragwort daisies, necessitating annual deflowering if you don't care
for them. I don't mind the flowers; they're an eyeful of sour yellow, it's true,
but I should tolerate far worse for the sake of the icing-sugar whiteness of
their stems and buds. The flowers are not really the point; it is the foliage
that matters – all snow and hoarfrost on 'Sunshine', but warmer on *B.
monroi*, with a cupreous tinge to the silver, like old Sheffield plate, on the
upper surface of the leaves, and thick ivory suede below, which shows in
titillating glimpses beneath the goffered edges. This colouring, like
lavender-blue, is a universal adaptor, looking appropriate and supportive
whatever its neighbours may be.

Lonicera nitida is another winter casualty, being just on the cusp of hardiness. Surprisingly, the plain green species seems the most sensitive, and the white-edged variety 'Silver Beauty' the most resilient. 'Baggesen's Gold' is threadbare pinchbeck here, so I no longer bother with it. I planted a little circular hedge of the species around the feet of *Davidia involucrata*, the fluttering handkerchief tree. The hollow between the two is filled with a giant form of *Hyacinthoides hispanica* that turned up under a holly tree in my parents' garden. The flowering stems grow up to 2 feet tall, carrying large bells of a lively blue. They are all over and done with before the davidia puts on a leaf, so each has the stage to itself, except for the quiet encirclement of the little hedge. That, at least, was the idea, but reality rearing its head made the arrangement somewhat less restful. Each winter the hedge would be killed to the ground in chunks here and there; never the whole lot, and never in one fell swoop. It would begin to recover by midsummer, and by summer's end I would need to be shearing it weekly to keep it looking presentable. Every tiny sprig dropped would root within half a minute, which seemed useful at first – to replace winter losses. I have never been an advocate of low-maintenance gardening, but when one plant requires so much assistance, and still looks miserable for most of the year, it is time to think again. The little rondel hedge has been transformed into box, which is like Bunyan's pilgrim – one here will constant be, come wind, come weather.

There are llamas in a nearby village but, as yet, no camels, so box (which is poisonous to them) was already well represented in the garden. The common *Buxus sempervirens* is grown in clipped balls that form a quincunx around the septic tank (on the principle that what can't be disguised should be emphasized). I grow *B. sempervirens* freeform as a large shrub too. This is good for cuttings, for its deliciously pungent spring flowers and for its protective mass as a windbreak. A slower growing, yellow-splashed version seems to be forming itself (with minimal help) into a small golden globule. A dual-purpose plant, this: clipping removes all the gingerbread gilding for midsummer, which makes it less aggressive with the adjacent mass of high-season colour; then the gold grows back again to grab the attention in winter among the dying-back tones of dun and umber and to chant in a springtime descant with the daffodils.

I do not grow the dwarf *B.s.* 'Suffruticosa'. It is not so hardy, and I have yet to succumb to the tyranny of edged beds. It says much for my brain or morals, no doubt, that I prefer a less compartmental approach, with looser edges. With the dreaded box blight marauding the country, it would be as well to stay loose, perhaps. If I developed a taste for the stiffened sinews of dwarf hedges, only to be blighted, I should have difficulty replacing them, as the standard shrubs for this are even less hardy than the vulnerable dwarf box. Is its predisposition to box blight anything to do with the fact that it is propagated entirely from cuttings, I wonder, leaving every offspring boxlet subject to its parent's diseases? I believe that this same vegetative identicality was the determining factor in the spread of Dutch elm disease, as elms grew almost exclusively from suckers.

The larger-leaved form, *B.s.* 'Latifolia Macrophylla' is markedly slow-growing and naturally pyramidal in habit, which makes for negligible trimming. This is all to the good, as its leaves, twice the size of the common box, show, too obviously, where they have been spliced, which detracts from their otherwise constitutional neatness. Mine, making a short, square hedgeling this time, surrounding *Chimonanthus praecox*, has an occasional shoot pinched when it steps out of line, but needs no actual shearing. This is taller than the davidia's encircling hedge, as a screen to keep away rough winds from the ankles of the susceptible wintersweet, which is as wary of draughts as Mr Woodhouse. The inner space has a sprinkling of delicate pink *Cyclamen cilicium*, then double snowdrops and ice-blue *Crocus chrysanthus* 'Blue Pearl' as company for the spicily-scented winter flowers of the chimonanthus, and a further dusting of *Anthericum ramosum* to solace its rather dull summer foliage. Above the shining box square the anthericum's tiny white stars float with ethereal grace.

B.s. 'Kingsville' (now known as *B.microphylla* 'Compacta') differs in habit from the stiffly upright carriage of these other forms of box. It is softer and more billowy in growth, not floppy exactly, but it reclines wantonly on its elbows and spreads out its skirts in a lax swirl of yellowish green, which adopts a distinctly rufous wash in winter. The leaves are small and ovoid, so would be clippable by those of a topiarizing bent, but mistakes would long be visible, with its leisurely rate of growth.

Along with box, I grow the other native evergreens: yew, juniper, holly, privet and ivy. Also, still in a pot, is a Scots pine, *Pinus sylvestris*, our only native conifer, which I grew from seed, and want to plant on the bank over a culverted stream at the far end of the garden, where it merges into woodland. My plan is to 'mound' plant it – that is, on top of the soil with its roots spread out decorously, then covered with good loam and anchored by stones to hold it in place until it has established itself. This is how the followers of the Georgian Picturesque movement planted those trees, whose serpentine surface roots look like Laocoön's struggles carved in wood rather than ancient marble. Shropshire, however, is not native pine country. So after all the effort (which it would be – imagine the stakes and guy-ropes necessary to keep it upright against gales for its first decade or so), my Charlie tree might look as incongruous as bagpipes at a cricket match.

But the other natives look right. Yew would give a good account of itself on the top of the pyramid of Cheops. Holly, somehow, would not, being perhaps too much associated with carols and cold weather. There was a small bush of holly in the garden – I presume the usual *Ilex aquifolium* – when I arrived here: a gift to my predecessor from a neighbour (now both dead). It has grown strongly so I have clipped it lately into a sort of dumb waiter or hose-in-hose lollipop. It fruits little and seldom, doubtless because I have seen no other hollies in the immediate neighbourhood. This is unusual, as traditionally they were planted in hedgerows to give an evergreen marker for land-drains. But I have just planted another in convenient flirting distance for my spinster-of-this-parish holly, which I hope will lead to a fruitful relationship.

My columnar junipers, *Juniperus communis* 'Hibernica', are Irish, of course, rather than English, and are among the loveliest things in the garden. They please me at all seasons, perhaps most of all in late spring, when their sea-green flush of new growth begs to be ruffled, but with care and the grain: it is as prickly as a bee with hives. I bought one to plant as an exclamatory eye-catcher at the head of some steps. Clumsily, I broke a piece off as I planted it, so I made the exclamation in stereo by pushing it in, as an impromptu cutting, on the other side of the steps. So now I have la Paix et la Prospérité, like all French peasant farmers (except, of course, that theirs are pencil-slim cypresses). Historically, la Paix never grows well, as there is so little peace in the world. I felt serenely peaceful when I planted mine, but rather poor, so it is la Prospérité which is the laggard here.

I dislike seeing those ugly, flat-topped, grimly wire-corseted Irish yews and junipers, unable to stand on their own and stuffed with dead leaves and mouse-nests. I am determined that mine shall not be wired, so I have started as I mean to go on – clipping the side shoots to keep them narrow but bushy, and sturdy enough to be zimmerless to the end. Already they have been sorely tried by gusting gales bending them into a capital C, followed by heavy snowfalls weighing down each strained branch. They have also been used as scratching posts by most of the cats in the county. So far, however, all is well for the sea-green incorruptibles and their statement is becoming emphatic.

Privet, *Ligustrum ovalifolium*, is another deciduous 'evergreen' here. A painfully slow-growing golden form was given to me as a cutting twenty years ago, and it is still under 3 feet tall, despite wall protection. It is a genial glimmer in clement early winters. Later it will be stripped to naked twigs, whose shivering is almost audible until it gathers sufficient energy to redress itself – usually not until May, often not until July. Poor thing, it has little joy in its life, and I am not very appreciative of the effort it makes. But it grows in a bone-dry spot, tight up against a windy corner, acting as a filtering buttress for the border beyond, so it is unlikely that anything else would do even half as well. It rests its case.

Ivy should be obligatory for all gardens, especially, as Michael Jefferson-Brown once said, as it is as hardy as a pig's snout. It pays its rent wherever it may be established and it is an essential plant for wildlife: holly blue butterflies use it alternately with holly itself for both egg-laying and food; late wasps and overwintering insects depend upon the nectar-rich, autumn flowers; clattering wood pigeons and bickering thrushes gorge on the berries. All common ivy, *Hedera helix*, will mature into a non-clinging tree form given time, but cuttings can be taken from these shrubby growths that will remain always in this grown-up, arborescent form. They're meant to be tricky, but I took mine before I knew that, so they rooted with ease: the confidence of ignorance can sometimes pay dividends. Personally, I like to see ivy mantling trees, although I know its weight can prove murderous, even though its aerial roots can't – it is not parasitic. Better still is to see it in hedges, where its weight cannot hurt (as it will support itself in tree form all the quicker for lack of a taller climbing frame). Its evergreen gleam will block all the gaps at ground level, and its sickly-sweet but evocative scent will be at nose level. Snug roosts and nesting platforms will then be available for birds, and also the mice which otherwise would disfigure your Irish yews and junipers.

I don't like to see ivy cloaking houses. Not because it damages pointing – it doesn't if the pointing is sound to start with – but because it holds so much dirt and dust, as well as most of its own dead leaves, so the ivy wallpaper, flocked with grubby spiders' webs, never looks pristine. It quickly reaches and grows into eaves, and still more rapidly starves the soil beneath itself. Besides all this, there are several hundred much more beautiful plants to grow on house walls that will benefit from the residual warmth – a luxury scorned by the tough pig's snout. Leave ivy for the wilder areas of the garden.

Having suggested the wilder areas, ivy can be magnificently formal too: arborescent forms can be clipped as rigidly as yew, like the enormous conical tree ivy at Herterton; still-juvenile forms can be trained and restrained over wires, like the dwarf ivy hedge at Preen Manor. Some need rallying rather than restraint, as development is imperceptible: the miniature *Hedera helix* 'Spetchley' has leaves of barely half an inch and an annual growth-rate to match. Some variegated forms are tardy as infants but, like most late-developers, they race ahead in adolescence. The frilly-edged forms behave similarly. There is a pretty one with pink tinges to its petticoats (although not all the time; some years blink and you miss it). I wish it were called Crispa Rosea or something equally descriptive and suitable to the ivy's dignity. Instead, blush to tell, it is called 'Pink 'n' Curly', which I despise most particularly for the abbreviated 'and'. How could plant breeders go down that Toys 'R' Us, fish 'n' chips avenue of illiteracy and gimmickry? The name is shamefully crass but the plant is good.

I like to thread ivy through low walls, and keep it clipped loosely as a ruffled hem. I plant it beneath evergreen shrubs, too, as a serviceable blanket for otherwise bare soil – the small-leaved, variegated forms are especially useful for this living mulch as they lighten what can be a rather dim oubliette. The dry conditions keep them compact. Most of my ivies are nameless, being liberated from the mixed bowls of house plants one is given from time to time. But three whose names I do know, which are staunch performers, are 'Buttercup', in lucent topaz-yellow throughout, 'Persian Carpet', whose gently lobed leaves with their strongly delineated white veins are (at a glance) indistinguishable from *Cyclamen hederifolium*, and 'Duckfoot', which is an accurate description of this polished, splay-footed little ivy.

Now Barabbas was a beech tree . . . robbing the soil around its own feet. I planted a young beech on the wall above the stream, as part of a ribbon of shrubs, mostly deciduous, for a windbreak (of course) but also to provide the eye with a natural barrier in summer rather than leave the border plants in front hanging in mid-air, and as a veil in winter through which to glimpse the water meadows beyond. Intermittently beaded upon the ribbon are evergreens, to cajole the eye and to give asylum to small birds. I thought that the beech, *Fagus sylvatica*, kept young and winter-brown by clipping, would contrast well with the deciduous stems and the rich lustre of holly and box. But the foxy foliage was invisible against the bracken-encrusted bank beyond the meadow, and nothing prospered beneath it, so despite the silken fans of its tender beechen-green that I loved in kindly springs, I changed it for yet more evergreen gloss. The only large-leaved evergreen (non-native this time) that laughs at the adverse conditions here is the Portugal laurel, *Prunus lusitanica*. It doesn't turn a hair and looks cat-sleek and content throughout the most trying winter. Its polished foliage is regularly mistaken for a camellia and, frankly, it would not surprise me if, one spring, it put on huge, double, striped camellia flowers: it is so capable and unperturbed by life, that anything is possible.

SPRING

SOME YEARS, SPRING ARRIVES in a quiet, conspiratorial fashion, unnoticed as it slips stealthily among the trees. There is no first day of spring, merely a growing realization that a mist of green is spreading and thickening, despite the weather: cruel gales batter the blossom that the frost has not already singed; early lambs flounder through blizzards; daffodils, spreadeagled by cascading rain, are gnawed by slugs before they can lift their heads again. I agree with Cowper that our severest winter is commonly called the spring.

Harsh weather is bad enough in winter's dormancy, but is far worse when delicate new growth has unfurled, only to be blackened and scorched. The effort to produce more may be made only at the expense of flowers. But the domino-effect of the frost can have far more serious implications than just loss of colour. Where new top-growth has been shrivelled, unseasonal exposure of the soil surrounding the crown will follow, so repeated frosts can reach to the heart of the now unprotected plant; sudden warm sunshine (the customary stalker of frost in spring) will dry out its roots; weed seed will blow in to compete for food and moisture; slugs have unrestricted access to the damaged crown and can smell rotting stems across three counties. All of these will weaken further the already vulnerable plant. Persistent frosts, at this time, with the sap rising, may kill hardy plants that have sailed through a ferocious winter.

There are days of despair, now, when I wonder why I bother. Everything is either eaten, smashed, dug out, ripped by gales, rotted by rain or tortured by killing frosts. The whole garden adopts a Mrs Gummidge gloom – all lone and lorn. And then I tighten my mental belt and look again. Always there will be something to rub off the rust and restore faith: a tiny bead of green growth appearing on a forsaken shrub, a blunt bulb-nose breasting the soil, viburnums tossing their scent abroad or the tattered splendour of an overwintered peacock butterfly.

Certainly this is a time when I need an extra hinge in my back as I quarter the ground with my nose 2 inches above the surface of the soil, questing like a truffle hound for signs of life. It is an exciting as well as a dispiriting time. The sound ore that has passed through the crucible of winter and survived (unaccountably, sometimes) always outweighs the dross that succumbs. But the victims are either young and new – so untried, and now, not to be given a chance – which is sad; or else they are old friends, which is worse. The past winter has been relatively benign, so I am not expecting any major losses caused by the cold, although there is still ample time for fathomless frost to deliver the *coup de grâce*. Hatching must be done, ere counting is begun.

This year, *Prunus mume* 'Beni-chidori' is swarming with sweetly-scented, deep-pink flowers where, normally, it struggles to make much of a show as plummeting temperatures trash the buds, then knock back new shoots after any blossom has faded. As a result, it is a poor shape, raw-boned and pinched, so its late-summer scragginess is screened a little by the climbing *Aconitum volubile*, with sapphire monkshood flowers. Late to shoot from its deep tubers, the aconite is still below ground when the prunus blooms. Warmer gardens, particularly those in urban surroundings, where the dazzling 'Beni-chidori' would look glamorous indeed against the white walls of Stucconia, can expect to see their *P. mume* flowers at Christmas, if not earlier. Mine will manage Easter, provided the paschal moon is favourably late.

Golden Numbers must also control the flowering of my *Prunus* x *subhirtella* 'Autumnalis Rosea' as, despite its common name, the autumn cherry seldom starts before Lent, here, and even then only when frosts permit. Although the pink-flowered form can be later to bloom than the white, I had hoped to counterbalance that by choosing a bush form rather than a single-stemmed tree: low, bushy growth is said to encourage more flowers. A further dissuasion: tree forms can be awkward to keep to an attractive silhouette ('prune us' is not an invocation; most of them despise trimming). They tend to be wide-spreading, which is not a co-operative contour in a small garden, whereas the V shape of the bush form allows close planting with access for light and rain. It is also more sympathetic to the support of a fairly sedentary climber, such as the non-clinging *Clematis* x *aromatica*, with intense purple stars, cream-stamened and hawthorn-scented, in late summer, or the cluster-flowered Rose 'Blush Noisette' (lately returned to its French roots as 'Noisette Carnée ').

Amelanchier canadensis is perhaps the comeliest of all spring-flowering trees. Its blossom is a better shape, and more substantial than a comparable single-flowered white cherry; its new foliage is caudled with molten caramel and honey. When grown on its own roots, it has an arching, thickety habit, so never looks stiff and gaunt, as do many of the prunus family. Nor does it suffer from the range of pests and diseases that martyr cherries and peaches. Amiable, graceful, it pays an annual dividend of unfailing fireworks in the autumn – by August, it will be spangled with sporadic scarlet leaves among the green; a few weeks later, it will be consumed in a pyre of coral and crimson.

Blossom, this year, on the bird-sown wild plums and damsons, is spectacular – a blizzard of snowy white. This happens so rarely that I notice it all the more. The dearth is always due to frost. I would rather it were bullfinches; a treeful would be better than blossom. Blackthorn foams from every hedgerow, parian-white. 'Sallies are wakin',' comments a neighbouring farmer, as the willows stretch their tasselled catkins. Yes, and so are the birds: a wren explodes into stentorian song each dawn from the hedge across the lane and a thrush croons the evening sun down. So, indeed, is the garden.

Apart from snowdrops, one of the first bulbs to waken here is the powder-blue *Scilla mischtschenkoana* 'Tubergeniana', whose flowers begin opening when still out of sight below ground, like someone beginning a conversation before they are quite in the room. The stems extend as the flowers continue to open, gathering attention as they increase. It is a pretty thing, and ease itself to grow, but is seldom seen in gardens. Being so early is a bonus but, along with many other blue flowers, it would be worthy of its small space at any time of the year. The colour blue is said to be favoured by freedom-loving nations for their flags, and perhaps for their flowers too: the bluebell has recently been declared the national wildflower of the United Kingdom.

Muscari, chionodoxas and *Scilla sibirica* continue the blue theme, although freedom to procreate is not encouraged – by the weather, mostly, which deters the bees; but by me in the case of the giant *Muscari latifolium*, which has no truck with self-restraint. Nevertheless, it is a valuable plant, its single leaf encompassing the emerging scape like a blue-green arum lily. This will extend to a sturdy 12 inches or more, with the two-tone blue flowerhead covering almost half of that. Mine are planted to box and cox with *Codonopsis clematidea*, still hibernating as yet, but whose rapid growth will hide the bedraggled bulb leaves of both the muscari and the later-flowering, raspberry-fudge coloured *Nectaroscordum siculum*.

Blended into this brew are clumps of fancy celandines: *Ranunculus ficaria* 'Tortoiseshell' has mottled leaves with a metallic bloom, and varnished yellow flowers; *R.f.* 'Coppernob' has flowers of glowing orange and leaves of dark, bitter chocolate. Celandine was a nymph spurned by all for being of too-easy virtue; but a change of clothes seems to result in a change of habit, as these coloured forms appear to be more circumspect than the wilding. Even that is not to be despised where its extremes of behaviour can be useful: the sparkling sheet of polished brass, with its ability to spread from wainscot to wall with joyous fervour, then its contrasting self-effacement for the rest of the year. I like to plant celandines around the slender springtime skirts of herbaceous plants that expand to a summertime crinoline. *Euphorbia palustris* is a particular favourite for this treatment, as it appreciates the same conditions of damp, hefty soil, and its sharp-yellow, spring-flowering bracts are timed and toned to perfection with the shining brilliance of the large shaggy flowers of *Ranunculus ficaria* 'Picton's Double' and the precise, green-eyed double pompons of 'Collarette'. White forms of the celandine surge from the base of a low wall that will be overhung, all summer, with *Polemonium reptans* and *Anaphalis triplinervis* – one of the few silver-leaved plants to thrive in torpid soil; unlike artemisias, which have the *outre-tombe* lassitude of the absinthe addict. A wall base is the perfect situation for a predella of primroses, but as they do most of their growing after they have flowered, instead of diving below periscope depth like the celandines, a wall beneath cantilevered herbaceous growth will not suit their thirsty souls.

Unsurprisingly, primroses do well here: rich soil, cool air and plenteous rain are all much to their taste. The wild primrose, *Primula vulgaris*, is better than many named cultivars, so I welcome its appearance wholeheartedly, wherever it may sow itself. The white form, *P.v. alba*, is not so vigorous, sadly, and my frequent supplications to 'make an effort, Mrs Dombey', meet with scant success. The double forms of the wilding, and of the white, have been failures too, whereas the coloured doubles are no trouble at all, particularly when grown in full sun. I leave them in peace, without the suggested annual splitting and replanting, until they show signs of requiring pastures new. The clump will become thinner in the centre and, on lifting, will fall apart into individual plants, to be tidied up and reseated in fresh soil with a marinade of muck. This seems much kinder to the plant than the aggression involved in tearing it out of the ground and carving into the crown with a knife; it is kinder to the indolent gardener too. Some need attention sooner than others: the old double 'Quaker's Bonnet'or 'Lilacina Plena' will want replanting every three or four years (on soil such as mine); the tea-stained pink 'Sue Jervis' perhaps a year longer. A small plant of the double white jack-in-the-green 'Dawn Ansell', however, was planted in 1996 and has had no further fuss since beyond a mulch of garden compost every couple of years. It makes a perfect dome 16 inches across with no leaves visible except for the small green ruffs behind each flower. It looks like a Victorian bride's posy.

These viviparous forms of primrose are especial favourites, with a good proportion coming true from seed and, periodically, disporting themselves spontaneously upon a plant of normal growth. When this happens I peg down the ruffed flower stem with a stone. Usually they will grow roots and flourish, even when severed from mama's apron strings, but so far they have always reverted to normal, ruffless growth the following year, and ever after. A shame, as the incipient jack-in-the-green forms of *P. denticulata* and gold-laced polyanthus were heart-warming. Margery Fish claimed she could never persuade them to root, which is surprising, as her skills were far superior to my botched efforts, and her soil rather similar.

Other primulas arrive unannounced, their parentage confused, but usually worth their space, often worth splitting to increase their contribution. One such is an engaging cross between the oxlip, *Primula elatior* and (I think) *P. 'Wanda'*, a tried and trusted charmer which an old friend called, not without reason, The Wanderer. My little hybrid has the same strolling habit and gnarled stems of its 'Wanda' parent, and slender, lopsided flowers, like a small oxlip, of a gentle, light heliotrope colour. Other *P. elatior* or *P. juliae* crosses occur with nankeen-cream or magnolia-pink flowers. All are delightful, as are the extempore cowslips, *P. veris*, which appeared unbidden, and have obliged me by seeding plentifully in a range of sunset colours, from palest terracotta to deepest blood-red, as well as the true bright yellow.

Spring flowers are spread over the whole garden, to further the plan of having something of interest in each border or area every month. Many of them, not just bulbs, spend the summer shrouded in the brown hollands of dormancy, so positions should be marked – with a stubble of labels, if your eye can reconcile borders *en brosse*, or in a horticultural Hansard if, like mine, it cannot. Or plant them where their vanishing act will be disguised by far-reaching summertime growth. Obviously this looks better than bald patches of soil and, more importantly, is ideal for woodland plants, as they are designed to spend teetotal summers beneath the panoply of deciduous cover. Many small bulbs come from rocky hillsides, parched in summer, so they benefit too, especially where drainage is not as precipitous as they would choose. The *primavera* pretties in the small border that (inevitably) I call Botticelli are arranged so that the leafy ones are at the front, and the invisible ones at the back where they are overlain by *Nepeta* 'Six Hills Giant' planted atop a short wall above them.

A brief intromission on nepetas, lest I forget them later in the year: cold, heavy soil nips them severely, so trial invariably brings failure as they rot over winter, despite my efforts towards improving the commissariat to something approaching catnip heaven. The standard *N.* x *faassenii* is hopeless in these conditions, as are *N. nervosa*, *N. nuda*, *N. parnassica* and sadly, as it is a beauty – looking like lamb's lugs gone to Hollywood – *N. tuberosa*. But there are two successes (besides 'Six Hills Giant', which would prosper anywhere) and luckily they are easily as intriguing as any of the above. *N. subsessilis*, a Japanese woodlander, has clusters of large (for nepeta) dark lavender tubular flowers in early summer, held at 14 inches or so, above large (for nepeta) oval leaves of a mat grass-green, with an intagliated maze of veins. It is quite unlike a catmint, looking closer to salvia or chelone. The second success is atypical too, this time from the Himalayas, also prefering dampish shade, and having sulphur-yellow flowers: *N. govaniana*, again, has a sagacious air, with broad green leaves, as dimpled as lychee skin, and delicately winged flowers held in pairs dangling from long, curving pedicels in late summer. It can grow to 4 feet, but mine is not yet that adventurous. Planted ahead of the sumptuous crimson Gallica rose 'Charles de Mills' and *Clematis viticella* 'Etoile Violette', it is a mouthwateringly full-flavoured group. This interlude has not been entirely unseasonal, as spring is the time to plant, split and move nepetas, and it is advisable to leave at least some of the previous year's stems over winter to be cut back in spring.

To return to Botticelli: the summertime invisibles concealed beneath 'Six Hills Giant' comprise a mixture of small bulbs, anemones and corydalis. *Galanthus ikariae*, with broad, shining green leaves, *Scilla bifolia*, whose outward-facing stars are a light saxe-blue, might seem a feeble 15-watt bulb unless planted *en masse*, and *Hyacinthus orientalis albus*, the fragile species from which all the fat hybrids have been bred, with sparse white bells on 6-inch stems. Threading among them are delicate white windflowers *Anemone nemorosa*, the exquisite *A.n.* 'Robinsoniana' in wood-pigeon lilac, the similar *A. appenina*, whose white daisy-flowers have sky-blue backs to their many slender petals, *A. ranunculoides*, with rounded flowers of buttercup yellow, and the creamy hybrid between the buttercup and the wind: *A. x lipsiensis* 'Pallida'. All have graceful filigree foliage that veils the ground lightly. Named forms of *A. nemorosa* with bigger flowers: 'Leeds' Variety' and 'Lychette' – or with coloured flowers: 'Bowles' Purple' and 'Royal Blue' – or with double flowers: 'Vestal' and 'Bracteata Pleniflora' – are planted elsewhere in the garden. But their bootlace roots are relished by mice and, when too greedily decimated, take time to build up reserves sufficiently to attempt any flowers at all, so I am unsure which remain and which have departed for ever.

The bulbous *Corydalis solida* has feathery, glaucous leaves, and cowled flowers of a steely, greyed-pink in the type, rose-pink on the sturdily growing 'Beth Evans', and a buoyant cherry-red on 'George Baker', whose vigour is a little less dependable. In comparison to the verve of these two colours, the type plant might sound second-rate, with an 'always the bridesmaid' air of inferiority. Not so; try it beneath the feet of *Daphne mezereum*, intermixed with *Chionodoxa* 'Pink Giant', for a first-rate symphony of pinks. Dry walls are the perfect setting for *Corydalis lutea*, as sour as an unripe lemon in colour, but insouciant by nature. Equally jaunty in such a situation is *C. ochroleuca*, in green-tinged ivory. Each will form a 12-inch bun of delicate foliage covered with intricate merrythought flowers from spring until autumn and, once planted, will look after themselves entirely, unlike the popular *C. flexuosa*, whose porcelain-blue flowers need more warmth than I can provide.

Planted beyond the tide-line of the nepeta, and camouflaged by the flowering stems of *Campanula poscharskyana* instead, are two American woodlanders with a summer dormancy habit. *Dodecatheon pulchellum*'s shooting-star flowers on a 10-inch stem have the swept-back look of a surprised cyclamen, but with a keen yellow beak between the brilliant pink petals. *Dicentra cucullaria*'s flowers are minute Dutchman's breeches in white, with a canary-yellow waistband and ravishingly ferny foliage of a gentle silvery-green in a 4-inch hummock. There are hepaticas near by in blue and pink – both startling in their intense colours, magnified by stark white stamens, and the tidy, semi-prostrate *Primula* 'Schneekissen', whose soft white blooms mingle with the Chinese-yellow strawberry flowers of the stoloniferous *Waldsteinia ternata*. This appliqués the wall with evergreen leaves. It is said to require shade, but I find it will bloom only in full sun.

On the other side of the border, beneath *Prunus mume* 'Beni-chidori' and flowering simultaneously, are clumps of *Anemone blanda* in deep violet and rosy pink, lilac-blue *Chionodoxa luciliae* and *Narcissus minor* in sunshine yellow, all of which make a jolly splash of early colour to dispel sullen winter. These, as they retire for the summer, are cloaked by the expanding aluminium-splashed leaves of *Pulmonaria* 'Sissinghurst White' and the infiltrating stems of a pale silvery-mauve seedling of *Viola cornuta*. I have planted *Iris histrioides*, whose early flowers are a vibrant purple, among the little bulbs, too, but so far it is reluctant to show more than leaves. Most of these small bulbous irises are non-performers here: slugs are waking hungry just as the buds form and birds shred the petals. *I. reticulata* 'J.S. Dijt', in strong reddish-purple, seems particularly slug-prone. The lapis and old-ivory 'Katharine Hodgkin' is irresistible to pheasants, although it is of such a strong constitution that it will carry a succession of buds, some of which escape the henpecking. It seems to develop flowering-sized bulbs quickly too, so will clump up faster than most. Why then is it so expensive? I no longer bother with *Iris danfordiae*, as slugs would destroy the few buds before they opened, and the tiny overwintering bulbils would never survive, let alone grow on. Many gardeners have the same problem, finding they are annual, at best. Lucky that Mrs Danford spotted them when she did; had she gone the following year, there would have been nothing to discover.

Keeping their leaves for the summer, so planted well forward, are two further enchanting woodlanders from North America: *Sanguinaria canadensis* f. *multiplex* 'Plena' and *Anemonella thalictroides* f. *rosea*. The latter has fragile button flowers, the pink of a kitten's paws – which Katherine Mansfield likened to unripe raspberries – and maidenhair foliage of leaden mauve-green. The double form of bloodroot is radiant; its glistening white flowers have a swan's-down purity, displayed above unfurling leaves of dense glaucousness. It has the look of a terrestrial water lily. As the flowers shatter (sadly all too soon, but not as quickly as the evanescent single flowers of the type), the leaves expand. By midsummer they are large and leathery, with scalloped edges that look as though leafcutter bees have been busy here, as well as on the Judas tree.

Hacquetia epipactis is a cheerful little umbelliferous woodland plant from Eastern Europe, with shiny fingered leaves forming a 6-inch mound, slowly spreading, and flowers that, at first glance, appear to be bright green daisies with warm yellow stamens in a central boss. Closer peering will prove the yellow to be the minute flowers, the green mere bracts, a family trait it shares with astrantias. Planted near to it, and enjoying the same light shade, is the amusing dwarf aroid from Italy, *Arisarum proboscideum*, whose ground-hugging spathes bow from the waist, and whose backs, therefore, present the rear view of chocolate-brown mice scuttling down their holes, long tails tempting a tweak.

Also in Botticelli, and seeding around usefully, is *Viola rupestris rosea*, a native violet, whose pink is that of mulberry fool – purplish, stirred with plenty of cream. Elsewhere in the garden, where their rambling habit can be better accommodated, are various forms of *Viola odorata* in deep purple, white, rose pink, and a murky pink, described as brown, and called 'de Bruneau'. There used to be double forms too, but they are neither as hardy nor as vigorous as the single forms, so they are short-lived at best and will not survive a normal winter if they have too much *parmigiano* in their blood. The toughest of all seems to be the so-called yellow *V. odorata* 'Sulfurea'; in reality, it is light apricot with a purple spur. All are sublimely scented, with the famously fugitive violet perfume. I find them most willing to perform at night, when a little Brannam-ware potful beside my bed wafts veils of violet — albeit intermittently. The rapidly spreading clumps are too boisterous for underplanting with small bulbs, unless they themselves are equally hoydenish. Bold yellow *Allium moly* (nicknamed Allium jolly) bounces through the violet verdure with great ease. Elsewhere again, but as fragile as *V. odorata* is bumptious, is *Viola jooi*, from the Carpathian mountains, with large flowers of a muted mauve, and fir-green leaves that are almost triangular.

Other spring-flowering alliums are less rackety than *A. moly*. *A. paradoxum* var. *normale*, from the Caucasus, has large snow-white hanging bells on 5-inch stems very early in the year. It is particularly useful for gardens with heavy soil, being impervious to cold and damp. Mid-spring is the time for *A. cyathophorum* var. *farreri*, with tiny, rich purple flowers held in clusters at 6 inches, above wiry leaves. The two greatest racketeers deserve a place in the Wilderness but nowhere more refined, as their multiplication rates could equal consumer debt: the Southern European *Allium triquetrum* has big white bells with green tramlines, held in cock-eyed clusters on 12-inch-long, tricorn stems. The late-spring-blooming *A. roseum*, from Turkey, has blush-pink stars in a domed head at 10 inches. Both are untrustworthy but beautiful, like all the best bounders.

Epimediums are plants of year-round interest and generous ease of culture. They come from damp woodland but, provided they are well watered until they are settled, I find that not only will they tolerate plenty of sun, they also parade their rich leaf colours with greater panache when grown in the open. Their rhizomatous roots clinch together tightly to form heaped mounds of mostly evergreen leaves, the quadrant-oval shape of a sea-bird's egg, and held on arched petioles in groups of three, displaying perfect symmetry in their arrangement, as the central leaf has equal lobes, but the secondary leaves carry extended lobes on their outside edges: near-side for the left, off-side for the right. Hydraulics or aesthetics? Polished moss-green all summer, sliding from springtime toffee to autumnal fudge, they scarcely need the intricate jingling jester's cap flowers held in sprays among the foliage. These range in colour from white, sherbet-lemon and lavender, to chrome-yellow, tangerine and crimson. Some flowers are minute – such as *Epimedium pubigerum* in cream and rose-madder; others measure more than an inch, from winging spur to spur, such as the citron-yellow *E. pinnatum* subsp. *colchicum*. Still others, newly introduced from the Far East, have hovering hummingbird flowers, twice as large, but, as yet, unobtainable. The standard advice is to remove the previous year's leaves in late winter to allow a better view of the shyly sequestered flowers. Here, such action allows merely a better view of frosted buds. Without their leafy protection, they stand no chance and will be blackened overnight, as will the tender new leaves forming later in spring. So the old leaves stay (to be snipped out bit by bit as they become too scruffy to endure and as the new leaves expand and toughen), and I hunt among them for the developing flower stems. These last well in water, so can be studied at leisure indoors.

The cruciferous flowers of honesty and lady's smock (sweet rocket, later, too) are favoured by the early butterflies – orange-tips and brimstones – so I try to add more each year. Although honesty's best policy is to demand sharp drainage, cardamines and the allied genus *Dentaria* do well here in the cold, clammy soil of the Wilderness. Their frail flowers are not long-lasting and their delicate colours are unexciting, at best, but as spring is such a blue-and-yellow time, it is a change to see some different, if quiet, tones: I should always want to grow them, even without their attendant zingy orange tips and sulphurous-banana brimstones. Lady's smock, both single and double, is an auld lang syne plant of sentimental memories – damp meadows with fragrant cows grazing knee-deep in them, milky-mauve, and swallows slanting through the glinting shafts of sunlight to feast on insects the cows disturb as they wade amid the flowers. The earliest here is the stark white *C. waldsteinii*, with nodding paper-lantern flowers and lustrous fingered foliage of dark bottle-green. Tones of cream and bronze on *C. enneaphylla*, pink and fern-green on *C. californica*; they are all similar, give or take an extra curve to the emergent stem, an upright or a hanging flower; they are all exquisite. Some have self-layering, rhizomatous stems. Lady's smock, *C. pratensis*, spreads itself by means of leaf cuttings; each broken fragment is capable of rooting so the cattle in my remembered meadow would have achieved the carpet of plants themselves, simply by walking among them.

Spring is a time of visible daily progress in the garden. One can smell the green growth; one can sense the life stirring. Insects become more evident as the sun's warmth increases. In dry springs the gaps between paving stones erupt with geysers of sifted soil as mining bees excavate their nests, doors gaping open in sunny weather but firmly shut with a disc of damp soil overnight and when it rains. Birds begin their exhausting work of nest-building. Sparrows turn somersaults in the rose on the front wall, as they tug at tufts of fillis and carry them off, in handlebar moustache-loads, to the eaves. Wood pigeons in the leylandii must start again, as crows have torn out their nest and wasted the eggs, lying dented on the ground. They have gone by the next morning, fortuitous bounty for a passing vixen, perhaps, scavenging for her cubs. But so, alas, have the pigeons. I shall miss their purring snores from the tree this summer.

As April slopes into May, the first of the big border plants will flower: *Thermopsis lanceolata* has startlingly navy-blue shoots as it bursts from the soil, and retains a hint of blue as the stems lengthen to 4 feet, turn sea-green and sport their elegant lemon, lupin-like flowerheads. It is the stay-at-home member of a peripatetic family: clump-forming rather than running, it is safe in the tightest border and is the vanguard of summer. Soon I shall be cutting the first stems of asparagus and making silky soups with the young foliage of buckler-leaved sorrel. Apple-blossom buds swell pinkly and rhubarb is almost ready for pulling – more signs of impending summer. But as the oak trees expand their gilded canopies, I notice the still bare branches of the ash on the bank beyond the stream, last year's keys dangling in dense black bunches like roosting fruit bats. Summer is not here yet.

Stercoration

TODAY I HAVE BEEN SPREADING muck on the Blue Border and in the front garden. It is luscious cow manure, so well rotted as to have no smell at all, beyond a rich earthiness, and so well chopped and turned that the straw content is of short staple and evenly spaced. So often, one finds either lumps of pure muck, turned to slime, with nothing to hold it, or hanks of straw with no muck to rot it down. Invariably it will not have been turned or left long enough to mature; more will have been added to the pile so that, although the lower regions will be as ripe as a ten-year Stilton, the top will be raw and reeking; and it will be this that will assail your throat and assault your tear ducts as you load your first forkful. But this is premier cru muck, with a cheeky little nose and a hint of hayfields, nettles and clover on the palate, with none of the ammonial aftertaste of non-vintage manure.

It is also weed-free, which is a blessing. That's not to say that I shan't be finding freshly sprouted meadow grass and fat hen seedlings later on: those are inevitable, no matter how well rotted, as the cow's digestive system works too efficiently to kill all of the seeds that it consumes with each mouthful. Like jays with acorns, cows are great gardeners, making sure that the biodiversity of their pasture continues: each seed is warmed to break any dormancy, soaked in acid to scarify tough skins and enveloped with fertilizer, which also acts as a deterrent to most seed-eaters and to the grass, thus giving the seed the equivalent of a circle cut out of the turf surrounding a young tree.

Hauling out seedling weeds later on is easy gardening – in a crowded border they can't get too big, being starved of light and air, so are simple to pull once spotted. What is far more risky, and indeed can become a disaster, is chasing one-inch slivers of couch or bindweed root in the muck as you are spreading it. Every lurking piece will achieve its ambition, if unnoticed, to manoeuvre that tiny root into the heart of each border plant, and get its toes down to the earth's magma before you have turned to collect another forkful. If you don't manage to extricate it at once – Action This Day – you might as well move house, or pretend, as do many of the afflicted, that you really love those beautiful white trumpets. A bindweed root is alien enough, in its albino brittleness, for even a non-gardener to take note. But most non-gardeners would not know a couch from a potato.

The Romans revered both Cloacina, the goddess of sewers, and Saturn Stercutius, who presided over the stercoration or dunging of soil. It is one of those rare jobs in the garden that is not only vital, but pleasurable too, unlike the equally crucial tasks of staking or tying-in thorny ramblers. 'For the soil is the stomach of the plant,' wrote Aristotle. It is said that women gardeners enjoy the process more than men: supposedly our nurturing needs are as satisfied by force-feeding the soil to Strasbourg goose proportions as they are by pushing just one more spoonful of milky rusk into a baby. Perhaps, by now, 'new men' are gaining on us, and will happily spend their paternity leave feeding either soil or babies.

My soil, being slightly limey, is a little pale when *au naturel*, so I like to see the enriched chocolate mousse colour and consistency of a newly mucked border. Within weeks it will be gone, dragged out of sight by hardworking worms; but one knows, deep down, that the soil must feel replete, deep down. Stand quietly and listen, and you will hear a burp of satisfaction, and a sigh of content.

The engraver Clare Leighton warned against dropping your coat on the ground during hot work: hungry soil would swallow it whole. Mine is not quite that starved, as the clay content holds on to nutrients as well as water. But it is greedy, and can consume vast quantities of muck, which in turn will improve the dense structure of the clay, opening it up to the air and allowing roots to penetrate deeper. Naturally deep-rooted plants are not necessarily just the biggest trees and shrubs – some alpines, growing only an inch above ground, will have roots reaching down to 5–6 feet. Some bulbs, too, put down droppers to over a foot, or they have contractile roots that can pull down the bulb to immense depths – camassias and erythroniums are capable of sinking to 14 inches or more and, it is said, will begin to flower well only when they have sunk to their preferred level. So it is essential to improve the soil structure as deeply as possible, to allow these basso-profundo roots to leave the upper ranges clear for the contralto and soprano roots.

Urging you to improve the soil deeply, does not mean digging down to the antipodes – do consider your aching back; nor does it mean rotovating – do consider the worms. If you cut them all in half with the churning blades, you are defeating the purpose of all your effort: dead worms mean dead soil. Worms have been cultivating the soil since long before Adam began digging. It is their sole purpose in life and, as they spend all their time doing it, whereas we spend only occasional Sunday afternoons when there isn't any football on the telly, it seems likely that they know more about it than we do and will do a far better job. So let them: spread the muck on the surface following a nice wet week, and go and watch the football. By half time the worms will have made a start, and by next week's return match they will almost have completed the work, without one tulip bulb being sliced in half, and without any damage to rose roots which might result in the sprouting of suckers.

Serious organic gardeners frown upon animal manure being used in the garden, unless it is from their own, certified organic and drug-free stock. Non-organic farm animals are fed doses of prophylactic drugs as a matter of course, so the resulting muck is full of antibiotics, hormones and steroids, which may or may not worry you. This is now known as 'conventional farming', which seems strangely inapposite when drug-infested animals and chemically-drenched crops have been the unnecessary norm only since the 1940s, whereas the organic system has been practised since the Stone Age. Doubtless 'night soil' is still used (particularly as septic tanks are so costly to have emptied) and will carry still more drugs in it, unless, like a friend of mine, you do not allow anyone near your loo who is on any form of medication. Given traditional Chinese medicine (and without going into the ethics of using endangered species for spurious aphrodisiacs), the famous Chinese night soil fertilizer should be relatively free of artificial chemicals, as opposed to the potent drugs obtained from plants. But do they still use it, or do they now, like everyone else, it seems, dump their effluent into the sea?

How easy it is to descend from manure to politics in one paragraph . . . and back again. There are well-documented tables explaining which manure is of most benefit to your particular soil or for the type of plants you wish to please. Horse dung was said, by the nineteenth-century garden writer Shirley Hibberd, to be good for cold stiff soil because it is hot – this, because of the horse's rich diet and smaller intake of water than a cow. Cow dung was regarded as cool, due to the diet of grass and copious water, and was used particularly for fruit trees. Pig dung was favoured for growing pineapples. Sheep manure was considered the most valuable, as it contains more nitrogen and phosphates than that of pig or cow. But then it was also stated that too much nitrogen fed to apple trees would make them flower earlier, thus risking frost damage, and that the resulting fruit would neither taste as sweet nor keep as long, as those from trees on a less rich diet. Excessive nitrogen can make growth on any plant, not just fruit trees, too lush to withstand either weather or pest attack. Aphids, particularly, favour over-sappy, weak-walled stems for their dining room/nursery: like a studio flat, the same square-inch provides simultaneous facilities.

The great rosarian Dean Hole applied a spring mulch of pigeon guano, bone meal and garden compost to his roses, followed by a liquid feed made from stored manure, which, he decreed, should be given 'weak and oft, rather than strong and seldom'. He suggested that clay soils could sanction newer, that is, less rotted, manure than lighter soils. This is fine if you are mulching with it in winter, when there is no new growth to be scorched by close association. Some plants cannot bear a whiff of muck near them in any season: the genus *Dianthus* will not tolerate it, nor will any of the hot-hillside, garrigue plants – rosemary, lavender, cistus and so on – although they no doubt endure their share of goat and rabbit droppings in the wild. Snowdrops, reputedly, die if they are mucked too heavily, and many shady woodland plants are better with leaf mould, if you can make it, or garden compost, than with manure. Most alpines do not enjoy lashings round their necks, but are more than happy to dabble their toes in it.

I believe that nearly every plant will benefit from muck under its roots at planting time – more for its soil-opening qualities than simply as fast food. But it must be well rotted (and preferably sterilized) or you might as well put the poor roots into the microwave. If it is not well rotted, don't, even if you have nothing else with which to offer hospitality to the new arrival in your garden. Not everyone lives next door to a farm or stable, and one must consider muck-miles, if one is environmentally responsible. Buying sacks of sterilized organic poultry manure, to be delivered to your door by carriers who would be passing anyway, is an excellent but expensive alternative. I use this in every planting hole (except those for bulbs), keeping local stable or farmyard manure for mulching the surface, where the weed roots are a little easier to control.

There is an even worthier alternative: good for the environment, reducing rubbish destined for landfill sites, better for those plants that prefer a vegan diet and best of all for your pocket, as it is free – garden compost. One of the immutable laws of gardening is that, no matter how many tons of compost you make, you never have enough. It works on the same principle as spinach: a colanderful, just picked, will barely squeeze into your largest pan but, once cooked, will scarcely stretch the resources of a tablespoon. I try to ring the changes on the borders: this year muck, next year compost as I think it helps to prevent a build-up of possible pests and diseases. The exception to this rule is Botticelli, with all its little spring-flowering woodlanders. Like Keats in his latter moments, it subsists solely upon a lettuce leaf, or, in this instance, solely upon garden compost. A vegetarian diet can be just as sustaining as meat. Nothing dies from boredom, at any rate.

Polar Bear

Neither a lamb nor a lion, March has come in like a polar bear, with the lowest morning temperature of the winter so far: 10°F shows that there is still a long, long road ahead before we arrive at spring. Snow is still clotting the shady corners, and is stitched by the little hopping birds into puffs of trapunto quilting, with zigzags of bargello-work embroidered by doves. All are set hard in the ice, as petrified as pacing dinosaur prints in Purbeck marble. (Are those still sold as birdbaths?)

Icicles dangle from grasses and tree-roots overhanging the stream, its flow jangling and clattering in a sharper key with the altered echoes. A paddling dipper bounces and curtsies to the rhythm, swaying its head to the icy music, unheeding the cold. In the garden everything is bowing its head, withered by ice, coated with rime. Snowdrops are flattened, crocuses wrung out, the early leaves of alliums blackened and limp; hellebores are frozen into croquet hoops; almost-bursting buds on winter shrubs are browned and blasted. But the pink light of early morning turns the snow-grizzled hills to sparkling rose quartz, so not everything reflects the boiled-spinach gloom of the Snow Queen's mirror. As Keats proclaimed, the poetry of the earth is never dead.

This has always been a time for enduring what we must and enjoying what we can until spring shrugs off its old grey-flannel shawl in earnest. But worthwhile effects are to be seen, even now, where the coloured stems of willows and dogwoods shine gleefully above the rebarbative slime, which is all that most herbaceous plants can show in such conditions. Forms of *Cornus alba* stride forth like Beckford's red-legged cardinals, whereas *C. sericea* 'Flaviramea' is as yellow-stockinged as Malvolio. *C. sanguinea* 'Winter Beauty' is more accurately served by its old synonym 'Winter Flame', as its smouldering stems range from scarlet through coral to orange, which is much more warming than beautiful; I find myself spreading my hands towards the heat as I pass. Just as blazing on sharp winter days are the blood-red stems of *Salix alba* var. *vitellina* 'Britzensis'; a young plant yet, mine is to be trained to shake out its streamers, as scarlet as sin, on a mezzanine half-stem above the ground-floor dogwoods. The blackish-purple stems of *Salix purpurea* and the cinnamon bark of *Betula nigra*, which in years to come should display shaggy curls as thin as liquorice cigarette-papers, form a mellow backcloth to the more dazzling winter stems. These trees have been planted close to the bank above the stream, where their roots will bind the earth – wearing the willow in mourning for the flood-washed edges. Dogwood prunings are pushed deep into the silty stream-bed, to be woven into a living hurdle to guard the bank. The thinnest wand will not bend as they are sunk, showing the springy strength that caused them to be used for spear shafts.

Already this purple willow is powder-puffed with pussies, which have a reddish tinge to the silver chinchilla fur. The native pussy willow, *Salix caprea*, is a little later, its gleaming catkins no more than a promise – a shining silver crack within the brittle brown bud. Neither of these has been touched by the searing frosts. All the coloured stems are accentuated by the ice-bleached soil, cappucino-pale, but the pussies are shown in greater contrast when melting snow turns the earth espresso-black.

A dogwood cousin, *Cornus mas*, has young stems of a gentle sage-green, but is more noticeable in winter for its mimosa-fluff of bright yellow flowers. These open from clusters of bobbly buds arranged around the naked twigs before any hint of leaf is visible. They have a light, tangy scent and seem impervious to the worst weather. It will grow into a large shrub, with far-flung arms, but its shade is not dense, so much can be grown beneath it, provided the soil is not so dry as to give the lion the only share. Planted here is the native herb Christopher, *Actaea spicata*, with creamy racemes of flower in early summer, followed by clusters of shining black berries (poisonous enough to make Mithridates smile) and the delicate filigree of foliage that is displayed by all the actaeas and the related cimicifugas too.

Hopefully, I have *Podophyllum hexandrum* there as well, although it is too soon to tell whether or not last year's planting has come through the winter.

Optimism impels me to assume that mine will have survived, even though all the other podophyllums in the country were killed outright. So I shall continue to presume that there will be lurid umbrellas of mottled black-and-khaki chintz unfurling in the shade, with fragile porcelain cups of shell-pink flowers. If the season and slugs allow, there may be large fleshy, deep red fruits, which should echo the autumn colour of the *Cornus mas* and its cherries. So far I have seen minimal colour and no fruit at all on the shrub. Gales account for the lack of seasonal fireworks, and loneliness, probably, for the dearth of fruit: the cornelian cherry performs best with a friend near by with which to swap pollen. Just as well, therefore, to concentrate the autumn interest on the herbaceous plants beneath.

Equally unaffected by the cold, growing in as much shelter as I can manage, is *Azara microphylla*. Its oval leaves are evergreen, but small, and glittering with polish, so ice-shruggingly capable. Beneath the leaves, sitting tight on the stems, are the minute flowers — mere tufts of tiny stamens that would be invisible if it were not for the delicious scent of vanilla, which pours from the plant, causing you to peer closely to discover the source. South American plants such as this do not settle here willingly, but the azara is planted against a south wall with windward protection from *Magnolia stellata*. Both shrubs could grow taller but, having low walls to port and starboard, they seem content not to see what goes on in the world beyond them. Also sharing this protection is a small *Leucothoe keiskei* 'Royal Ruby', a present from a friend who was assured by the nursery that it loves lime. It does not, as they must very well have known, but such is commerce. Nor does it like wind, hence the shelter, which means that it stays republican green instead of blushing regal red. It has thickened stoutly, but it attempts very little in the way of flowers, and is not so happy as to incite much praise, but is attractively lustrous in wet summers.

Much safer, in these conditions, if a trifle tame, is the stalwart evergreen *Mahonia aquifolium*. This is not one of the tender, glamour-puss mahonias, with arching racemes of lemon flowers, stimulating scent, and gaunt parasols of stems and leaves; this is a cosy, cottage loaf of a shrub, plump and *bonté*, laughing at the weather. Mine were grown from seed, specifically to do a tough job: to sucker into a steadily thickening windbreak in an area of soil which is full of tree roots and land-drains, open to all the weather in winter but bone dry and concealed by tall herbaceous plants all summer. Planted small, as it was impossible to dig much of a hole, they have got their toes down now, are growing away strongly and beginning to flower prettily too. These are rather blobby little racemes in comparison to the elegant plumes of *M. japonica* – like the Prince of Wales' feathers on a debutante's head – and the scent is not so insistent, but is still attar of lily of the valley, and readily appreciated when the soil has a bone in it strong enough to bear, unflinchingly, my footsteps across the wide border.

Mahonia aquifolium will grow anywhere, but the poorer the soil, and the stronger the sun, the richer the bull's blood gleam to its shining holly-like leaves. This effect is particularly obvious in winter – just when we need all the colour we can get – and is striking in contrast to the soft lemon flowers which appear in late February in mild winters. These are followed by bloomy blue-black beads, Oregon grapes, that make fine jam, I am told, if the birds allow such spoilage of their harvest.

The genus was named after a nineteenth-century American horticulturalist, Bernhard M'Mahon, so perhaps it should be pronounced 'marnia'? This is another of those celebratory names that has been botanically Latinized, like deschampsia, kniphofia, fuchsia, and menziesia, which, by their Anglicized pronunciation, have become simply plant names, rather than a remembrance of the person who inspired them.

Brandy-Nan

'KING ALFRED' DAFFODILS ARE NO more welcome in my garden than burnt cakes. But the genus *Narcissus* is well represented nonetheless, especially the ancient hybrids and the species that come mostly from Spain, Portugal and Mediterranean North Africa. Queen Anne's double jonquil, *N. jonquilla flore pleno*, is such a screaming yellow, it hurts to look at it, as does the new spring foliage of *Valeriana phu* 'Aurea'. This quietens to a light apple-green for the rest of the year, but is timed to cacophonous perfection to partner the jonquil. Both must have full sun to give their brightest foliage or sweetest scent, so plant near to a passing nose. The jonquil is a tubby star of double petals with verdigris-green, slender leaves. The combination is splendidly rich and baroque and Brandy-Nan-ish, and was planted at the newly built Blenheim Palace. It all fits so well; but now I have read that it was not our Queen Anne after all, but that of Austria. Still baroque, though, so that's all right.

The Queen of Spain's daffodil, *N. x johnstonii*, is quite different – pale and drooping, like an infanta shut up too long in the Escorial and never allowed to see the sunshine. There are two flowers to each stem, with long, pendulous trumpets, all in milky-primrose with the merest squeeze of lemon, reminiscent of the wigs worn by the infantas in Velasquez's portraits: silvery-blonde and hanging on either side of the face in bell-shaped tresses. Here, she knows she is slumming, but is too well bred to complain. But she doesn't thrive, she merely survives, and endures, as court etiquette demands.

There is another royal bulb: Queen Anne's double daffodil, *N.* 'Eystettensis', which adds to the confusion as this is said to be named after another Anne of Austria, who married Philip II of Spain as his fourth wife (Mary Tudor was the second). But is she the same Anne of Austria after whom the double jonquil is named? I believe this Anne is a later Spanish princess, who married the French king and became the mother of Louis XIV. But if the two Annes are the same – the earlier princess – one must consider that she may be the eponymous Queen of Spain also, thereby having three distinct narcissus bulbs named after her. All for one or one each for all, let us hope the flowers gave Queen Anne some solace in the difficult life of a pawn princess, married for political gain.

I tend to buy the bulbs for the romance of their names, so the older varieties are the best for me. No one would call a daffodil Primrose Peerless now; it would be Pale 'n' Wan, or Jaundice, probably with an exclamation mark to add to the banality. Primrose Peerless itself is a delicate beauty that flowers late in the season. As its botanical name *N. biflorus* suggests, there are two, slightly nodding flowers to the stem, each with a white perianth and primrose-tinted, flat crown. Its scent is sublime – peerless, indeed, although Parkinson refers to it as 'a sweete but stuffing scent'.

Another late-flowering narcissus is the double pheasant's eye, *N. poeticus* 'Plenus'. When it does flower, it looks like a gardenia or a ruffled, double white rose; but, although it has the rich and dampish conditions it enjoys, it is not always warm enough here to ripen the bulbs sufficiently to flower well. Often buds will appear to be forming, but the inflatable paper bags of their onion-skin spathes stay empty and blind, and another year will pass without their spiced-lemon scent.

The single-flowered variety, *N. poeticus* var. *recurvus*, fares no better here, for the same reason, which is sad, as it is an elegant beauty. More so than the double, in one respect: it does at least have an eye to justify its name. The double should perhaps be called by the other common name for this species: the poet's narcissus – a double poet, along the lines of Elizabeth Barrett and Robert Browning, or Sylvia Plath and Ted Hughes, sits better than a binocular but blind pheasant.

Narcissus 'Barrii Conspicuus' won an award in 1886 and is still worthy of its place in the garden. It is not listed in the *Plantfinder* so perhaps, by now, it is available only in anonymous mixtures. I presume that was how it arrived here, before my time, in a job lot of mostly large-headed, long-shanked daffs. I have given some of them away, but I have kept many, ostensibly for picking although, being top-heavy and weak-kneed – like all too many hybrids – they are always the first to be bowed to the ground by heavy rain, so suffer dirty faces and slug-kissed cheeks. Originally, they had been planted all along the top of the retaining wall above the stream and probably made a jolly splash of bright colour before the lupins and the lilac got going.

Healthy neglect, as long as it doesn't go on for ever, is no bad thing for daffodils such as these; they are tough, and inexacting enough to thrive, regardless. Over the years prior to my accession, birds, roosting in the alder trees overhanging the daffodils, dropped the seed remains of many a tasty meal: goose-, snow-, black- and raspberries aplenty, which germinated and grew on into a tangle of nettles and scrubby saplings of bullace and alder (which, by the by, have startling royal-blue shoots in early spring). All but one stand of the wild plums were removed. These had grown into sinuous, multi-stemmed trees, which made absorbing patterns with their swooping curves, like the swan-necked trunks of gum trees, against the water meadow grasses beyond. With hindsight, I see that this was a case of practicality sacrificed for effect, as their suckering roots pop up all over the border in front, relishing the improved soil. Seedlings, so far, are not a problem, as the blossom rarely manages to show even a smattered confetti of white, during its early-blooming period of severe frosts.

Tucked tight in among the plum trees' roots are the *Narcissus* 'Barrii-Conspicuus'; they are so tight that I cannot extricate even one bulb to start another colony in roomier surroundings. I doubt there is any soil there at all by now, as not only are the poor bulbs being squeezed and squozed by the plum roots, but they are being squoozed, also, by land-drains immediately beneath them. Indeed, the plum roots divide around the drainpipes, giving the same incongruous effect to the eye as those odd windows set above fireplaces, with a divided flue on either side. None of these deters the pretty little narcissus, though; it covers the base of the trees with its small banana-yellow flowers, with their puckered lips edged in vermilion and their rich, fruity scent.

The first flowering of *Narcissus* 'Telemonius Plenus' was recorded in 1620, in the London garden of Vincent van Sion, whose name it also bears. Despite its great age, it appears not to have shed any vigour with the centuries; mine multiplies profusely, and is probably the easiest and most contented daffodil here. It is a hard, strong slash of brilliant yellow, of which one would not want too much at any other time of the year. But with the fresh spring light and newly laundered greens with which the garden abounds at daffodil time, it is a joyful sight. It has the sense to flower quite early, too, so one is not yet suffering yellow-fatigue from the mile upon mile of daffodil-stuffed road verges around every town, not to mention all the forsythias in every garden. On 'Van Sion' the doubling occurs only within the trumpet. The perianth is untouched, so it does not become a muddled gardenia-flower. Nor does it grow too tall for its stem to support the heavy head. For those who like doubles, and I do, it is the perfect daffodil.

Another old double, but star-flowered this time, is 'Double Campernelle', a form of *Narcissus* x *odorus*. It is likely to be a near contemporary of 'Van Sion', if not even older in cultivation. This yellow, though bright, is softer in tone than 'Van Sion', so may be more appropriate for your garden scheme. It is slighter in growth – there is delicate jonquil blood in its ancestry, which accounts also for its delicious scent. I find that it does not romp in my garden; the jonquil family needs more sun and warmth to do really well.

One that does succeed here is the Tenby daffodil, *N. obvallaris*, which, I am told, still has one or two wild stations in Shropshire. It is a charming little daffodil: small and neat, a good bright yellow and an equally good constitution. Both this and *Narcissus pseudonarcissus*, the Lent lily, look right in the wilder, meadowy areas of the garden and cope well with the competition from grass. I do wish that these two were used more for road verges, whether council or private, instead of the gross 'King Alfred' and 'Carlton'. No doubt I am in a minority with this request, as most seem to like the vivid waves of tartrazine-yellow; but a worthwhile doctorate could be concentrated on their hyperactive effect upon motorists on every town by-pass.

With the real tinies, I do less well. They seem to miss their Iberian homeland too much to be really comfortable here. *Narcissus minor*, itself, is an easy guest, but its early flowering form, 'Cedric Morris', is reluctant. This is not helped by pheasants, who nip off the few flower buds before they open, so I have yet to see it in bloom. *N. rupicola* – whose name points to its dry habitat, meaning rock-dweller (just as sylvicola means living in woods, and pepsicola means living in cafés) — does not achieve even that amount of success: it regularly manages one leaf, but no more. I see one or two flowers on the hoop petticoat daffodil, *N. bulbocodium*, but they are youngsters yet, having been grown from seed, so I shall hope for better things in future. They rot, here, if planted in their preferred damp soil. So I keep them a little dry, which no doubt retards the flowering. I am trying *N. cyclamineus* from seed too, because the price of bulbs is even more prohibitive if you suspect, as I do, that either they would rot, or else succumb to the excess lime. *N. asturiensis* (syn. *minimus*) is a success with which I am thrilled, as it is an exquisite little poppet — a true miniature trumpet daffodil at only 4 inches high. So far, the pheasants (maybe the eyeless ones) have ignored its buds, although the sailing is not yet all plain, as a mole has been busy in that bed.

Wilderness

TACITUS WROTE THAT WHEN THEY make a wilderness they call it peace. The development of my Wilderness is still immature, but it is progressing slowly towards a peaceful conclusion. The balancing act between my effect upon the garden versus the garden's effect upon me is becoming less implicitly weighted on my side, as heavy-booted clearance and large-scale planting gives way to hand-fork weeding. In the early stages of garden clearance, parity on this issue is paramount in any area designated 'wild', but the scales must soon be tipped in the garden's favour if your aim is for it to be as self-managing as is feasible. There is no such thing as a low-maintenance wild garden, nor an eternally peaceful one, now that the sigh of the scythe has given way to the banshee-strimmer. With this in mind, as well as the high fertility of the soil, I decided against a wildflower meadow, and have chosen instead to plant my Wilderness as a mixture of shrubs, herbaceous plants and bulbs – rough scrub rather than hayfield.

First consideration had to be given to the fragile, oft-flooded stream bank, so anchoring willows, river birch and shrubby cornus were planted, interspersed with *Iris pseudacorus*, osmunda ferns and the native sedge *Carex pendula*, whose baited fishing-rod culms dangle enticingly over the water, like angler-fishes' lures, jiggling in the downstream air currents. The parasol leaves of *Darmera peltata* make a stimulating contrast, although its blush-pink periscope flower stems are too-frequently torpedoed by early spring frosts. Male fern seedlings, their crowns like clenched fists, and surplus roots of mint, particularly the buddleia-flowered *Mentha longifolia*, are pushed into the side of the stream bank for their roots to sink or swim.

Other surplus plants from elsewhere in the garden are transplanted on to the higher ground away from the stream, which makes a convenient Botany Bay for all the thugs too pervasive for border hugger-muggery, such as double soapwort, Japanese anemones, lysimachias and adenophoras. They can be given a free rein for a few years. Other plants with indefeasible roots are encouraged to grow with the handbrake pulled on, in the driest, concrete clay over the shallow roots of a long-established alder tree, rather than the free-draining moisture they would prefer. These include *Sinacalia tangutica*, whose bright yellow plumes in late summer look as though its groundsel parent has been dallying with an astilbe, and *Symphytum tuberosum*, a miniature, but determined, comfrey with creamy-yellow flowers in spring followed by summer dormancy. Shorter, tighter: they are idling phlegmatically. So where plants exceed their brief by growing gluttonously and sprawling wantonly on the rich diet near the stream, such as the lemon-puff *Thalictrum isopyroides* and *Sanguisorba armena*, the melianthus lookalike, they will be given another chance in the alder-root, concrete-boot-camp, to toughen their sinews on the short rations. Giants are fine, provided they stand up, as this is no place for staking — aesthetics and ethics backed firmly by laziness; these two were as heavily horizontal as a reclining Buddha.

When clearing any area, I dig out a small plot very thoroughly, chasing every dropped or turned root and weed. Once certain that it is clean, I plant immediately, before clearing any more. If the plants are not ready to be moved into their new home, the ground is not cleared: there is no point in uncovering the soil and leaving it bare, as the weather will cry havoc and let slip the dogs of rain to poach and leach, and wind to blow both the surface away and weed seeds in; your work, and the soil texture, will be wasted. An area like this, edged with a stream, is bound to lose nutrients constantly from bare soil, by flood inundation, as well as drainage, so ground-covering plants are vital to gobble up and hold on to the available food. Weeds are just as efficient at the job as chosen plants.

Another point to consider is that the higher the lime content, the paler the colour of the soil, so the more it will reflect, rather than absorb, heat. It will be slower to warm and quicker to cool. Clay soil exacerbates this, as it holds greater quantities of water than, say, sandy soil, so it will be even quicker to cool, and will stay frozen for longer periods, and to a greater depth. Ground-cover, whether weeds or pretties, is essential. Covering clean ground with a thick mulch, to be dug in later when you plant, is a good plan where the soil is starved. Here, the fertility is too high for that. I should be battling with weak, jungly growth on everything planted, like the flopping thalictrum and sanguisorba; winter losses would be cruel with such soft living; and any further nutrients added would quickly drain into the stream. Increasing pollution is not an option I am prepared to countenance.

So it is important to do my homework first: deciding what is to be moved, what planted and where, that the process may run smoothly, without logjams of plants waiting in a lay-by and forgotten, or worse: bare-rooted plants being hawked about the garden in want of a home. Notebooks are vital, although many gardeners are disciplined about writing in them but less so about reading them. I find a jotting notebook essential but, for my riddle-brain, it must be belted and braced with a daybook of plantings, reciting full name, provenance (in case I have forms from more than one source), the border or area where it has just been planted and all its neighbours, starting at eight o'clock and circling clockwise; also the date of planting. Further files record plants alphabetically, with more information, such as the date of acquisition or sowing, price paid, any further moves or, with a large cross, its death. These pipe rolls are updated each year, so that changes of neighbours are recorded and comment made upon any aberrations of growth or delinquencies of habit. It may smack of trainspotting, but it is unfailingly useful, both now – writing the names settles them firmly in my mind and allows my garden to be label-free – and in the future – those tempting gaps when I am bulb planting should remain as unpestered dormancy for plants that have returned to their roots for the summer recess.

The Wilderness, then, is the same as any other part of the garden, in that it is planted for year-round interest. Coloured stems on dogwoods and willows palliate stern winter, when the skirl of the spate dulls the senses into requiring something cheerfully obvious to attract the attention away from all the truculent gloom. Sprinkles of snowdrops lift the heart; *Symphytum grandiflorum*, with its corner-shop habit of being open all hours throughout the year, brings more colour. Known as cherubim and seraphim, it has the red and blue of angelic wings marking its cream bells, held above a blanket of coarse comfrey leaves. It will flourish in the worst soil, tight up against house walls as well as over tree roots; its lax stems will clothe manhole covers and are easily, if scratchily, tugged away when necessary; it is the last word in dry-shade ground-cover.

The lesser celandine made a sheet of gold among the reedy tussocks before the ground was cleared, and its nubbly clusters of tubers were ignored during clearance. I am happy for it to stay and multiply; it is such a jolly start to spring. More have been added, including *Ranunculus ficaria* subsp. *major*: the contradiction of the greater lesser celandine makes me think of a baby giant panda, but it looks like a young kingcup. This is confused still further by *Caltha palustris minor*, the lesser kingcup, just planted, which, no doubt, will look like a large celandine. Kingcups, globe flowers and buttercups are perfectly at home in these conditions. *Caltha palustris*, its white form, the green-eyed double form and its astonishing deep red form from China, *C.p.* var. *barthei* f. *atrorubra*, line the shallow nullah that channels storm-water from the lane. *Trollius europaeus*, the native lemon globe flower, has been joined by the ivory-pale *T.* x *cultorum* 'Alabaster', whose constitution is equally pallid, sadly, and the smaller but tougher, lime-yellow *T. pumilus* from Nepal.

If the prevailing weed in these damp conditions had been the bulbous buttercup, I should have concurred with Reginald Arkell's declaration that 'In the end we all agreed/A buttercup is not a weed.' Instead, I am plagued by the creeping buttercup, a truly pernicious weed. *Ranunculus repens* is proscribed, and, although eradicated on sight, it seeks sanctuary on the stream bank, where animal tracks pan the soil to polished marble, and tree-roots forbid easy extraction. Here, the rights of vert and venison are reversed, and they have the upper hand.

I have flooded my own market, albeit inadvertently, by planting the double form of the creep. It was bought as *R. constantinopolitanus* 'Plenus', a stout, clump-forming buttercup with big double flowers. The double *R. repens* has small bobby-button flowers – enchanting but deadly. Much safer is the double form of the meadow buttercup, *R. acris* 'Flore Pleno' – equally enchanting but sedate, or the buttermilk satin, single flowers of *R. acris citrinus*, which, for me, rarely sets seed. For cautious gamblers there is the lemon syllabub-coloured *R. bulbosus* 'F.M. Burton' (*R.b. farreri* appears to be identical). Self-sown seedlings revert to bright yellow, but are easily removed from damp soil, having no flotilla of infants attached by flimsy painters. *R. aconitifolius* 'Flore Pleno', with double white pompons, should find the silty soil much to its taste, but my single plant, elsewhere in the garden, is too small yet to divide. Somewhat surprisingly for a buttercup, it is yawningly slow to establish and multiply; as a direct result of this recalcitrance, it is expensive to buy. Being double and thereby sterile, seeds are not an option.

H.E. Bates' flecks of earthbound moonlight are apparent in most months of the year: primroses seed in from the road verges and hedgerows and are always welcomed; cowslips too, most likely carried in on root clumps of transplants from the main part of the garden. Divisions of the lemon-eyed, pale lavender primrose, *Primula vulgaris* subsp. *sibthorpii* – Tradescant's 'Turkie-Purple' – have been added too. But springtime's most noticeable primula is the shocking-pink *P. rosea*, which continues the nullah-edging with the simultaneously startling kingcups, and Mary Webb's yellow cradles of mimulus. Such a rasping conflict of colour can be enjoyed as an early-spring slap in the face, although I plan to add the perennial marsh forget-me-not, *Myosotis scorpioides*, in propitiating turquoise. Near the stream are swathes of candelabra primulas in whorls of glorious colour: pink-eyed white, flesh, apricot, yellow-duster-chrome, tangerine, coral and carmine. Now that they are beginning to seed around, I shall begin to move the infants forward, to be intermixed with aquilegias and ragged robin, *Lychnis flos-cuculi*, with feathery tatters in light rose-pink. The later-flowering candelabras are joined by *Primula florindae*, in primrose-lemon, butterscotch-buff and garnet, with dangling bunches of bells. All are refreshingly scented, and all carry a dusting of lemon farina on their 3-foot stems, which reminds me of rosin-powdered ballet shoes. Like foxgloves, *P. florindae* wear their heart on their sleeve, by previewing the depth of their eventual flower colour on their leaf stems.

The melancholy thistle, *Cirsium heterophyllum*, is a plant that needs plenty of room for its thick, spreading roots, and its long, spineless leaves with a silvery reverse, that give the plant its common name (according to Geoffrey Grigson) of fish-belly. Its thistly, pinkish-mauve flowers, on 5-foot silver stems, make impromptu mattresses for sleepy bumblebees all summer. For cold soil, it is a worthy visual substitute for cardoons and globe artichokes.

The native valerian, *Valeriana officinalis* (not to be confused with *Centranthus ruber*, also known as valerian, the red, pink or white froth that floats over walls in the West Country), is a good bee plant too. Its blush-pink cymes are held on 4-foot stems (these are blackish-maroon on the form *V.o.* subsp. *sambucifolia*) above curving glabrous basal leaves. Its roots are like small starfish, and are strongly scented of violets, detectable through the soil. This was a fortuitous squatter on the stream bank, which I am happy to encourage, as was the tiny *Adoxa moschatellina*, or town hall clock, which describes the four faces and roof of its cupola-like flowerhead. It is a creamy green, with feathery glaucous foliage, like a miniature corydalis.

Another elderly resident that now takes advantage of the sheltered housing is the meadowsweet, *Filipendula ulmaria*, swaying arm-in-arm with the valerian, and my introductions of rosebay willowherb, *Epilobium angustifolium*, in its immaculate white form, and 'Starl Rose', a delicate shell-pink. I have added other species of filipendula, including the single and double forms of dropwort, *F. vulgaris*, with feathery, fir-green leaves, like a clump of carrots, and fluffs of cream flowers opening from red-tinged buds. It likes drier conditions than the other filipendulas, such as *F. rubra* 'Venusta', known as the queen of the prairies. Despite its dewy soul, I have planted this one dry too, so its vigorously spreading roots will be checked, as is its height: flowering stems of 8 feet are not unusual, but here, dry, it satisfies itself with 5 feet. The flowers are like a giant raspberry-pink meadowsweet, as are its leaves – bigger and red-flushed. Varieties of *F. palmata* have also been planted in shades of pink, from creamy-magnolia to almost-magenta, with heights varying from 3–5 feet and, unsurprisingly, almost palmate leaves.

On such heavy soil, both *Lactuca perennis* and *Cichorium intybus* are soundly monocarpic, which is sad, as their lavender-lettuce and cerulean-chicory daisy flowers are charming in early summer. Still more annoying is that their seeds rot before germinating in the soil, so I must remember to collect and sow them inside. I am trying the blue-purple *Cicerbita alpina* this year to see if it will tolerate the cumbrous conditions any more willingly. This used to be known as *Lactuca alpina* but now calls itself a sow thistle rather than a lettuce. From a packet of seed only one germinated, so I am hoping that the trend will continue, as basking sow thistles could stuff a silk purse with surplus seeds.

At the higher, drier end of the Wilderness are two more English natives: sainfoin and field scabious. Sainfoin, *Onobrychis viciifolia*, is a classic meadow plant, supposedly contributing a sweet scent and flavour to hay. Indeed, a traditional belief is that it lined the Baby Jesus' manger and is thereby known as holy clover. It is a beautiful plant, with silvery pinnate foliage and terminal racemes of rose-pink pea flowers, veined with purple and paint-box green. It grows to almost 3 feet and remains true to its hayfield habit of sprawling, especially when transplanted to drawing-room conditions in the border. *Knautia arvensis*, the field scabious, makes a basal tuffet of variable leaves – entire, lyrate, and pinnatifid, all jumbled together – and thin, wiry stems to 4 feet or more, with lilac scabious flowers of short ruffled petals encircling a domed centre. These are larger than the intense crimson blooms of *K. macedonica* but smaller than the chalky-lemon flowers on the related *Cephalaria gigantea*. Another cousin is *Dipsacus inermis*: teasel by name, but more like a scabious in looks, with small cream flowers. It likes hefty soil, so has made ample clumps of contentment here. Similar in colour is the giant Hungarian clover, *Trifolium pannonicum*, with 4-inch creamy-yellow flowerheads above sturdy, bushy growth.

By August, autumn's long lineage of yellow is beginning to warm the leaves, both here in the Wilderness and, as the picture strays over the edge of the canvas, in the surrounding countryside. But it is not all foliage, and no filberts: the chimera of flower colour continues. Two species of aster fit well into the *modus operandi* of the Wilderness, with a self-reliant habit and the artless look of the wilding, although these two display flowers of a creditable size, unlike some nugatory species. *Aster diplostephioides*, from Kashmir, has large, lavender, needle-rayed daisies on 14-inch stems in late summer. It is unusual in having rusty-brown centres, the disc-florets that gradually turn to the orange-yellow of mango flesh. The North American *Aster divaricatus* has a mass of white daisies on 3-foot, branched black stems and large heart-shaped leaves – again, unusual for an aster. It flowers all summer and waxes fat on the lush soil, whereas *A. diplostephioides* might appreciate rather faster drainage.

Perhaps the most comfortable genus planted on the Wilderness is *Persicaria*. The annual native knotgrass and the perennial redshank were, and still are, growing here abundantly. I have added the larger-flowered form of the native bistort, *P. bistorta* 'Superba', which has distinguished itself by blooming from April to November, with its fondant-pink, fat pokers above curled reddish-green foliage. Two species from the Himalayas have been planted: *P. campanulata* flowers from midsummer until frost explodes its 4-foot cage of intertwined and self-supporting stems, with sweetly-scented panicles of tiny bells that look like polystyrene bobbles. These will be white, pale pink, dark pink and almost crimson, all at the same time on the same plant. The leaves and stems are flushed with pink, too. Similarly long-winded is *P. amplexicaulis* 'Atrosanguinea', with narrow, cherry-red tails on branched, 3-foot stems of fox-brown above russety foliage. Each makes a spreading plant, emanating from a small crown, so is a good candidate for underplanting with spring bulbs, such as *Fritillaria meleagris*, which will relish the same alluvial soil. *P. polymorpha* and the similar *P. weyrichii* have been added this year. They will reach 6 feet or more and have foaming cream flowers in branched panicles. Their first tentative sortie, this summer, looked a little too much like Japanese knotweed for comfort, so I hope they will settle into their proper stride before I live to regret a planting that may return the whole plot to true wilderness. *Plus ça change, plus c'est la même chose.*

Euphorbias

I HAVE OFTEN WONDERED what style of bonnet Mrs Robb was wearing as she strolled through the Balkan woods and discovered *Euphorbia amygdaloides* var. *robbiae*. Legend claims that she stowed the plant in either her bonnet or the bonnet box, which seems an odd thing to be carrying on a woodland ramble, unless she used it habitually as a sort of vasculum. I imagine her in a calash hood stuffed with moss and scraps of plants, like an Edward Lear caricature. I suppose if the euphorbia's discovery had been delayed until the 1990s, it would be known as 'Corporal Robb's cartridge case', instead of Mrs Robb's bonnet.

Euphorbia amygdaloides var. *robbiae* was one of the few plants (as opposed to rank weeds) growing here when I came to the garden. Probably everyone I know has had bits of it since – it is such a good plant, and will do well anywhere. Or so I thought until recently, when mine was killed by prolonged double-figure frosts. It will be easy to replace, as I need only scan my address book: that is one of the many benefits of exchanging plants. But I wonder whether to do so, or if it has joined a long list of other unsuitable euphorbias, if such a contradiction can be entertained.

The paradox is concerned mostly, but not entirely, with the weather: interminable ice and cold, heavy soil are not conducive to the ultimate happiness of many of these handsome plants. *E. mellifera* struggled for a while, as did *E. characias* subsp. *wulfenii*, *E. myrsinites*, *E. corallioides* and even, suprisingly, *E. hyberna*. But they all succumbed in the end to euphobia – the dread of dank soil.

I regret *E. mellifera*'s demise, as I should have enjoyed the wafting scent of honey had I lived in warmer climes. *E. corallioides*, of the flamingo-pink legs, is beginning a second trial after some free seeds of it came my way. The snakily reptilian *E. myrsinites*, more gorgon than gorgeous, lived for years with my best drainage on the edge of a wall, but it remained with only the same two armadillo-plated stems that it had when I bought it. They grew longer and longer and looked like two grey plaits hanging down the wall. I cut one off, to see if it would sprout some more in replacement. It died. I believe that *E. hyberna*, the Irish spurge, must be short-lived; possibly my conditions curtail it still further – two to three years being the maximum. It seeds itself around and, if the seedling happens on a sheltered nook, it will manage three and grow to a useful 2-foot mound, but more usually they will grow weedily and die annually.

Euphorbia characias, in all its similar forms, has become the ultimate designer plant. It is green, which is the new white, or the new black, as the more excitable magazines explain, and has the faubourg mentality that makes a good town-garden plant. I mean by this that it looks its best bulging from a corner between walls and performs best with the added warmth of urban surroundings. Given this clemency, it will do well even in shade, with which closely packed, tunnel-like town gardens are apt to abound. Like *Fatsia japonica*, it can look incongruous other than in an urban setting. Certainly it is inappropriate in the midst of a herbaceous border, where its formidable size will cause concern to its neighbours.

But it is not all gloom and euphobia; there are many more spurges – euphorias – which relish the moisture, and shrug off the cold. It is these on which I concentrate here. *Euphorbia palustris* is one of the best. In fact, even if I could grow *E. characias* subsp. *wulfenii* triumphantly, I think I should still choose the marsh spurge, as it is the perfect plant. It is all ease and amiability from seed (whence mine came), sturdy, reliable . . . I am making it sound like a well-meaning social worker, but it is much more exciting than that. Early in the spring, stout ruddy-bronze noses will push up through the ice and snow, and by April they will begin to open inverted saucers of acid-greenery-yallery that set off the daffs so well. The flower stems then perform their circus trick – as when, to the astonishment of all onlookers, and the strains of the William Tell overture, a few invisible tears are made in a tube of paper, and a paper ladder is pulled from the centre of the tube. As the flower stems extend like the paper ladder, the leaf-stems develop too, eventually overtopping the fading flowers by late summer, to reach 5 feet or more. The weight of these additional stems pulls them down into a cumulous curtsey, making a vast billowing cloud of willowy leaves. The stems shine through, a dazzling pink, which is but an *amuse bouche* for the next course, when painting frosts dab each leaf with crimson, each vein blood-red. Then a hoar frost will powder the leaves with crystals before they fall, leaving the arching stems, that ripen to a rich, polished cinnamon. Yes, I know, too lyrical by half, but this plant is poetry.

Euphorbia amygdaloides 'Purpurea' is another splendid spurge that tolerates cold air with stoicism but would prefer somewhat lighter, leafier soil than mine. I give it the best drainage in the garden, yet still it dies off in chunks in wet winters. But what remains is magnificent, particularly in early spring, when its tonsilitis-red foliage is at its most startling. The contrast of this colouring with the acid-yellow flowerheads (large bracts, minute flowers) is not for those of a nervous disposition, especially as it is evident for months, before the flowering stems fade and are cut off. (Watch out for the milky sap on the backs of your hands, as it can irritate if, like me, you are susceptible to allergies.) Once again the paper ladder trick evolves, but in miniature, as the new foliage extends to its overwintering hassock of 12 inches or so, dressed in bloodstone-green tinged with crimson, until cold nights strengthen the haemoglobin levels again.

Equally not for the faint-hearted is *Euphorbia polychroma*, a screaming yellow acid-head, whose springtime bracts are of the same migraine-inducing sharpness as the aforementioned *Valeriana phu* 'Aurea' and some daffodils. They all look marvellous at that time of year, when the light is so fresh, but would be indefensible at any other time, especially if anything pink were close by. This makes a small tuffet to 10 inches or so, and, after its portentous offering in spring, it settles down to a quiet forty winks in the background for the rest of the year. That's not to say it is dull: its summer foliage deepens to the family colouring, described by Margery Fish as 'lovebird green', which is a restful accompaniment to every other shade.

Euphorbia griffithii 'Fireglow' has overweening territorial ambitions. It will romp in any soil and keeps its colour well in dim light so, as a result, tends to be pushed into uncongenial corners, where it repays me more than I deserve for such cavalier treatment. Given the damp, robust soil that it would choose for itself, it will grow rain-bowingly tall to 4 feet, causing its burnished copper bracts to be seen only from a worm's-eye view.

I have two forms of *Euphorbia dulcis* 'Chameleon': the true scheme of bright pink and ripe mulberry, and a second, obviously seed-grown and so not true, which I call Mock Chameleon, as not only is it falsely attributed but it is also a mocha mixture of *café au lait* and chocolate. They are both worthwhile plants, although martyrs to mildew, where air cannot circulate with ease in crowded border conditions. But by the time the spores manifest themselves, the early-flowering show is over anyway, so spent stems, mildew and all, can be removed to make way for clean new basal growth. The tiny flowers on this species seem particularly beady-eyed among the richly coloured bracts, as, unusually for a euphorbia, they show no variation in tone from the foliage. This monochromatic scheme gives an added depth to the hummock shape, that is a decisive foil to all the spiky-leaved, spring greens about at the time.

Euphorbia-like in form and colouring is the genus *Bupleurum*, which, like the spurge, has annuals, herbaceous perennials and woody-based sub-shrubs in the family. I grew the annual *B. rotundifolium* from seed several years ago, so I welcome the odd self-perpetuated seedlings that continue to turn up occasionally. Also grown from seed is *B. falcatum*, a valuable perennial so far, although I have heard it described as annual. It can best be illustrated as the result of a marriage between euphorbia and crambe, having its father's glaucous foliage and citrus flowers but its mother's ditty flowerheads in an exploding firework display of froth at 4 feet or so, in late summer and on into autumn, when it makes a refreshing change from the ubiquitous daisy shape.

The annual, *Euphorbia lathyris*, the caper spurge, was growing here when I came, and still turns up, intermittently, to my great pleasure: a well grown plant (all credit to itself) is a spectacular sight. Three seedlings spaced closely like a multi-stemmed tree, appeared on a newly constructed raised border a few years ago. They were the finest specimens I have ever seen, reaching 5 feet tall and, together, at least triple that in girth. The raised bed is 2 feet high, so it was quite an experience gazing up into their canopy as one walked beneath. When the seeds began to ripen, I had to move my favourite seat, rather than risk a volley of buckshot every few moments, as the caper-like seed pods burst open in the hot sunshine, and flung away the seed (also, reputedly, why cannas are called Indian shot). Surprisingly few germinated, and none showed the stature of its magnificent parents, but that's genetics for you.

Seeds

AS WITH PUBLIC LIFE, which Saki said was knowing when to stop and going just that bit further, so with seed orders: there are good things offered that I want to try, others that are old friends and worth growing again, and still others I have never heard of before and which sound intriguing. Some of these may turn into time-wasting kittle-cattle; yet more will be ground-absorbing weeds; but one seed might grow into the best plant in the garden – so going that bit further can be politic.

Descriptions woo me far more than glossy photos, so the seedsmen who grow their own, study the plant in growth and describe it with accuracy in a simple list, are the ones I favour. Their seeds should be fresher, too, if they have been gathered and packed on site. Despite all the thermostatically controlled storage systems keeping seeds at the correct degree of dormancy, once they leave the suppliers they are at the mercy of heated delivery vans, draughty or stifling shops and unscientific (if not downright careless) storage in the average house. To hold infinity in the palm of one's hand is miraculous enough: that it should survive our fumbling attentions is the stuff of legend.

My seed packets are kept in shoeboxes in the larder. As this was the old dairy, facing north, with slate shelves and stone floor, its temperature is a steady 40–45°F, winter and summer, which encourages little action from me, let alone from dormant seeds. I attempt to sow all those I have acquired in the current year, plus as many older ones as space allows, but I never clear the backlog completely. If I live to be one hundred, I plan to spend that birthday sowing seeds for the future. It is a good way to celebrate a birth, too: I sowed *Davidia involucrata* on the day my goddaughter was born; they are both taller than me, now, and although one has been blossoming every day, the other might begin to flower in a few more years' time.

Some seeds will snooze contentedly in a cool shoebox for many a long year, then leap elastically to life when eventually they are sown. Others will have died of old age before the spring following their collection: hellebores and primulas are seldom worth ordering other than from merchants who pick, pack and post before autumn is over. This is also the case where seeds require a period of frost (sometimes more than one) to break their dormancy. Sowing in autumn to allow winter to do its work will tend to give better results than the artificial stratification recommended by the seed distributors who send your order in spring: six weeks in the fridge, two in the airing cupboard, and three more in the fridge. Either the salix will be tossed with a salad or the linum will muddy the linen. No, I prefer to keep them all in the shed, where a Socratic field mouse can nibble my hemlock seeds in peace, also aconitum, colchicum, digitalis and the prussic acid-filled kernels of prunus, seemingly, with no ill-effects. Perhaps a little *Atropa bella-donna* for pudding, sir?

It may be that the field mouse's immune system is no more potent than the seeds themselves: umbellifers, such as hemlock, are notorious for their two seconds of viability – it is suggested that damp kitchen paper should be spread beneath an uncut, but ripening seedhead, so that seeds falling on to it may be germinated before sowing. I can appreciate that nurserymen might benefit from such fiddling but, for the rest of us, it is easier to leave the plant to arrange its own sowing-bee (most umbellifers manage this with superfluous ease) and then remove the excess. Some years, when a long, freezing spring succeeds a deluging winter, there will be barely enough; heavy soil is slow to warm and seeds rot before they can germinate. I look upon anything self-sown as a minor miracle rather than a dependable occurance. *Angelica sylvestris* 'Purpurea' manages to keep itself going; being biennial, it is in its own best interests, as I doubt I should bother to sow it every year. Even so, it is necessary to haul out the green-leaved seedlings, whose flowers are a dirty off-white. If left, these would squeeze out the purple form, with its dusty-dusky pink umbels. A little selective weeding is necessary with self-sown infants of the perennial *Anthriscus sylvestris* 'Ravenswing' too, as some will show more affinity to a magpie's Black Watch-green wing than to the bitter chocolate that is meant to represent a raven. Anything budgerigar-green has flown in from the hedgerows but, as exquisite as it may be, I have no craving for wild cow parsley to fill the borders. The Wilderness is a different matter.

These diaphanous, feathery-leaved umbellifers: foeniculum, selinum, ferula, meum, with their attendant taproots, are not inclined to mistake my soil for Cloud Nine. If I can encourage them to grow at all, they are, at best, short-lived and, to all intents and purposes, barren. I cannot collect seed, as they seldom flower, clearly believing that what passes for late spring, here, is still winter, so are firmly wrapped in dormancy until too late for buds, let alone seeds, to form. Buying seed, with its low viability, is a gamble I should be prepared to take if I knew that any resulting seedlings would bask in their surroundings but, as it is, the quaintly named bald-money would be simply waste-money.

Seeds used to be the cheapest way to fill a garden with plants; not any more. When a packet of seed can cost more than a standard-sized herbaceous plant that can be split into two or three plants within a few weeks of purchase, it seems thriftless to expend further money on seed compost, vermiculite, labels, pots, not to mention time, heat and water – and still manage only two or three seedlings, which must be nurtured, potted-on and generally fussed over for possibly another year or two before they can be fed to the slugs in the garden. By that time, the purchased plant will have been split again, the excess given away or sold for church funds (no, of course I am not suggesting any infringement of Plant Breeders' Rights).

But economics never had much to do with enjoyment, and seed-sowing is hugely enjoyable. The whole process, from start to finish, never ceases to thrill because of the inexplicable magic that a speck of dust can transform itself into a forest tree, or a cabbage, or a gentian, despite our feckless interference.

So both economics and enjoyment are spoiled when nothing comes up. This is not always due to clumsiness on our part, although it is true that in general seeds are buried too deeply. Some will cope determinedly and rise above the avalanche, lifting it with them, occasionally, like caryatids supporting a stone entablature, but most will not. Instead, it could be due to our impatience: many seeds will take their time – up to five years for the genus *Paris*. But if several germinate, almost any delay is acceptable: they are expensive plants to buy and their parasol leaves studded with delicate emerald, star-pointed flowers look best in a crowd – paris is worth a mass. Peonies take two years, putting down a root in the first, balanced by a shoot in the second. So it pays not to fiddle, nor to throw away a pot before it has had its chance. But few greenhouses are large enough to accommodate geriatric pots in quantity, and the third cause of non-germination may be to blame: dead seed. Dead seed is what makes it expensive to attempt to fill your garden with seed-grown plants, as it frequents seed orders like Banquo's ghost.

Even so, we go on sowing, always expecting Micawber-seedlings to turn up, and invariably they do. I am in no hurry to start the process each year, as I rely on sun-warmth rather than a heated propagating unit. There is no point in incubating your babies unless you have a suitable weaning area of slightly less warmth to which your delicate seedlings can progress, for the weeks of fattening before the weather allows them to be planted in safety. Besides, I rarely sow or grow half-hardy annuals, which need heat to germinate, as they are caught by growth-curtailing frosts in June, and by flower-killing frosts in September. Even hardy annuals are a gamble, as their sowing (inside) must be late enough for them to germinate and grow on quickly, but early enough to give them a decent run at flowering once planted out – the season is too short for sequential buds to continue performing. The steadily increasing plants take up more room inside than their usual poor display can justify, so I sow very few, rather resentfully.

Biennials are better, provided they are doughty enough to survive the winter. I am fond of the very dark form of honesty, *Lunaria annua* 'Munstead Purple' and the white-flowered form with white-splashed leaves, *L.a.* var. *albiflora* 'Alba Variegata'. They need to be big burly plants to withstand both slugs and ice, which they never achieve if left to their own devices. Having released the large seeds from their sandwich of communion wafers, I sow a few in spring most years – one to a 3-inch pot (as Churchill said: solitary trees, if they grow at all, grow strong) then potted on into 5-inch pots to fill with roots before launching in August. The good thing about biennials – foxgloves, Canterbury bells, wallflowers and so on – is that they start flowering early enough to set and ripen seed. Annuals are less obliging: even nasturtium seed must be bought and sown

in pots inside. They are considered more as superb foliage plants —
particularly the dark-leaved *N.* 'Empress of India' — with the few flowers a
bonus not to be relied upon.

Borage, *Borago officinalis,* is another hardy annual that needs the fuss of
pricking out and potting on in order to achieve well-furnished plants. Even
so, it will always be reduced by frost to dripping, blackened slime when still
at the peak of flowering. The white form, *B.o.*'Alba', is ravishing,
unexpectedly so as, prior to seeing it in a friend's garden, I had failed to see
the point of a white form of anything whose total glory is its blueness. I
was wrong; there are times when the white can make the blue look coarse
(I mean the flowers; the plants themselves are unremittingly coarse).
Sometimes I follow the early demise of *Aconitum napellus* with an
interplanting of steadily encroaching borage — the aconite's dying stems
will lend support (very soon hidden) to the brittle growth of the borage.
Originally from the south of France, self-sown borage has gone native. It
is referred to as a British casual, which makes me think of it as the
informal, summer equivalent of the British warm.

Most of the seeds I sow, then, are perennials, plus a few shrubs and
trees — although lack of space must begin to quell my ardour for these.
Bulbs from seed are a smaller alternative, but are not for those who want
instant colour, as they can dally for years at the single thread-like leaf stage
and must be safeguarded the while from the attentions of a whole bestiary
of pests. I never prick out seedling bulbs, but pot on the whole potful each
year, until they have grown sufficiently to be planted out. It saves on space,
as well as suiting the seedlings, which appreciate the lack of disturbance.
As soon as the leaves die back I reduce watering, so that they are kept
completely dry over winter.

Seeds of herbaceous perennials can be just as inexacting, or devilishly
intractable. Whether you persevere limitlessly with them depends much
upon your available time, temperament and blood-pressure. Gardening in
an equable climate, and studying the phases of the moon might help. Far
more efficacious is to find a dependable seed merchant and a good brand
of seed compost — neither of which is as easy as it should be.

Many find the process of sowing and pricking out daunting, when deft
fingers and keen eyesight are distant memories. Certainly some seedlings

will germinate into your huddled masses yearning to breathe free and require the Statue of Liberty's exclusivity to develop strongly. Others, gregarious plants that thrive in close company, such as carpeting campanulas, tiarellas or asters, can be potted on as small clumps of seedlings (in the same way as bedding-plant suppliers deal with lobelia) by those who find pricking out a carking chore, and grown on to be split again if necessary. It seems not to deter the plants; indeed, it may be beneficial in a sluggy garden, where surfing pests home in on a single green life-raft in a sea of brown soil, but will ignore some, if not all, of a flotilla of plants. Apart from a few cactuses and beech trees, most plants grow naturally in tight proximity to others, their roots locked, their stems supporting each other. Meadow and prairie plants will germinate in minute spaces between sturdy grasses; woodlanders will create an ever-thickening ground-covering rug by seeding among themselves; bog-plant seedlings must compete with the enormously lush growth of their neighbours. Seedlings do not necessarily need oceans of space.

The societies that distribute seeds to their members are a useful source of general and specialized seed. They usually send small quantities, which is preferable, I believe, to the overstuffed packets of some of the glossier seed companies, although I frequently hear moans about the paucity of seed in packets these days – no doubt the seedsmen are tired of the diverse arguments too. Ideal for me, with perennials at least, are half a dozen seeds in a sensibly priced packet, of which at least four will germinate, giving me three plants, with one to give away now (as an insurance policy – if I lose mine I can claim a friendly replacement) and probably more later, if they bulk up well, or if I find I can garden quite contentedly without them.

With annuals I might require a larger number. If I am growing them for a potful of, say, incense-wafting, carmine *Cuphea procumbens* beside the front door, then one plant will do. When I want nasturtiums to plant over red tulips in the Noon Border in order to continue the scarlet sizzle (if it is a warm summer, and flowers appear) and to close the gaps with glaucous saucers, then three plants will be perfect. Or if I want a mass of delicate pink *Claytonia sibirica* in the damp soil beneath the amelanchier, then there would be room for a dozen or so. In no instance, however, do I see myself ever needing two hundred opium poppies or snapdragons, much as I like both plants. Seed counts can be off-putting, even though the plants are enticing.

Then there are the Ganymede seeds: carried into the garden on the feet of birds, or the wind or floodwater. They can easily be overlooked until they surprise me with flowers. Many would be viewed as weeds in smarter gardens, or indeed, in mine, had I no Wilderness on which they may romp. Mullein, *Verbascum thapsus*, needs a great deal of space, as its biennial leaf rosette, which, like Belloc's llama, is a woolly sort of fleecy hairy goat, can be cartwheel-sized, and its flowering stem pitchfork-tall (it is a very rustic plant). *Hieracium spilophaeum* can cover twice that space with wind-sown seedlings, as it flowers for months yet takes about a minute from dandelion-yellow bud to powder-puff fluffy seedhead. But its foliage is a striking crimson speckled with grey and black, as obvious as semaphore flags when weeding. *Circaea lutetiana* appeared on the stream bank one year in a tiarella-foam of white flowers. It is known as enchanter's nightshade, which gives no clue as to its habit of infiltrating the roots of every surrounding plant. A variegated form is being sold in nurseries as *C.l.* 'Caveat Emptor', which must surely have been a warning rather than a name. I suggested this to a puzzled nurseryman who offered it. He said he thought it meant 'lives in a cave', so had suggested to each buyer that it needed damp shade. Oddly enough, it does. Primroses, cowslips, ferns, bugle, geum – all turn up in places best suited to themselves and, occasionally, with interesting colour forms, or narrower leaves, or larger calyces and so on: interesting to me, although I am aware that few, if any, are swans. But then, I am rather fond of geese, and there are degrees of gooseness.

America

FROM THE UNASSAILABLE POSITION of the English garden, it was considered, patronizingly, that American gardens and gardeners were not, generally, among the best. Never the whole truth; America, as in all things, covers both poles of excess – all too many of the very worst gardens, yet an increasing minority of the very best. I can't say if that trend is followed wholly by America's garden writers, but several are included within my pantheon of excellence: in particular, Eleanor Perényi and Henry Mitchell, whose acerbity is most agreeable when one is feeling all's-wrong-with-the-world-ish.

American plants are indispensible, whether your preference is for coniferous trees, tender salvias and dahlias, prairie daisies or the exquisite wildings of the forest. Mine is for the latter. My only regret is not having acres of deciduous woodland to plant: imagine sheets of trillium, erythronium and mertensia; swathes of uvularia, jeffersonia, phlox and synthyris; drifts of sanguinaria, viola, maianthemum, shortia, dodecatheon, anemonella . . . the list is as boundless as the American wilderness itself. To sink from such sublimity to the bathos of a small, damp border in the shade of an old quickthorn hedge is hard enough to bear, but add to that the ineluctable slug and you will understand why my garden will never respond to the wild cry of the Appalachian forest. A minor whimper can be achieved with the least fussy of these beauties, but they will never sigh to the sound of wolves, alas.

For the American plants of the east-coast woodlands (as Christopher Smart would have begun) are accustomed not only to less lime in their gin, but to more 'duff' with their plums. That is to say, they grow in damp, but free-draining, acidic leaf-mould. They enjoy the protection of a duvet of deep snow cover for months each winter, followed by copious snowmelt, then steady dry heat beneath summer's leaf canopy. None of this comes remotely within the menu that I can offer: limey clay, unyielding and cold with sluggish drainage, warm sunshine in winter, frosts in summer . . . a more realistic gardener would not even try.

If these tenacious plants can survive all that and push their springtime noses above the covers, they must then face an equally persistent and formidable foe – the slug. Acidic leaf-mould discourages slugs; stiff clay seems to breed them. Months of heavy snow kills them off, whereas our stop-start winter merely sharpens their appetite. So my mertensias are still there – in root at least; they grow and spread and attempt an enfilade here, an encirclement there, like a determined guerrilla brigade. But the army of grazing slugs sweeps down like the Assyrian horde upon the fold each night, and mows them flat with scythe-like jaws.

No, I will not resort to poisons, neither slug pellets nor powders. And nematodes work only when the temperature of the soil reaches a certain height, which occurs here for about half an hour on a warm afternoon in July, by which time the spent woodlanders have retreated to their summertime bunkers below ground anyway. Besides, nematodes are alien species, introduced by man. And we all know what happened to rabbits in Australia and blackberries in New Zealand.

So I shall keep trying with the trilliums and persevering with podophyllums. Success or failure is largely dependent upon the weather: seldom will success be more than modest; all too often failure will be total. But one must plant hope with each hepatica and patience with every phlox, so that in future springs there may be swathes of hepaticas and oceans of phlox. (Or should that be phloxes? Are the plural plants still phlox, in the rangy sportsman's lingo of wildebeest, elephant and duck; or phloxes in the nursery idiom of fishes?) Time should heal still more of the problems: increased shade as trees grow stronger, resulting in a healthier humus content from all the extra leaves, and consequent improvement to drainage. Then there is just brother slug . . .

Lamiums

LAMIUMS HAVE LONG BEEN REGARDED as mere spear-carriers on the garden stage. They rarely feature in glossy photographs, other than in the sort of mugshot used for identification parades: armed and dangerous, keep your distance. Mention lamiums and the immediate response is 'Aren't those nettles?' followed by 'They're very invasive.' Not necessarily. They are certainly not stinging nettles – those are *Urtica*, usually with an 'H' in front, and although some spread usefully (they are among the more attractive of all easy ground-covering plants), others grow in sedate clumps. Lamiums do not deserve the bad press ascribed to them by gardeners ungrateful for their generosity.

To distinguish them from their cousins the stingers, lamiums have long been known as dead-nettles, a sobriquet unfitted to their lively grace. Even *Lamium album*, the native white dead-nettle, has a decorative quality, in its pristine white and downy silver-green, that fits well in the garden and not just in the wilder areas. It makes a long-armed clump shinning through shrubs and lightening the gloom where it weaves through hedge bottoms. I should like to plant it as a *petit-point* carpet, mixed with its cousins prunella, nepeta and stachys in a swirl of misty colours around the feet of a grove of Judas trees.

The Mittel-European *Lamium maculatum* is the most obliging species for ground-cover. Its badger-faced leaves make an evergreen patchwork quilt if several different forms are planted in swathes. They layer themselves as they go, but in a desultory way, with shallow roots that are readily removed with a twitch of the hand, making weeding very simple. The richer the soil, the faster they sprint, so I should not be tempted to waste their qualities on soil that would suit other plants, and your time, better. Save *Lamium maculatum* for bone-dry problem areas, which it will cloak with ease. I planted a clump of roots in the parch beneath a Portugal laurel fifteen years ago and have never touched it since. In such conditions it loiters with deferred intent. At planting it covered about a foot of soil; now it measures 3 feet of soft silver and green, year-round, with sullen-pink flowers from late spring, and off and on all summer.

There are better forms for colour, in both flower and leaf. I have another nameless one, begged from a neighbour, with starkly striped leaves and larger-than-normal magenta flowers. 'White Nancy' has leaves almost entirely silver-plated and small, sugary-white flowers. This struggled in flea-bitten misery here until, wanting to spread its aluminium haze between a sandwich of *Rubus* 'Benenden' and *Narcissus* 'Actaea', I found, by chance, 'White Nancy' heaven – as well drained as it can be, here, rich soil and full sun. The pastel variety 'Pink Nancy' was given the same plate of food and promptly died. Such is gardening. *Lamium maculatum* 'Aureum' is said to require full shade and damp feet or it will scorch and shrivel. Twice I tried it as recommended and twice it succumbed to mildew and aphids. Now I have it growing successfully in dry soil over the roots of a large, free-range, shrubby box, facing full south but partially shaded by herbaceous plants in front. Its foliage is acid-yellow with a narrow white arterial stripe; its flowers are a good purple.

The native yellow archangel, *Lamium galeobdolen*, used to grow on road verges near by and was a timely reminder that bluebells would be at their best, so a woodland pilgrimage to pay my devoirs was due. But I have failed to see the archangel's buttery spires for the last two springs. It seems extraordinary that such a strong plant could vanish so completely and so quickly. One root of *L.g.* 'Variegatum' (now known as *L.g.* subsp. *montanum* 'Florentinum') was evacuated from a London garden twenty years ago, and has repaid me ever since with unstinting spontaneity: grasping stream banks, leap-frogging through rough grass and pointing wall-bases with unexpected winter colour – when the silver and green splashes are steeped in vinous purple. Its creamy-yellow flowers in late spring are fleeting, alas, but this is its only fault in my eyes. Even its lasso-stems can be useful, where rough cover is needed. Where it is not, they are soon removed – again, rooting is shallow to facilitate weeding. The variety 'Hermann's Pride' is from the same stable but increases slowly in a single clump with no infiltrating insurgents on leading reins attached to a stalking-horse parent. Its variegation takes the form of a distinct white reticulation of veins over fir-green but it contributes nothing over winter, as it retires below ground completely. The flowers are the same light yellow (although mine seem a little shy) but start later and last profitably longer.

A more unusual lamium hails from the Mediterranean: *L. garganicum* subsp. *garganicum* is named after Monte Gargano in Southern Italy, although why twice I know not, unless it is found on both sides of the mountain. It is a pleasing and undemanding plant, which should be seen more often, growing contentedly in sun or shade, requiring only reasonable drainage. It is clump-forming, with lax stems spreading to 16 inches or more, clothed in ashen-green, silky-soft leaves and – from early summer onwards – gentle lilac-pink and white flowers that have a maiden-aunt delicacy allied to the usual hidden agenda among maiden-aunts: indomitability. It makes a balanced partnership with old roses, sharing both their fortitude and their soothing colours.

Nor does *Lamium orvala*, from the Balkans, have the attention it deserves. Where *L. garganicum*'s sweet-pea colouring lulls the senses, *L.. orvala* foments them with its dusky tones of chaffinch-pink flowers and crimson-flushed foliage. Louring from the shade or kindling in full sun, it is equally easy to please; growing stiffly upright to 14 inches or so, its large, shining leaves half hide its modest, coppery flowers. Mine marches with the bletted-mulberry tones of the Californian Hybrid iris 'Broadleigh Rose', both flowering in late spring. *Lamium orvala* grows easily from collected seed, but I have never yet found any self-sown plants. There is a white form, with lighter green foliage, which I have not yet grown, mistakenly believing that it would be too similar to *L. album* to afford it any of my rapidly diminishing space. I was wrong; the seed is being sown, a space is being cleared.

Lamium in all but name is the allied genus *Meehania*, whose one representative in my garden, *M. urticifolia*, from damp woodlands in China, was obliterated by a gaggle of half-feral hens bent on hysterical attack before scorched-earth retreat. So I cannot comment on its large purple flowers, or its ease of culture in this damp garden, until I track down another. First catch your plant; not always as easy as one imagines.

Another seldom-seen lamium relative is *Melittis melissophyllum*. It is an English native that suffers from the common name of bastard balm, which is unfairly damning when one considers the weediness of melissa, the legitimate balm, in both invisible flower and incontinent seed, compared with the stance, foliage, chastity and impressive flowers of melittis. The lemon balm, particularly in its golden form, deserves a place in the kitchen garden, but the uncharitably smeared melittis is worthy of front-row placing in any border. It is not quite so stiff in habit as *L. orvala*, to a foot in height, and its purple-flushed leaves are somewhat smaller. Where the lamium's flowers have a small lower lip but an extended curve to the upper petal, like the projected shell canopy over a Georgian front door, the melittis has no canopy to speak of, but a splaying perron beneath the door, for its pendulous lower lip. The steps are red-carpeted too, as the petal has a loud splash of deeper colour: mauve-pink over pale rose on one plant here, but shrill magenta over clear white on another – sticking its tongue out in defiance of its ignoble common name.

Where lamiums are reviled as weedy nettles, their ajuga relatives are inveighed against as invasive thugs. But, once again, their roots are shallow and easily dislodged, whether stoloniferous *Ajuga reptans*, as unruly as strings of puppies on extension-leads, or the clump-forming but equally land-grabbing species *A. pyramidalis*. Even in a small garden, I grow several, as their willingness to clothe the worst situation and soil with a weed-suppressing brocade of rich colour encourages me to respond positively to the call of the bugle.

The sturdy 6-inch spikes of labiate flowers are a compelling sapphire on the native, bottle green-leaved plant, but are experimental in spirit with useful variations on the blue theme – in cobalt and a light sky-blue, as well as the pure white and rose-pink. Foliage tones are speculative too, showing liver, bronze, silver and variegated forms in cream and green, the tortoiseshell-brindle of 'Multicolor' and the pink-splashed 'Burgundy Glow'. I am rather proud of a lavender-flowered form, with almost black, bronze foliage, which turned up here. Where a mixture is grown, surprises are apt to result. A pale blue form of the green-leaved native appeared in the thick of a redundantly placed clump. Not only did I fail to weed out the type-blue rosettes around it while they were still in flower, but I managed to forget it completely once the flowers had gone over, and hauled out the whole clump. It was the Last Post for that bugle.

Boraginaceae

My AIM IS TO MAKE THESE blue remembered hills still bluer by adding to the garden as many plants of the family Boraginaceae as I can. It's true that some are coarse, such as borage itself, and some are short-lived (as short as flaky pastry on heavy soil), such as anchusa, but they are as blue as a jumbly's hands, so they are worth a little effort. Blue, Presbyterian true-blue, is such an encouraging colour in the garden. There are few other shades that will not be enhanced by its close proximity. It zips along with hot colours and contributes to the quiescence of gentle tones without maundering into the range of gutless pastels. It can be as rasping as a glittering peacock or as pellucid as a kitten's eyes, starry midnight-deep or pink-washed dawn-soft. Good enough to eat, in fact, like borage itself.

Most of the family will flower in the first half of the year here, although the alkanet (naturalized in England, but originally from Portugal), *Pentaglottis sempervirens*, carries flowers as well as leaves throughout the year. Before you rush to acquire it, consider the quantities of seed this habit will encourage, and the stubborn taproot on barely visible seedlings. Perfect if you have large areas of rough ground to clothe but not entirely house-trained for a border unless you are a determined deadheader. Its long leaves are silver-dimpled and coarsely bristled. This leitmotif is recurrent in the borage family; indeed, the name is said to come from the Latin word *burra*, meaning a hairy garment. It has simple flowers of brilliant ultramarine on branched heads to 2–3 feet. Growing strongly, and soundly perennial even on heavy soil, it is an easier option than the similarly coloured *Anchusa azurea*, especially as it needs no staking.

Brunnera macrophylla will throw flowering stems throughout the year too. It is usually known as the perennial forget-me-not, but the turquoise of its flowers is much sharper than myosotis sky-blue, and there is no tentative pinkiness about opening buds. Although there is a delicate chalk-white variety, *B.m.* 'Betty Bowring', pink is not, so far, a brunnera colour, unlike the forget-me-not again, which has all three shades in its make-up box. The rough cordate foliage on brunnera, however, does attempt to widen its repertoire, with conspicuous variegation of milky-lemon and grey-green on 'Hadspen Cream', nearer ivory on 'Dawson's White'. These can suffer sunburn, so in warm gardens they would need the sort of woodsy position that would suit the Yonghy-Bonghy-Bo unless, like a Japanese emperor caring for his azaleas, you can command little boys to hold paper parasols over your susceptible plants. Less troublesome are the silver paint-splashed leaves of 'Langtrees'. I am sorry to see that the name of this renowned garden is being superseded by 'Aluminium Spot', in some garden centres. 'Langtrees' is not difficult to pronounce, nor does it need a translation. Dr Rogerson introduced this brunnera and other good plants from his North Devon garden, Langtrees, including varieties of dicentra, nerine and francoa. Taxonomists are constantly finding earlier references to genera and species, so must alter well-known names accordingly – the earliest name must prevail. Should not this ruling cover cultivar names too? The silver and bottle-green fretted leaves of *Brunnera macrophylla* 'Jack Frost' have a houseplant air of tropicality about them, making it look like a temporary, out-for-an-airing visitor. Silvers that tolerate these conditions are rare, so I am trying to value it, but I'm not sure that I do.

Assayed-silver leaves of *Pulmonaria* 'Cotton Cool' thrive on the edge of a dry wall above the pearly-white *Narcissus triandrus* hybrid, 'Thalia'. Another lungwort, *P.* 'Majesté' is not such a sterling sheet, having almost joined-up dots and an edging; nor is it such a doughty performer. There are now dozens of named varieties of the old boys and girls with which we all grew up. Although many are no better than seedlings that will turn up in your garden, some are delicious, in coral-red, opal, white and a warm pink that stays pink without the slide into blue of the original lungwort, *P. officinalis*. This nails its colours firmly to the fence, unsure, like many an MP, on which side of the gangway it really wants to sit. Its names, both common and botanical, arose from the suggested similarity between its spotted leaves and consumptive lungs. The pulmonaria that I like best is the species *P. angustifolia*, from Eastern Europe, in a good deep cobalt blue, very early in spring, with unspotted leaves the green of a cooking apple. Unlike most lungworts, whose foliage grows into profuse hassocks for the summer and autumn, to be replaced in early winter by new young shoots to partner the flower sprays, *P. angustifolia*'s leaves stay small and disappear completely by late summer, to emerge, just ahead of the flowering-stems, in spring.

Where most pulmonarias have creeping rhizomes, the similar genus *Nonea*, from the Caucasus, has widely spreading stems from a single crown. Having said it is similar, it occurs to me that the main, if not only reason for growing nonea is to accentuate its differences from pulmonaria. First the single crown, then colour: *N. lutea* surprises visitors, unaware of its name and presuming it is a lungwort, with its primrose-lemon flowers. *N. intermedia* has bells of a sultry plum-red blooming in midsummer – another significant difference. Both have narrow, unblemished green leaves. Yet another deviation is that *N. lutea* is a hardy annual, which makes it a most useful spring bedder, over tulips perhaps, or cascading from window-boxes, as its flowering period begins in early March and continues on ever-lengthening stems – eventually to 12 inches or more – until late May. Then, collect seed, sprinkle if your soil allows such liberties or sow inside and plant out as your tulips begin to wake up and guide your trowel the following spring. The nonea will be in flower by then, but still small enough to have remained in a 3-inch pot, taking up little room in your overwintering cold frame. If you choose the indoor-sowing method, rather than *in situ*, it will allow you to cover the tulip plot with summer bedding, whether planted or in large pots.

Similar in habit is *Borago pygmaea* (syn. *laxiflora*). The synonymous name is more descriptive, as it is certainly lax in flower, but, as its arms extend to 2 feet eventually, it is scarcely a pygmy. It is commonly termed the perennial borage; doubtless in hot, sunny, well-drained gardens, whose conditions are reminiscent of its home range on Corsican hillsides, it would correspond to this epithet, and would seed around sufficiently to mask its naturally short life. Here, inevitably, it cannot manage more than an annual whimper, not even that if left to the mercy of slugs. Winter damp seals its fate, and that of any brave seed. It has nodding bells of a lucent aquamarine, among leaves and stems stamped from grey-green sandpaper.

Trachystemon orientalis, from the Caucasus, would also prefer a more sheltered Sargasso than I can provide, as its early spring flowers are pulped by frost too often or perished to purple, rather than deep royal blue, when they do manage to run the gauntlet of minus temperatures. The flowers are held in large clusters, with white borage-beaks, but more slender, Turk's cap petals. The 18-inch stems are borage-like too, wherein lies the frost susceptibility as, being hollow, they hold a quantity of water, which expands and shatters the brittle stems in icy weather, turning them to black slime. As I lose the flowers so often, it is fortunate that the trachystemon's foliage is valuable. Coarse, certainly, like most of the family, it expands throughout the season too, another family trait. As a result, it fails to protect the earliest flowers and swamps their later efforts with its vehemence. Eighteen inches long and twelve inches wide by midsummer, grass-green with darker veins and held on arching stems emerging from its doggedly-creeping rhizomes, they make impressive rough cover in damp soil, and thrive on neglect.

The genus *Omphalodes* is another member of the borage family whose flowers pop out in all seasons, although, once again, the main flush in spring manages better here after a mild winter. *O. verna*, which grew in the woods at Schönbrunn, was said to be the favourite flower of Marie-Antoinette. As it has Sèvres-blue flowers on a plant with polished manners masking a steely will of iron, it seems an appropriate choice. The white form is as guileless as Le Hameau: superficially ingenuous, that is, with a self-interested determination; they are uncompromising territorialists. Less greedy of space, and with significantly bigger flowers, is *Omphalodes cappadocica*. On the variety 'Cherry Ingram' the flowers are an intense sapphire blue, in spring, on 6-inch stems above deep bottle-green creeping foliage. I cannot please this beautiful plant; it endures, but I can see that its teeth are gritted. The shade it favours is too ice-bound here in spring; the soil is claggy, rather than the loose leafy litter it would prefer. Planted with better drainage, it dries out and shrivels to nothing. In full sun and silty soil on the Wilderness, where its shallow roots spread slowly, it will flower reasonably well following less intractable winters, but the blooming is brief and it does not enjoy its fling. I hope that the texture of this soil will improve with time and continued leaf accumulation among the herbaceous plants. Earlier, wind would scour them away before the soil could benefit. We shall persevere. One of the most delicate annuals is *O. linifolia*, with silvery foliage and chalk-white flowers that look as though they are cut from *broderie-anglaise*, complete with embroidered eyelet in the centre: the navel that gives them their name. Pure innocence, rather than Trianon-gimcrackery.

Buglossoides purpurocaerulea is another lowly ground-covering plant that excels in well drained shade. Its flowers, of the pulmonaria persuasion, are deep violet from pink buds, held above silvery-green, willow-like leaves. It used to be known as a lithospermum but, unusually for that genus, comes from limestone areas of Europe, including several native stations in Great Britain. *Cynoglossum nervosum*, from the Himalayas, needs good drainage and full sun. On heavy soils it can be short-lived and flop-stemmed, but so far so good. Its simple flowers are a tropical turquoise-sky blue, on branched 2-foot stems above a basal swirl of strappy leaves in a light Adam green. The biennial *C. dioscoridis* makes a bigger plant, almost pyramidal in shape, to 3 feet, with a soft, muffled appearance, as though veiled in mist. Its foliage is an ashy grey-green and its sprays of flowers are a 'Patty's Plum' greyed crimson – subdued but sensitive. Determinedly perennial, with large sprays of ultramarine blue flowers, is *Lindelofia anchusoides*, from Kashmir. Mine is planted rather dry, in full sun, so its 3-foot stems are almost self-supporting; it flowers at midsummer.

Symphytum officinale grows in the hedgerow ditches around here, a very comfy comfrey, displaying its unfurling crozier flowerheads in countless shades of whey-white, washed-mauve and slatey-blue. It is not a plant to die for, but is worth growing nonetheless for two reasons: firstly, you will have deeply contented bees, and secondly, equally serene compost. Adding comfrey leaves to an active bin is like giving it a shot of Prozac. It will help the compost to relax into friable filaments, rather than the usual taut wodge of depressed slime. So a row of comfrey roots in your kitchen garden will ensure your bins resemble Fortunatus' purse: the more they are emptied, the quicker they fill again.

Some species of comfrey are scarcely to be trusted other than in rough areas of the garden: they run about voraciously. But there are two clump-forming beauties that would grace any border and would look equally at home in woodland clearings, too. *Symphytum orientale*, from the Caucasus, has soft, heart-shaped leaves of a light pea-green, and 2-foot stems of lime-wash white flowers from spring to early summer. It is staunch in dry shade, lightening any gloom with its calm colours. Mine is planted in just such a sequestered corner, so I am lazy about cutting it back after flowering. As a result I have been blessed with a couple of seedlings, which can stay and add to the effect: nepotism in progress. I have read that it can seed about too much; perhaps that happens if grown in rich soil. As it does so well where few other plants will thrive, such hospitality seems wasted. *Symphytum* 'Rubrum' is equally easy to please, but its brilliant ruby-pink flowers are so rewarding that it should be given a seat in the dress circle. Mine is next to *Papaver orientale* 'Raspberry Queen', whose colour is a good match for the comfrey's early summer efforts. If cut back as these flowers finish, it will retrick its beams and produce a second flush in late summer, toning well with *Fuchsia magellanica* 'Versicolor', whose flowers are the usual ruby and violet, but whose foliage has pink swirled into a creamy grey-green. Near by, *Penstemon* 'Garnet' and *P.* 'Rich Ruby' continue the jewelled setting. *Symphytum* 'Rubrum' grows only 12–15 inches tall, its roots are well mannered and, being a sterile hybrid, will not embarrass you with self-sown ardour.

Two more good plants are not members of the borage family but of the Solanaceae, the potato family; I include them here because their looks and habit are close enough to have the root of the matter in them, if not the genes. *Physochlaina orientalis*, from the Caucasus, has hairy oval leaves of a dim lavender-green and clusters of pulmonaria-like flowers in spring, of a curious steely-mauve colour. It is said to grow to 2 feet, but mine stays at about 9 inches. It likes well-drained soil and is happy in sun, but I feel that its *triste* tone is more suited to shade. It disappears completely by midsummer. *Scopolia carniolica*, also an unlikely potato, except in that it shares the family preoccupation with poison, comes likewise from the Caucasus, but from damper areas of woodland. It pushes blunt blue noses through the soil in early spring from black, brittle rhizomes, which open into mat green leaves, distinctly netted with veins. Among these leaves, in spring, funnel-shaped bells appear on slender stems. They are glossy chestnut-brown outside with an ochrous mustard interior. There is a greenish-yellow form (sometimes said to be a separate sub-species, *S.c. podolica*) and a deep violet variety 'Zwanenburg'. They make a slowly creeping hummock, about a foot tall.

Finally, there is an ambition, rather than just a plant: *Eritrichium nanum* is probably the smallest member of the borage family, and certainly the most difficult (verytrichium) to please. It is also one of the most beautiful, with its silver tuffet of leaves and empyreanly blue flowers, as unlike the rough-hewn trachystemon as a delicate harvest mouse differs from the giant capybara. It is one of the plants I should like to grow before I die. Known as the King of the Alps, and found only on the highest, cleanest and generally most inaccessible mountain ranges, it would be utterly impossible here: an alpine house must be built to attempt to suit its exactitude. But as I always muddle tufa with tofu, not to mention humus with hummous, my soil recipe might not suffice, although, come to think of it, they are rather similar.

EARLY SUMMER

IT IS A WARM EVENING IN EARLY SUMMER, and the air is a thick mayfly soup, with flickering wings and curved tails glittering in the soft westering sun. A swift swoops through them like a basking shark sifting plankton, and carries its haul to a hole beneath the eaves where its sitting mate greets her supper with a wheezy squeal. All the gold of Golconda glistens in the ash tree, each leaf newly burnished like the dripping foliage in a John Sell Cotman watercolour. From its heart, the liquid mellifluence of a garden warbler sighs the sun down, with a blackcap from a nearby wire taking, like Frank Churchill, a slight second.

The golden velvet light glints through the creamy bells of an erstwhile allium, now *Nectaroscordum siculum* subsp. *bulgaricum*, turning the internal stripes of quiet murrey to a rich raspberry pink, echoing the taffeta petals of an oriental poppy beyond. A week or so ago, the nectaroscordum's buds stood like cormorants sunbathing, beak-high, their heads held obliquely to the sun. Bursting from their papery caul, the opening bells hung down on agile stems. Now, as pollinating wasps and bees work over them, the spent flowers lift again to form the seed heads: a cluster of pepper-pot turrets like the cities of the plain in an Edmund Dulac illustration.

Above my chair a honeysuckle pulses with bumblebees: *Lonicera* x *tellmanniana* has no scent but delights the eye, at least, with bunches of large amber bugles set in perfoliate saucers of glaucous green. At its feet are clumps of *Geum rivale* 'Leonard's Variety' and an unnamed, early-blooming day lily with tidy 16-inch stems of slender trumpets. Each plant bloomed in a blush terracotta that harmonized well with the lonicera, displaying a contrast of foliage and flower in both shape and texture. This year, on a whim, the day lily has sounded its trumpets in a much deeper key of burnt Venetian red, and splayed open to reveal a brazen-orange throat. Odd how day lilies manage this — is it due to water content in the soil, or some volatile mineral, or temperature, or just a genetic weakness? I have noticed it before when they have been moved and, indeed, when newly planted, causing me to wonder if a nursery has supplied the wrong variety. My *Hemerocallis* 'American Revolution' (described as 'blackish-maroon, narrow trumpets') was a coarse orange with a scanty red lip the first time it flowered, but certainly the right shape — like that of the beautiful *H. lilioasphodelus*. So it was banished to the kitchen garden, pencilled-in until it proved its identity, before being inked-in permanently in any border. Two years on, I am still waiting for it to flower again: it has buds forming; this is its last chance.

Later: the flowers turned back on themselves, like Turk's cap lilies in a pedestrian red, still with the stolid orange throat. Enough; it is time for the day lily to kiss hands and relinquish office. A small garden is not licensed to carry passengers. It is vital to aim for the best forms of each plant, but this does not necessarily mean the accepted best or the best as recommended by anyone else. It means the best for you, in your garden, in your circumstances. Gardeners often lack the confidence to wade against the tide, opting for safe, accredited dullness, rather than trusting themselves out on their own slender, audacious spar.

The accepted theory of the colour wheel points to orange as the natural contrast to blue, it being a blend of the second and third primary colours, red and yellow. With respect, I prefer orange with purple, instead of the latter's official contrast yellow, which can look insipid when both are light in tone, and too raucous for my taste when each is rich in hue. There are few pure orange flowers; most of them have yellow mixed in, like pot marigolds, or brown, like crocosmias, or else are horribly acrylic, like the chemical orange of day lilies. Nasturtiums can be a pure orange; *Geum* 'Borisii' shines cleanly, albeit briefly. But the best orange of all are the button-headed daisy flowers of *Anthemis sancti-johannis*, which would look splendidly opulent beside the sort of imperial purple that you see on certain clematises or on the old *Phlox* 'Border Gem'. As none of the anthemis family performs well in cold, heavy soil, showing bald etiolated stems, all rickety knees and elbows, and rotting over winter — gone, alas, like our youth, too soon — I gave up growing them too long ago to remember whether either of these suggested partners will coincide in their flowering with no more than elementary tinkering. Almost as pure in tone (if slightly on the vermilion side of orange) is the annual *Tithonia rotundifolia*, the Mexican sunflower. This will coincide, but, at 4 feet tall, needs to be behind the phlox, with a shot or two of *Clematis* 'Polish Spirit' splashed over it, perhaps. On my soil the tithonia needs to be staked, else its top-heavy daisy flowers, with their curiously swollen stems, as thick-necked as a Bismarkian general, will crash down and ruin the artistry. Being half-hardy, tithonias are a risk, here, proved by most summers to be not worth the taking.

The rule of contrast is useful for those nervous of colour, or of their own sensibilities when using it; but it can be self-conscious and easily becomes hackneyed when the same old clichés of chosen contrast – *Cotinus coggygria* 'Royal Purple' beneath *Robinia pseudoacacia* 'Frisia' or golden conifers with purple berberis – are repeated in too many gardens. How much more harmonious, but still arresting, would be the pewter *Rosa glauca* with the cotinus and *Ceanothus* x *delileanus* 'Gloire de Versailles' beneath the 'Frisia'.

White is considered the ultimate contrast to leaven the border, but should be used, I feel, as sparingly as yeast. Big blocks of white can kill by the severity of the contrast. I have a large swathe of the native stitchwort, *Stellaria holostea*, around a gatepost, where its infiltrating roots have spread through the shallow soil over the concrete footings, and under the gate itself, to give a year-round covering of its, candidly, unedifying and frugal foliage. Not that I am complaining; it does a difficult job admirably, and is not there to be noticed, necessarily, until it flowers in early summer. At this point, nothing could be prettier, more delicate or more suitable. To enhance all three attributes, it has invited forget-me-nots to co-habit, and their *ménage* is entrancing: simultaneous flowering of turquoise and chalk-white, on matching 12-inch stems, which are then tugged away to tidiness for the remainder of the year, as taller neighbours draw the attention. The white works here as, despite the large number of flowers, they are individually small with slender, ribbon-thin petals that look like a species of dianthus – in fact they are cousins, and in this situation the stitchwort is the very pink of perfection. The bright myosotis blue is a definite contrast but there is plenty of gentle silvery-green to suspend the sequins of disparate colours. A similar effect could be achieved with other natives:

sweet woodruff, *Galium odoratum*, for a fastidious perennial froth at ground level of tiny white flowers held above whorls of bright green leaves, which throw an undemanding coverlet over snowdrops. Or the white form of herb Robert, *Geranium robertianum* 'Album', which, although annual, conducts its own right of succession with ease and constructive stage management – always sowing itself into what looks like a carefully considered picture: sparkling in the shadow beneath a large fern, through which it insinuates itself with merit to both parties; or beside the front door to lounge against the old bricks and share a little of their colour as summer leans on autumn.

To return to the colour wheel – or my heterodox version of it: rather than conformist purple, I prefer my yellow with blue, by which I mean true blue, such as gentians or borage, and not nurseryman's 'blue', which is invariably a mawkish mauve – blue sells, mauve does not. Whether navy aconite or sky-blue echinops, yellow is the perfect complement. My own choice leans more toward lemons than egg-yolks, *crème anglaise* rather than Bird's custard. But that's not to say that any yellow is excluded purposely from my garden: if it is a good plant, I am happy to grow the eggiest cowardy-custard of all yellows, such as *Crocosmia* 'Golden Fleece' (now sheared of its familiar name, and rebranded as 'Coleton Fishacre'), provided there are no pinks near by. That, to my eye, would be a contrast too far.

Blue and yellow are the predominant colours now, in early summer, in a large border, facing sou-sou-west, whose focal point is a brace of silver birch trees, the native *Betula pendula*. These were grown from seed and planted at about 5 feet, seven years ago. Now they are well over 20 feet tall and their trunks have shed their juvenile tan, like peeling sunburn, to reveal a crepuscular silver creased with black, carved in cameo upon the yew hedge behind. I prefer these delicate native trees to the popular *B. utilis* var. *jacquemontii*, whose dead-white trunk makes me think of a flayed snake pinned out on the dissecting table. Silver birches are not, perhaps, the best choice for the middle of a border, as their roots are greedy, and their lower branches, waltzing with the wind, can lacerate surrounding plants, and your own face as you move among them, with their whippy stems. Spare the birch and spoil the plant, but any lower-limbing should be done in autumn when the sap is no longer rising, or your birch can bleed to death.

The border is roughly triangular, the right angle being formed by the yew hedge and the wall above the stream. The latter is thickly-shrubbed (to dissipate both frost and wind) with rugged evergreens such as box, *Mahonia aquifolium* and *Berberis* x *stenophylla*, interspersed with equally staunch deciduous shrubs: an unnamed variegated forsythia — for early colour, enough said — and *Philadelphus coronarius* 'Aureus', planted in the half-shade beyond the silver birches so that its leaves are not scorched by the sun and its ormolu will lighten the blackness of the surrounding evergreens. It works magically. On the strength of this success, I have added more shrubs with yellow foliage in front of the evergreens. This deepens the border by deepening the shadows. It accentuates both textures and colours, as the golden foliage tends to be thin and mat, whereas the evergreens are thick and shiny. *Physocarpus opulifolius* 'Luteus' has the peeling bark and palmate leaves of a currant bush, but not its vigour, alas. Coming from eastern North America, it might prefer a more neutral soil, and its dry dock (tree-shade as well as tree-roots) will make this worse. As a result, its leaves are smaller than normal, its growth tighter. *Sambucus racemosa* 'Plumosa Aurea' seems unaffected by the arid soil. Its foliage is as lavishly feathered and gilded as one could wish, although its shape is now awkward, as the third arm of a well spaced fan was found snapped off one morning. A year or two of judicious pruning should sort that out.

All of these yellow shrubs age to a light lime-green as summer progresses, but are at their sharpest in May and June when the mainly blue herbaceous plants in front of them form delicate patterns like shot silk — revealing then veiling the golden background. Great stooks of deep blue *Camassia leichtlinii* and the powder blue *C. cusickii* contribute strong verticals as a *clairvoyée* before the billowing shrubs. Airy aquilegias in matching powder-blue and in milk-white, with bright yellow foliage or with variegated foliage, allow similar glimpses of gold and gleaming green between floating bonnet-flowers and dainty basal leaves. Richer blue polemoniums perform the same service. *Iris sibirica* 'Summer Sky' (the name is perfect, unlike many sibiricas, particularly those described as pink, when the nearest they ever manage is a bluish-mauve) is a fine plant, unfailingly floriferous, early and not too tall. Its large, light-blue and crisp white flowers are of good proportion — again, unlike many that have paltry blooms on lank stems and bushels of untidy leaves that age poorly over a wearily long period of late summer.

Harmonies of tone, as well as pigment, are necessary: deep and light, clear and clouded. A border of perfectly complemented colours, with no tonal range, can look as banal as supermarket advertising. Colours blended with subtle tertiary tones or curdled with white, tip the complementaries slightly off-balance, creating less patent foils. So by adding tobacco-amber-demerara sugar colours, I am nodding toward both orange and purple, but the nod is firmly nonconformist. Thus the arching, 3-foot stems of *Lathyrus aureus*, from the Urals, with clusters of ambrous pea flowers, curve behind 'Summer Sky', and help to disguise the ragged remains of the camassia's spent blue stars and obsolescent bulb leaves. More verticals are provided by *Digitalis parviflora*. Grown from seed, mine show two distinct colour forms: milk chocolate and the warm chestnut of Pears soap. Their tightly packed narrow bells surge to 4 feet or so above gleaming dark-green, strappy leaves. The brown form of *Bupleurum longifolium* has tiny flowers of tobacco-brown set in flaring, honey-coloured bracts above ample glabrous foliage also steeped in honey. It grows to 3 feet and looks like a wide-eyed euphorbia, but has a better temperament than many of those, in my conditions. Bronze fennel, *Foeniculum vulgare* 'Purpureum', attempts to luxuriate near by; it never manages more than a couple of weedy stems of ill-polished spelter ware, but gilt-bronze *Carex dipsacea*, from New Zealand, kindles merrily at its feet. On a small hazel wigwam *Clematis fusca* dangles its tactile bells, made from thick felt, with the teardrop shape of an upturned pipkin pot and the colour of freshly ground coffee. It is a world away from 'Marie Boisselot' and the 'Duchess of Edinburgh', but worth growing if your taste veers away from the obvious. All of this metheglin richness turns the eggshell delicacy of the blue and yellow to an earthy majolica in the caressing sunshine.

Nearer the path, where smaller plants can be seen in detail, is the miniature goat's beard from Korea. *Aruncus aethusifolius* makes a bun of finely cut foliage that changes from spring gold to fresh green for early summer, on to copper by late summer, then as red as a herring for autumn. Its feather-duster flowers are briefly cream on 10-inch stems, then toasted walnut for the rest of its season, and on over winter, if it is not too gale-blown. Next to it grow two early summer-flowering beauties: a short form of *Veronica gentianoides* from the Caucasus and the enchanting Himalayan blue buttercup, *Anemone trullifolia*. Each is an exquisite larkspur-blue, like a clear morning sky seen through a wisp of organza cloud. The 6-inch tall anemone sits tight in its sunny, not-too-dry position; the veronica needs frequent division – at least every other year – to keep it happy. This one grows to only 8 inches or so, but another, elsewhere in the garden, rushes up to more than 2 feet. This tall form was acquired at a village fête, labelled 'Aster – blue'. One can only wonder at so grotesque a blunder.

Early summer is still a good time for planting. Most of the bulbs will be evident in either post-blooming disarray or pre-blooming beakiness, so gaps should not be tempting disaster, except where arisaemas are lurking – some species can delay their arrival until July. Anything planted now should get away fast in the warmer soil, soon showing its true colours, which, hopefully, will not spring an unwelcome surprise that must be lived with for the season, before another move is possible. More irritating is a horticultural equivalent of *esprit de l'escalier*, where I remember, too late, what it was that I had meant to plant in a space just filled by something less suitable. The only thing that stops planting is the probability of damage: the borders are filling up too much now to allow easy access with either a spade or successive watering cans.

So planting must stop and staking take over – my least favourite job. Must I do it? Sounding like an Anthony Trollope title, it is my annual soliloquy at this time. And yes, on the whole, I must, until I hate the chore enough to stop growing susceptible plants. A chummery of close planting does not help, as plants in a party-wall dispute are just as likely to push each other over as to prop each other up; altruism does not proliferate in the border. Had I the sort of soil that would accept brushwood I should find pleasure in the construction of lobster-pot domes of twiggery, with an Arts and Crafts' pride in the doing as well as the done. But my method must be more Heath Robinson than Morris, as my heavy soil requires strong canes hammered as deeply as stones allow, at the latest possible moment in the plant's growth. If this is done too soon, particularly in wet summers, gales will rock the canes until they are loosened, even lifted out of the ground, just as the plant reaches full size; too late, and I am struggling to lift right-angled stems back to vertical – most will retain a cricked neck to the end.

The majority of plants need to be poussetted with string around their total girth, then crossed through the centre to stop all the stems leaning on those at the front. Ideally, I will time it so that one length of string will be all the restraint necessary. But keen to have a disagreeable job finished, I will always do some too soon, so that as they grow taller, another girdle must be added. This must be done with care, as it will alter the poise of the plant and can leave the first string redundantly slack, or else truss the plant like George IV in squeezing corsets and strangling stock. Being congenitally mean with string, I save and re-use all I can from one year to the next. Tugging will expose the rotten ends, but inevitably there will be a collapse or two, as pieces I should have discarded give way. Birds tear at it for nesting material; animals blunder through and break it; gales cause the plants themselves to rebel against their captor. Deadheaded, and thereby shortened, plants may need their surcingles resited, canes too – although in drought years the soil shrinkage around the stakes makes them impossible to remove until soaked repeatedly to the base. Visible stakes are a distraction from what should be holding the eye – the plants themselves. The only time I like the sight is over winter, when all are safely gathered into sheaves stored in tall coal-hods in the garage. They look as ready for action as the shocks of militiamen's pikes hoarded, against invasion, in old churches; and, in winter, thankfully, about as likely to be used.

By the middle of June I hope that frosts are lessening enough for me to be placing the more intrepid plants in pots out in their summer positions. Lilies can cope with low temperatures but not with slugs, so they are guarded until almost flowering before staying out at night, especially in wet summers. Penstemon hybrids vary in their hardiness: a general guideline being the larger the leaf, the more tender the plant. Such dauntless old favourites as 'Garnet' and 'Hidcote Pink' (or Hideous Pink, as the donor of mine called it) have stood outside for the last two winters with minimal damage, so I am planting them in the borders this summer to take their chance on a third lenient winter. Insurance cuttings are growing apace. These and newly acquired penstemons stay potted and inside over winter. Much as I admire their generous flowering season and flamboyant colours, the strident red of 'Rubicundus' is too bellicose for casual placing. Its long-snouted bugles remind me of the flared, red-painted nostrils on a rocking horse.

Large pots are planted up with annuals to stand on the gaps left by finished bulbs; some grown from seed, others bought, if the garden centre display takes my fancy. This year I bought *Mimulus* × *hybridus*, in a coruscating mixture of scarlet, cherry and citrus yellow, which has been a *tour de force* swaggering over a 16-inch terracotta pot – big enough to prevent them drying out too quickly. At a village fête last year I bought two young plants of the biennial *Campanula pyramidalis*, intending to grow them on to flower this summer as matched footmen flanking the front door. They must be picked over for deadheads each day, unlike those grown *in locus classicus* beside the empty summer fireplace, where, with no bees to ravage them, each flower lasts for weeks.

Other pots stand in groups on a sunny terrace in the centre of the garden where an armchair is surrounded by three small borders facing east, south and west, planted in the colours of the dawn, noon, and sunset. Thus a pot of the delicate *Fuchsia magellanica* var. *molinae* 'Sharpitor', whose flowers are the palest shell-pink, and each leaf a *parterre de broderie* of grey, green and cream, stands by the Dawn border, beside *Convolvulus cneorum*, from the Balkans, with cloth-of-silver foliage and carmine buds spiralled like narwhal tusks. As its flowers begin to unfurl, the pink shows only as narrow spokes on the back of the petals, like mother of pearl sticks on a fan of white silk. There is also the Tasmanian *Diplarrhena moraea*, an iris relative, from whose stiff grassy leaves arise 18-inch stems of enchanting white flowers: a triad of curved petals arranged around a central knot that is lightly fretted with lilac and pale yellow. It is more like a seashell than a flower, the petals having a nacreous iridescence. All of these plants are too tender to withstand a normal winter here, so their pots must be kept in the shed, as near to bone-dry as idling evergreens will sanction.

In the primary-coloured Noon border, above tulips, stand other generous pots: of the mimulus already mentioned; *Nasturtium* 'Empress of India', with vermilion horns and verdigris cymbals, and *Commelina tuberosa* Coelestis Group, from Central America, which has been hardened off gradually, in relative shelter beside the front door, an extra hour each day.

It began in spring as a handful of roots, each like a grey rubber octopus, which were planted in a capacious pot (so that their eventual requirements should not be stinted), but kept inside and dry until the days became warmer and watering could commence. It is well worth what might appear to be a lot of fuss: 2-foot culms, short-jointed and bamboo-stiff, are topped by large bud-cases shaped like birds' heads, which split across the top, like gaping pitta bread, to reveal a mass of buds that open in sequence throughout the summer into three-petalled flowers of a celestial curaçao-blue. The tuberous octopuses should be treated like a dahlia over winter.

Eucomis bicolor and *E. autumnalis* are grown in pots here too, which are stored inside, dry, for the winter. Beginning watering in spring can be hazardous, as they are naturally late to appear. If I water too early and a long cold spell returns immediately afterwards, the bulbs will rot. But if all goes well, the heraldic pineapple-buds with their top-knot tuft of leaves, looking like a ceremonial mace, will be opening by late summer. *E. bicolor* is a green satin Tudor doublet, padded and puffed, piped with cherry-red and sprinkled with pearls. The smaller *E. autumnalis* seems to be carved from ivory. Both, after what can be a wobbly start in a cold season, are the very pineapple of politeness. Slugs find them irresistible, chewing holes in the wall of the hollow stems, so they may slime their way inside and live in their own larder.

Another pot holds the tender bi-generic hybrid x *Pardancanda norrisii* (or Whatcanda, as a friend insists), a cross between iridaceous cousins pardanthopsis and belamcanda, the latter sometimes called the leopard lily. Its purple-freckled, red flowers are similar in style to schizostylis, but its leaves are pure iris and scruffy to boot, where slugs have been attentive. Also like schizostylis, it flowers too late in autumn to succeed each year, when frost will burst buds before their debut. A safer bet is *Cistus* x *loretii* (syn. *C.* x *stenophyllus*), whose tissue-paper flowers continue all summer. They are white with a maroon blotch at the base of each large petal, around a central boss of sunshine-yellow stamens. The foliage is a gleam of bottle-green, pungently aromatic and sticky. My favourite cistus, *C.* x *purpureus*, with expansive flowers of deep rose-pink taffeta with a big purple thumbprint at the centre, has grown out of its pot so, as with the penstemons, I have planted it out this year, with the usual insurance policy of cuttings taken. Cistus are simple indeed from cuttings, taken now if you rely on the sun to warm the pot, or in autumn if you have artificial heat. They put weight on fast, provided they have plenty of water in the growing season. Winter drought is their ideal where temperatures are as cold as this.

As the days lengthen, and warmth becomes palpable, frogs begin to creak in the dry walls, and insects are suddenly more evident, both visually and aurally. White-painted windowsills act as electric under-blankets for bees and butterflies needing a boost of heat. Less safely, so do tarmac roads. Exotic ruby-tailed wasps favour the old wooden gate, gathering in twos and threes, their hummingbird suits of emerald and ruby lamé dazzling in the midday sun. Neither mayflies nor maybugs restrict themselves to their eponymous month. I have found mayflies clinging ruefully to the back door on sunny days in February and November, all purpose thwarted. Maybugs used to crash against the lighted windows (picking quarrels with the quarrels) throughout the summer months, two or three every night. Now, I am lucky to hear one over the whole summer. Closely akin to cockroaches, but more attractive in their pinkish armour, edged with a ric-rac Greek-key pattern, one would imagine them to be just as indestructible, but clearly something is happening to the absurdly bombastic maybug.

Wasps appear to be nesting in one of the compost bins. It is almost full anyway, so can be left to prove, with or without wasps. *Laisser faire, laisser passer.* And bumblebees have been excavating their nest in the dry soil beneath a small pile of stones on the Wilderness. I watch with delight their comings and goings: each arrival is greeted, each departure waved-off by a friendly group of bumbles, who hang in the air around the entrance and around me when I am weeding close by, floating up to hover on a level with my face — studying me, as I study them — murmuring gently, then floating off again. There is no aggression, just benign curiosity. After a week or so of this graceful behaviour, they feel like old friends, and I am listening hard to try to detect recognizable differences in their hums. Then, one morning, molehills have appeared around the nest. The bees are interested, but calm, and endless site meetings take place. The following morning, disaster: something has dug down into the soft soil of the mole tump, and there are bees crawling everywhere, clearly in great distress. Their nest must have been in an old mouse nest, as shredded plastic has been disinterred and strewn about and the bumbles are trying to drag it all back again. Perhaps the mole disturbed it sufficiently to release mouse scent to whatever dug it out – badger or fox. Torrential rain on the following night spells doom. Three dazed bees remain. Next day, all are gone. Weeding is not so much fun now.

As cow parsley spumes from every hedgerow and a tide of bluebells rolls over the bank beyond the meadow, curlews fly overhead, their plangent cries winding up to a crescendo, then winding down again, like a clockwork toy. They lay their eggs on the ground in the high pastures, so many must be lost each year. But one glorious August, nine curlews flew in convoy over my garden, heading south after a successful breeding season, each bird a rippling resonance, scimitar-beak agape. A single curlew sounds like a sob of despair, but a group – surely their collective noun should be a cadence of curlews – sounds like a joyful proclamation.

Cuckoos are now as rare as magpies are common; it used to be the other way round. Much as I regret the cuckoo, I have a sneaking fondness for the magpie, whose *joie de vivre* is as infectious as their cannibalistic beastliness is indefensible. In their tight black breeches and shot-silk cut-away coat, they are the epitome of the roistering Regency buck. Clearly all magpies belong to the Hellfire Club.

Early summer is a coat of many colours. Foliage is at its best, new-minted and gorged with richness. To describe it as green is to call a prism white. Textures vary more at this time, too, having just left the drawing board, as per spec. Like children lately arrived at the party, plants are still clean and tidy, before rumbustious horseplay – the pushing, shoving, pinching and pulling away of the chair as one sits down, that is life in an average garden – takes its inevitable toll as summer heightens. The pristine colours tarnish, velvet leaves become pilled, the gloss dims. But time marches onwards, and the midsummer pomps are listening for their cue.

Poppies

BY THE TIME SUMMER HAS set in with its usual severity, oriental poppies will be bursting into bloom. The earliest to flower here is *Papaver orientale* 'May Queen'. Flowering in May, its ragged blooms are untidy doubles that look like a kindergarten craft class's effort with orange crêpe paper. Indeed, the whole plant is an old man of Thermopylae, who never does anything properly. Its flowers are a mess, of an uncompromising orange, lasting for half a second before the sun bleaches and scorches them; its stems are incapable of growing straight – whether staked or left to themselves, they always spiral and plunge like a fly-fishing line; its roots are dogged runners, unwavering in their ambition to win the hearts of every surrounding plant. Why do I bother with it? Because it has the most beautiful buds of any plant in the garden: the silver-furred stems arch gracefully at this moment in their career, topped with the drooping, swan's-necked, downy buds, as supple as a ballerina's arched wrist, as limpid as a sleeping kitten's paw. Circled with a halo of captured sunlight or sprinkled with a shimmer of dew, they attract all who see them. As soon as these buds are past their best, I rarely wait for the anticlimactic flowers to finish, but cut them all back to base. Gone to earth, for another year.

No other oriental poppy of my acquaintance has buds like these, nor shares the quirks of character of the maverick 'May Queen'. Normal oriental poppies grow in sedate clumps and have upright, green, bristly buds on straight, wiry stems. And of course it is the flowers that count. The flowers are the only point. I have never seen a malevolent meadow of somnolent opium poppies grown for trade, so it is oriental poppies that evoke, for me, the title Lords of Lethe and recall Virgil's poppies drenched in oblivion.

Drooping like the daughters of pleasure, was how Mary Webb portrayed day lilies; but oriental poppies are a closer fit. They have such an air of ennui, such world-weary languor; they make me think of drowsy old courtesans, powdered and rouged, sipping tokay, playing piquet, comparing past conquests. They are self-conscious plants, with yet a hint of restraint – no poppy is scented. Thorough sensuousness would have provided a heady, something-of-the-night perfume, to be pollinated by moths, instead of bumblebees by day, scrambling through the *chevaux de frise* of purple chenille stamens.

Some oriental poppies have less romantic connotations: *Papaver orientale* 'Helen Elizabeth' is the chemical flesh-pink of a 1960s Bri-nylon cardi. Grief failed to prostrate me when it appeared to succumb to winter rot, which happens sometimes in very wet seasons – the crown turns to smelly brown slime, in turn attracting slugs to finish the job. Most recover, but take a year or two to return to former glory. In the case of 'Helen Elizabeth', only one small shoot resurrected itself, so it was three years before it flowered again. Perhaps my memory, sight, or sensibilities have failed me, but the revived plant seems to have shed the worst of its synthetic prawn cocktail-sauce colour, and has emerged more the hue of a Hollywood dawn. It shocks me less than it did.

P.o. 'Juliane' is a rosy shrimp-pink, with shallow blooms lacking the central henna-rimmed, odalisque's eyes. This gives the flowers a pearly translucency that looks best with other light colours. It is slight in growth, too, so may fit well into schemes where the big poppies, such as 'Graue Witwe', would be overpowering. Its alabaster blooms open to 8 inches wide by 4 inches deep and makes a proportionately bosomy clump, with flowering stems to 4 feet. Bigger still is 'Beauty of Livermere': 5 feet tall and with deeply cupped flowers of gleaming blood-red, further embellished by mascara'd black satin centres. On my plant, the petals are rather floppy, curving inwards before bellying out. This crimson cave reverberates with mumbling bees, making it the noisiest oriental poppy.

'Patty's Plum' must be too well known, now, to require a description of its muted murrey. It is a fine plant, and the colour is a splendid catalyst between so-called purple foliage – in reality maroon – and dusty pinks and greys. It looks surprisingly good with khaki-browns, too, such as the moody (in both senses) *Aquilegia viridiflora*, or the intermediate bearded iris 'Shampoo', whose gilt-bronze matches the contemporaneous new shoots on the yew hedge beyond. Other poppies of that ilk, but less well-known, are 'Lilac Girl', whose name fails to describe the pewtered cherry of its large blooms, 'Royal Chocolate Distinction', a cumbrous name for an umbrous carmine poppy that, with me, is not vigorous in growth, or 'Indian Chief', which is a soft mulled red.

'Watermelon' exactly describes its luscious, deep pink blooms; 'Raspberry Queen' is a similar colour, so its name is not so accurate as to the shade of pink. 'Cedric Morris' is the palest greyed pink – what 1920s fashion designers called ashes of roses. It is later to bloom than most, so chimes well with the first flowers of *Campanula lactiflora* 'Loddon Anna', in a toning lime-washed pink. Most oriental poppies will throw secondary blooms throughout the summer – not necessarily a blessing: odd flowers look lopsided and, in wet summers (worse still, after early frosts), will dissolve blackly. To me, they are not the sort of flowers that need to repeat themselves – we hear it all, loud and clear, at first utterance, so repetition is superfluous. One huge blow-out of bloom, in early summer and as many colours as the garden can hold, is what I want from oriental poppies, then quiet tuffets of silvery-green foliage sitting demurely for the rest of the year.

This fleeting season means that even the tall poppies can be planted well forward in the border: you need to be able to gaze into those luscious blooms and, being so temporary, they can steal all the thunder for a week or two without hindrance, before settling back to anonymous clumps again. Their roots, apart from the wayward 'May Queen', are well-behaved enough to allow semi-detached planting of annuals around their crowns, or the standing-out of pots – of lilies, perhaps – for high summer, as well as a surrounding sprawl of early bulbs for spring, whose terminal foliage will be hidden by the expanding poppy leaves. Oriental poppies appreciate reasonable drainage, preferring to be drier over winter than I can always manage: those fat storage roots are a sure sign of drought-tolerance. Hotter gardens than mine might find that the petals scorch in full sun; 'Beauty of Livermere' seems especially susceptible, even here, so a position in half shade might be beneficial and would increase the Richter scale of colour intensity, too.

Heavy, wet soil would never be first choice for any self-respecting poppy; only the toughest survive here for, at best, an abridged life. Self-sown plants seldom prolong the transience, and, as poppies resent disturbance at every stage of their lives, I sow very few. Sir Cedric Morris also developed a strain of field poppies, *Papaver rhoeas*, in shades of pink, grey, and white, that would follow spring bulbs with grace, had I the well-drained soil they would accept. I've tried too many times with these, and the saturnine inkiness of the darkest, double forms of opium poppies (now suffering the euphemism of 'peony-flowered poppies' to guard us from a naughty word); I must accept defeat.

Other members of the family Papaveraceae would be similarly browbeaten by the cold soil: *Romneya coulteri* is tricky to establish even in ideal surroundings of warmth and sharp drainage, so I have continued to deny myself the pleasure of its creased paper-taffeta blooms. Successful growers bemoan its ability to sprint out of any chosen border, and push its way up through tarmac drives and concrete, even, I have been told, through encaustic tiles in the hall of a Victorian rectory.

Less groundbreaking, but running neck-and-neck, is the Chinese poppy of the dawn, *Eomecon chionantha*. It is said to be reluctant to flower even in its native haunts of shady stream banks. Here it makes an attempt to flower most years, but is thwarted by spring frosts when still in tight bud; the blackened, limp stems still showing streaks of mandarin-orange sap through their papery skins. As delicate as the white flowers might be, it is for the foliage that I grow it – dense, glaucous hearts with crinkle-crankled edges, on 8-inch stems, sitting flat, and overlapping where the roots are running freely. It would make impenetrable ground-cover in sheltered, leafy soil, but has its knuckles rapped by frost too often, here, to become a menace. Similar in essence is the North American bloodroot, *Sanguinaria canadensis*, although it is stouter-hearted against the cold, as well as being stouter of growth, with bigger, thicker leaves and shorter, sturdier flower stems – more red-blooded, indeed, in every way. A rather more leisurely traveller, it will continue to flower reliably if its ambling roots are divided every few years. I grow only the double form, *S.c.* f. *multiplex* 'Plena', whose fastidious ice-white pompons look as though they have been primped by a champion grower of show chrysanthemums.

As the Himalayan *Dicranostigma lactucoides* pushes through the soil in early spring, it looks like its cousin corydalis (another, if unlikely, poppy), with nubbly, brittle brown shoots opening into lobed and feathered leaves. As it continues to grow to a 12-inch mound and begins to open its buds, it shares more with another cousin, the Welsh poppy, although its chrome yellow flowers are much harder in tone. Its seedpods are entirely its own design, being fat and fleshy, and covered in dew-encrusted down. They dangle pendulously, 2 inches long, in a faintly greenish cream, the colour of home-made mayonnaise.

Welsh poppies, *Meconopsis cambrica*, are willing to share their favours with every gardener, and it takes a harder heart than mine to rebuff their overtures entirely – they are joyful plants. The zest-yellow of the type plant is like a personable bachelor – welcome everywhere, as it is such an easy mixer. I hear the 'easy mixer' chestnut most often from gardeners whose every border is overrun with the progeny of this fertile gentleman. Rough areas of scrub and woodland are the perfect habitats; elsewhere, if you insist, fervent deadheading and weeding should keep you busy. Even the amusing doubles set viable seed, not all of it resulting in more doubles. You have been warned. I need the warning myself, but shall certainly ignore it – deadheaded Welsh poppies are as angular as Mr Grewgious. The bland, not-quite-orange form is the busiest seeder here, and my least favourite; life's little ironies are no less hesitant in the garden than elsewhere. I wish that instead of concentrating their efforts on dwarfing delphiniums, plant breeders would develop a white Welsh poppy. It should be possible, as the *Meconopsis* genus is one of the few that include all three primary colours in its flowers, and white too; so is not averse to adventure. And while we are on the subject of man-made plants: a 10-foot wisteria and a pipless lemon would be more useful than a blue rose.

A blue meconopsis is not just useful, it is essential, in the way that none but the sheerest luxuries are essential. The Himalayan blue poppies display a magnetic nabob-glamour, but with no hint of ostentation; indeed, like Clive of India himself, they stand astonished at their own moderation. They are not quite believable – a mass has a mirage-like shimmer in the airy, dappled shade they require. One of these decades I shall have a copper-sulphate lake of them, but for now I am proud of my single clump – unhelpful soil and persistant slugs make it a high-maintenance plant, here. I believe it is a *Meconopsis* x *sheldonii* hybrid, but I have no idea which, nor does it greatly matter. Once the flowers are out, one pays little attention to the foliage, but it is worth more than a glance: large paddle-shaped leaves in a curious yellowish pea-green, covered in soft brown hairs that glow goldenly in the evening sunshine.

Despite my uncongenial soil, I try more papaver species when I can, and continue growing those that mind the conditions least: *Papaver rupifragum* 'Flore Pleno' has done so well that I now treat it mean by growing it in partial shade, where its not-quite-apricot ruffled flowers on 2-foot stems last into the late-afternoon, rather than shattering by noon, as they do in full sun. The plants themselves last a year or two less, grown in this gloom, but they are quick from collected seed, and always double. I deadhead assiduously, so they flower from June until the frosts, their slender stems waving above relaxed tussocks of a burnished-bronze form of *Carex comans*.

And while there is room in the garden, I shall go on adding to the orgy of oriental poppies. The latest is one called 'Beauty Queen', from the mail order nursery of Elizabeth MacGregor, whose catalogue descriptions are unusually accurate, unlike the siren-strains of many. She describes it as soft amber, which sounds most exciting. Next year should show whether the Marches' light and cold soil will chill the beauty queen's ambrous pallor into a deep-brewed, orange perma-tan.

Alstroemerias

SO FAR, I HAVE MANAGED TO GARDEN without alstroemerias. The lure is strong, I admit, especially of the species, but even of the common orange Peruvian lily and the more subtly tinted *A.ligtu* hybrids in their fleshy carmine and golden buff. There is an Inca savagery about them, which appeals fervently: the call of the condor, the shriek of the howler monkey. (On second thought, the howler monkey always reminds me of Jonathan Jo with a mouth like an O, so perhaps the growl of the jaguar would fit the bill better.)

I did succumb briefly to *Alstroemeria psittacina*. Too briefly, alas, as once planted it was never seen again. My winter temperatures would not encourage it to stay; indeed, my summer temperatures might give it pause for thought. Either way, its parrot-green and ruby could not fly free over my particular rain forest.

Ray Brown's list of Chilean alstroemerias makes my mouth water. But I remind myself that my garden is too chilly for Chile, and that, if I start on this gaucho-trek across the pampa, I should begin with the hardiest and cheapest, and see how that does before I indulge any macaw-flights of fancy. This means *A. aurea*.

Of course, it might do too well: I am told that bindweed offers a more easily controlled alternative to a happy alstroemeria. But those rich tangerine bells and waxy foliage might be worth the risk. Except for one problem: the fact that alstroemerias, even when sublimely happy, die back to base very early and extremely untidily. By midsummer, just as everything else is excelling, you have gaping holes yawning from the border instead of satsuma trumpets.

The trick, apparently, is to plant the thick tuberous roots at least 6 inches deep (which helps to keep them out of frost's way too), so that when the disappearing act occurs, you can safely plant annuals above them to fill the gap. I am also told that, once planted, alstroemerias should be left entirely alone: no digging up or splitting or carving off bits for friends. Fine; but what of their invasion tactics, which would make butter on a hot plate look tentative?

Perhaps, after all, I shall continue to resist temptation, and console my alstroemeria-lust with an occasional bought bunch. I once saw them advertised outside a florist's shop as 'Ulster Marys', but surely that's a bar in Belfast?

Irises

VIRGIL TELLS HOW JUNO GOADED the Trojan women into burning Aeneas' fleet: her messenger ran down her bow of a thousand colours. Irises are well named, showing the traditional seven rainbow colours, pure white, and coal black – the latter, in velvet, sets off the emerald satin of *Hermodactylus tuberosus*, whose maiden name was *Iris tuberosa*. But the gradation of tone and hue between those nine colours could exceed even the goddess Iris's thousand-banded rainbow. Think of the skim-blue bearded iris 'White City', or the slatey, bruised-grey of 'Langport Storm' and the sloe gin of its sibling 'Langport Wren', the dried-blood brown of the Californian Hybrid 'Broadleigh Dorothy' or the cherubic pink of the old bearded iris 'Vanity'.

Gardeners who admire the bearded iris as the essence of prismatic colour do not always esteem its notoriously scraggy foliage. But some of the species have really fine foliage, like the evergreen mass of glossy strap leaves on *Iris innominata* or the equally evergreen, but less demanding, clumps of *I. foetidissima*. The six-petalled flowers present a surprising array of shapes: consider the great underhung lip of *I. laevigata* or the arched falls of *I. kerneriana*, like a high-stepping horse, the perky standards of *I. spuria* and the classic curve of *I. pallida*, like capital Rs back to back. Equally variable are flowering times and habitat: in sheltered nooks, *I. unguicularis* can be blooming for Christmas, provided its plate is more like a colander – letting excess moisture and nutrients drain away fast. Conversely, *I. pseudacorus*, up to its ankles in water, will go on flowering until late summer. Heights will range from the 3-inch *I. winogradowii* (creamy-yellow, well-drained, in March), to the 6-foot *I. orientalis* (white, with yellow thumbprints, moist, in June). Fragrance shows diversity, too – many of the bearded irises, as well as some species, are paradisically scented. Colour seems to be related to intensity, so that *I. pallida* varieties have the light freshness of lemon sherbet and sweet-peas to match their delicate lavender colours, whereas the midnight-deep, black-purple 'Sable' has a heavy perfume as rich as arabica coffee beans.

I am besotted with bearded irises, but it is a largely unrequited passion, as my heavy cold wet soil is anathema to them. Rhizome-baking summers followed by indulgent winters happen all too rarely here, so I am backing a non-starter. But I persevere, offering libations of molten-muck and weathered ashes, and covering their roots with flat stones – to cosy them by absorbing summer warmth, and by deflecting a little of winter's iron frost. Even when the iced surface, as tenacious of its stone as a cling peach, first sticks to, then skins, my fingers, it will be a milli-degree warmer beneath. Some years the insulation works well, and I am rewarded with sumptuous flowers. 'Caliente' is the lustrous red-brown of a conker, with deeper shading like the burr-walnut contour lines on the conker's polished flanks. It has an intoxicating scent and the texture of silk velvet, cool to the touch. 'Kent Pride' is tortoiseshell, buhled with both silver frettings and brass. An old, nameless iris from my parents' garden is a florid peach with drizzlings of melba sauce. Another from there is an ethereal dove grey, with tissue-thin petals and a ghostly grey beard.

I cannot say that I love all bearded irises as, once again, breeders have meddled too much: increasing the tonal range, certainly – some of the colours are wonderful additions but others are chemically coarse with a flother of nylon petals. Either way, the classic double R shape has been choked by all the frills and frolls, and by the arms-akimbo stance of the lower petals – falls no longer. They lack the languid droop of the old purple flag, *Iris germanica*, once seen in every village garden, or the silvery-white 'Florentina' which grew in olive groves on Tuscan hillsides, and gave its dried rhizomes to the perfume industry as orris root.

Modern bearded irises have little affinity with the fleur-de-lis, but much with the Lollo Rossa lettuce. It would be helpful if introduction dates were included in catalogues, to give warning of the dreaded flounce. Most tall bearded irises bred before the mid-1960s escape it, as do many of those classed as Intermediates, bred since then. Names can give sound clues: 'Peaches 'n' Topping' is likely to be after that date, 'Mrs Horace

Darwin' before. But I am generalizing and guessing – I have no idea what either of them look like, and I could be entirely wrong. A more ominous clue catches the eye as one scans the lists in the *Plantfinder*: death knells could be ringing for all those irises stocked by only one nursery. Buy them now, or the next edition's entry could read 'Last listed . . . '. Serious gardens are about style, not fashion, so let us not lose these classic old irises, let them not become horticultural dodos.

The older varieties are easier plants, not only on the eye, but for maintenance, too. Their flowers, being well proportioned and designed to shed rain from their narrow-necked, pendulous falls, are less likely to become top-heavy or to need staking. Their rhizomes, like old swollen fingers, gnarled and dropsical, grow shorter and fatter, so store more food for the plant and clench together into a weed-defying fist. As a result, they need less frequent division. Those with *I. pallida* blood have strong greyish foliage that holds its shape – like the goddess's winged heels – more conspicuously than many of the flop-leaved modern weaklings, whose thin-walled stems are more likely to be wreathed, like her caduceus, in entwining slug-serpents.

No iris can be guaranteed to escape the attentions of slugs, although growing the wet-bobs in water will help, particularly if your pond has a healthy quota of frogs. A wrinkle worth smoothing under your belt is that water-loving irises have dots on their foliage that are visible when a leaf is held against the sun. This does not preclude you from growing them if your garden is pondless; my best clumps of *Iris ensata* grew on the arid edge of a dry-stone wall, flowering enough to pick greedily. Fool that I am, I moved them; there were no flowers at all this year. *Nil desperandum*: irises will take their time about settling into a new home; roots are more important than flowers. It is the anticipation of future glories that keeps us keen.

A friend has *Iris pseudacorus* 'Variegata' growing in a shady border with heavy soil – dampish but not wet, as there is a comfortable lupin growing there, too. The iris's green, canary and cream striped leaves sparkle in spring (they age, later, to a light lime-green) and the early summer citrus-yellow flowers crowd the 2-foot stems – shorter than normal, and no bad thing. I planted the piece she gave me in full sun and hefty soil, but, although the leaves are enticingly pyjama-striped, it neither burgeons nor blooms. Similar disappointment occured with the green-leaved type plant, the native yellow flag, until I moved it from its damp, shady, flowerless spot to the winterbourne stream bank in dappled sun. Now it blooms from May until the end of July, at a lofty 4 feet. It is beginning to spread, to hold the bank with its tough roots, and eventually, I hope, make a fringed eyelash to the watery eye.

Ten feet to the drier side of the same area grow clumps of *Iris sibirica* 'White Queen' and *I.s.* 'Butter and Sugar'. I despaired of inducing them ever to flower until they were moved into this rich silty soil as a last chance. They have been magnificent. The Stygian gloom of the far stream-bank hedgerow behind them throws their clear white into sharp relief, with the buttery falls of 'Butter' scrambling the egg yolk-yellow of nearby candelabra primulas. Sibirica leaves are too messy for neat borders once they begin their slow collapse. Here, on the Wilderness, I can leave them as a frog-concealing heap all winter.

Iris sibirica 'Summer Sky' flowers extravagantly in a dry, sunny spot elsewhere in the garden, as does the old variety 'Caesar', with its feet in damp shade. The latter stands proud, almost 5 feet tall, in the murex-purple with which imperial togas were edged. Sibiricas can be fickle, so it pays to try another location if they are not performing up to par at first. You'll find they settle quickly if you can move them as the leaves begin to flop in late summer. Trim the tops'l of unruly foliage back to a couple of inches from the crown, so that they are not inclined to attempt to revive them. Split them only if they are barely flowering and too big to move in a lump. I have had good results from single roots planted about 8 inches apart – they will have joined up again within a couple of years – also, conversely, from liftable clumps simply reseated in fresh, well-fed soil. But the usual method of digging up, chopping into three, and replanting, will cause them to sulk for a year or two before they get back to business. Multiplication is not always the result of division. Either way, remember their greed and be liberal with their rations. I must move the sibirica acquired simply as 'grey-flowered' to the Wilderness. It is slow and rather feeble in habit, but the small, ash-grey flowers have the gentle grace of the peerless *Iris* 'Florentina'. A season or two of Lease-Lend on the mudflats of the Wilderness should help to bulk it up before putting it back where I have it now – with 'Robert le Diable', the muted-mulberry Gallica rose, and the misnamed *Papaver orientale* 'Lilac Girl', which is the clouded-carmine to which 'Robert le Diable' fades, particularly in hot summers. The iris cuts the deck between the two, blooming with one, or the other, depending on the season; once, delectably, with both.

Iris spuria, I. setosa, I. versicolor and the latter's hybrid with *I. virginica*, named *I. × robusta*, are tone poems on a theme of purple. There are white forms of all but the hybrid (so far as I know) and varieties of *I. spuria* that offer a range of colours, including the exotic 'Cinnabar Red', whose spicy burnt paprika smudged with turmeric is bracing beside a butterscotch form of *Primula florindae* and *Uncinia rubra*, a 12-inch grass from New Zealand, whose early-summer newness is the red of rosewood veneer. All of these irises like dampish-to-wet soil but will give an excellent account of themselves if grown dry; they are easy, good-value plants requiring minimal fuss. Particularly fine is *Iris versicolor* 'Kermesina', with distinctly marked flowers of a striking red-purple. (Insects living in galls on the kermes oak were used to dye cloth this colour, commemorated also in *Clematis viticella* 'Kermesina'.) *Iris × robusta* 'Gerald Darby' is another generous plant, whose violet flowers, emphatically veined over blotches of clear yellow and white, are held on dashing navy-blue stems – especially obvious when the flowers are still in bud. At the same time, the base of the leaf-fan shows a hectic flush of crimson lake.

While these four species make sturdy clumps with abundant foliage, a further four are more refined: *Iris chrysographes* occurs in the wild in damp pastures in Western China, with small purple or yellow fragrant flowers, but is more often seen in gardens in one of its almost-black forms, such as 'Kew Black', or 'Rubella', the violet-crimson of blue-blood. It grows easily from seed, so unnamed (or misnamed) blacks and quasi-reds proliferate – some sensational, others dingily mediocre; it is well to buy only in flower. The best forms, as its name suggests, have doodles of gold scribbled over their dusky velvet falls, as prominent as a papal chrysobul. Although of similar size and urbanity, *I. fulva* differs unequivocally from the doleful restraint of *I. chrysographes*. There is not a dram of sobriety about the riotous, fresh rust colour of its flowers: terracotta glazed with scarlet, scintillating with silky honey-smoothness. As an iris colour, it is unique. *I. fulva*, which flowers in mid-summer, comes from steamy Mississippi swamps, so is an unlikely candidate for success in my garden, but so far, so marvellous.

The two slender irises, *Iris forrestii* and *I. wilsonii*, remind me of the slabs of marbled banana toffee one could buy years ago in a little tin tray with a steel toffee hammer – a most useful piece of potting-shed equipment; it is ideal for tapping pot-crocks to a manageable shape. Each iris was introduced from wet alpine meadows in China in 1909; each is light yellow, pencilled with brown; each is said to be 2 feet tall, flowering in early summer, but *I. forrestii*, for me, is earlier and shorter. Each is a delight.

Yellow, brown and purple are the colours of two good hybrids: *Iris* 'Holden Clough' is said to be a cross between *I. chrysographes* and *I. pseudacorus*, which improbable partnership brings to mind King Cophetua and the beggar-maid. It is a pushy clump-former, with branched stems to 2 feet or more, of early-summer blooms with plum-purple standards and custard-yellow falls closely engraved with purplish-brown hatching. Low-key, but intriguing. There must be similar bloodlines in the background of *I.* 'Berlin Tiger', but its English mustard-yellow flowers are inscribed with Dijon mustard-brown. They make an interesting partnership, although 'Berlin Tiger' is taller, at 4 feet, and has jungly-lush foliage – surely the largest of any iris. Despite their aqueous ancestors, mine are doing well in a bone-dry border, in full sun.

Near by, in the same conditions, is *Iris graminea*, whose leaves are indeed grassy, to 8 inches in height. The bright purple flowers nestle among them, beginning to open buds at ground level in late spring. They are worth a kneeling search, as this is known as the plum tart iris, on account of its crisp, fruity scent. Some say it smells of pineapple, others of greengages. A friend always refers to it as the hot plummy tart, which brings to mind something quite different. This year I have noticed its seedpods, which are segmented like miniature green pumpkins, but inside-out, with the seams showing.

The Californian Hybrid irises grow to only 12 inches in height, but spread willingly, if slowly. I am thrilled that they are such a success here, as when I started to buy them, they were said to need warm, sandy, acid soil, so were a gamble. Now, of course, it is recognized that where their ancestors, *Iris innominata*, *I. tenuissima*, *I. douglasiana*, *et al.*, were exigent, the hybrids are forbearing. This knowledge lessens my self-satisfaction, but increases my pleasure. Their colour range is as broad as that of bearded irises, with moody kilim carpet tones of browned carmines, smoky lavenders, and burnt caramels, as well as clear yellows, violet and white. The Broadleigh hybrids and Banbury hybrids are perfectly beautiful: try 'Banbury Melody' with the similarly coloured, but a tone greyer, *Papaver orientale* 'Patty's Plum', whose buds pull the ripcord and shake out their creased petals at the same, all too brief, moment in early summer. Or try *Geranium phaeum* 'Rose Madder' and *Anthriscus sylvestris* 'Ravenswing' with 'Broadleigh Rose', for a polished alloy of copper and bronze. Wherever you plant them – neither too dry nor too shady – try to get it right first time, as they resent disturbance to the extent of refusing to flower the year following your foozling. This means that you can be grudging without guilt to mendicant friends. Nurserymen will like that. Bought plants will take a year or two to settle and must not be allowed to dry out the while. After this slight period of watchfulness, they get the bit between their teeth and trot on, taking full responsibility for themselves. There is nothing for the gardener to do, ever after, but gloat.

Another independent plant is *Iris latifolia*, known as the English iris, although it comes from Spain. Most gardeners are familiar with Dutch irises, *I. xiphium*, sometimes known as Spanish irises, although they come from North Africa; not that I am trying to confuse you. This, the Dutch, is the florists' iris, whose bulbs are available in every garden centre, in a mixture of clear colours. They can be attractive in the garden, but are not long-lived, even where the soil is light and well-drained. Here, a ukase has been issued against further acquisition, as they are mostly blind, and scruffy for too long in dying leaf. English irises, however, were born for hefty soil, despite being bulbous. They increase steadily, have good reedy foliage, and flower late, in July, thus avoiding competition with any others, unlike the Dutch, which bloom among sibiricas and beards, and suffer by the candid comparison. *I. latifolia* would stand comparison as well as it stands on its own feet – it never needs staking, as its bulbs drop to a stabilizing counter-balance: in trying to dig one out for a friend, I went down over a foot, and still failed to trace the bulb which had been planted at about 4 inches deep only a couple of years previously. The flowers are big and important in their magisterial purples and violets – pure, decisive tones, well-flashed with white and clear yellow. There is a lilac-pink variety, 'Isabella', that has yet to flower, here. I hope it will be right, and not the isabelline colour, like tinned salmon, that earned its name from the unsavoury results of a vow made by Queen Isabella of Castile not to change her linen until a siege ended. It is one of the reasons why I don't grow eremurus.

Gardeners tend to be sniffily disdainful of the native *Iris foetidissima*, or gladdon iris. Its flowers are derided as dull and insignificant. They are modest in tone, certainly, being an off-white veined with buff and light purple; *I.f.* var. *citrina* has a slight primrosy tint to its base colour. I am always rather pleased to see them in flower and make a purposeful stop to study their quiet charm in close detail. It is a different story in autumn, when the heavy pods begin to burst open, revealing rows of dazzling orange, pea-sized seeds. Picked before slugs disembowel them, and hung upside down to strengthen the stems, they make a showy addition to arrangements of berries and evergreens for Christmas (always including litigious leylandii, whose foliage, in a warm room, is spicily redolent of 'cedarwood' pencil sharpenings). The iris seeds persist for long enough to outlast the rest of the arrangement and be reassembled with pussy willows for spring. These seed pods are the only reason why some gardeners grow the gladdon iris but, even if you care little for the flowers, the sheaves of evergreen leaves make a sprightly contribution, particularly to the winter garden, and are a panacea for all dry shade problems: *Iris foetidissima* will grow anywhere, no matter how gloomy and root-ridden. *I.f.* 'Variegata' has sleekly white-striped leaves. It seldom flowers, and is by no means such a romper as the type – mine is so retiring I forget it is there, until winter clears the decks around it. The white seeds of 'Fructu Albo' are truthfully a jaundiced-cream and parsimonious in production, but they are very stylish with black mondo grass and the ivory water-shoots from a variegated holly, for arty decorations at Christmas, where traditional greens and reds are considered too corny: a form of horticultural measles to which, I find, I am not always immune.

Codonopsis

THE BELLFLOWERS IN THE FAMILY of Campanula ring a complete peal of shapes and sizes, from the tiniest sleigh bell to the great bell of Kiev. Codonopsis, a cousin-german, rings a flourish of its own, from the Treble-Bob-Major of the star-shaped climbers to the Grandsire-Triple of *Codonopsis clematidea*, which, being the species most frequently encountered, will make the most sensible starting point to raise the bells.

Codonopsis clematidea always astonishes visitors to my garden who are not familiar with these striking plants. These poor, benighted people form a large majority, as codonopsis in general are not among the most popular attractions at your local garden centre. I imagine this lack of retail appreciation is due to two factors: firstly, they are of brittle and somewhat spindly growth, making them difficult to display to advantage, and almost impossible to transport, from supplier to garden centre, without considerable injury. This leads directly to their second retailable fault: a strong smell of ripe fox, particularly when damaged, but also when merely touched, often when simply approached. Some are worse than others, certainly, but in most well-fed gardens, pungent smells abound. Many urban gardens, and even some rural ones, are visited regularly by foxes, so you'll probably not notice any difference. Frankly, even if you do, the beauty of the plant far outweighs any nasal challenge.

And the bells on clematidea are exquisitely beautiful. They are large — at least an inch and a half long by an inch wide; the pointed lobes flick back, as do the dusty, ashen-green calyces. They are the soft, grey-blue of an English sky, pearly and lucent. On the outside they are as demure as Little Dorrit; the inside, seen against the light, is a rose window, stained with tangerine, crimson and green, leaded with circles of deepest black. Add to all that extravagance an astonishing cantilevered and buttressed construction of stamens and stigma, made, it seems, from crystalline marzipan, and you will begin to understand, perhaps, a little of their charms. I grew mine from seed a dozen years or so ago, and it is now well established on the top of a dry wall, where the drainage is reasonable. It grows in a tousled mass to about 2 feet, half-supported by, and hiding the legs of a 'Buff Beauty' rose. It can grow taller than this in favourable conditions, which to a codonopsis is soil that is sharply drained, but never completely dry. They are totally hardy, coming from the fairly high altitude woodlands and stream banks of the Himalayas, China and Japan. Some have nut-like, tuberous roots; others, including clematidea, have great starchy fangs. These do not transplant well, so your first choice of position must be for better, for worse.

The new shoots pushing through the ground in late spring have a lapis-blue tinge, and are much beloved by slugs in infancy, less so in foxy adolescence and beyond. So keep a watchful eye in the first couple of years and cover the emerging shoots with a timely jam jar to foil the molluscs. The early summer flowering species, such as clematidea, shut up shop pretty fast afterwards: the top hamper will turn yellow by late summer and within a couple of weeks will have severed all connection with its root, so can be lifted away and composted. This leaves a gap which can or needn't be filled, according to its position and your reputation. I don't bother at that end of the proceedings, but I do underplant for early spring with small bulbs – *Chionodoxa luciliae*, *Crocus chrysanthus* 'Gipsy Girl' and *Muscari latifolium* – and fancy celandines, *Ranunculus ficaria*, in varieties with orange flowers, or with dark foliage. All of these are happy to dive beneath the covers when the codonopsis envelopes their air space. On lighter soils than mine the celandines might not be so content.

Having found such delight in clematidea, I determined to grow more of these enchanting plants, so acquired as many different seeds as I could. This brought more disappointment than I had anticipated, as all too many of the seeds, no matter what they called themselves on the packets, turned out to be yet more clematidea, and usually a poor form to boot. *Codonopsis mollis*, *C. ovata*, *C. bulleyana* – all clematidea. Buying plants from reputable nurseries became a similar minefield, particularly when they had acquired their seeds from the same sources whence mine came: *C. meleagris* and *C. cardiophylla* – both clematidea – and washy forms at that.

Further seeds were not, for once, *C. clematidea*, but neither were they what they said they were: *C. pilosula* seeds brought forth *C. mollis*, which is possibly a more entrancing plant anyway, so I am not complaining, except on principle. These codonopses will require several years of growth before they flower in order to prove their identity or their worth. It is maddening to have wasted all those years, and the intensive care they needed in infancy, on a poor form of something you have already in abundance. It is worse when seedlings turn out well but, because of the wrong description, are planted in an unsuitable place. After three years or more, it may be risky, if not fatal, to move them.

Codonopsis mollis has ice-blue bells (somewhat smaller than those of clematidea), which have been gargling with mulberry juice. My plants grow to only 14–16 inches. This is shorter than normal, as they should reach up to 3 feet. But expecting them to be *C. pilosula*, which twines to 5 feet, I had planted them in the rain-shadow of the small shrub *Diervilla* x *splendens*. This is of the weigela persuasion, but with clusters of tiny, butter-yellow bells and a suckering, thickety disposition. It has rich, russet foliage, which is especially startling in spring but has a warm glow for most of the year, which I thought would look well with the greenish-cream bells, flushed with maroon, of the anticipated *Codonopsis pilosula*. Planting it slightly dry was deliberate: to reduce its vigour, so as not to swamp the diervilla. Not being the right codonopsis (experience stamping firmly upon the corns of hope, as usual), my plan has not worked. *C. mollis* is too short and is rendered still shorter here by its arid dining room. Dilemma: do I risk a fatal move, or do I spend further years on the insurance policy of starting again from collected seed?

Another wrong 'un was meant to be *Codonopsis lanceolata*, which mutated into *C. viridiflora*. Although different in colour scheme, they are at least similar in habit and vigour, both twining to about 6 feet, so a move need not be contemplated. I have it surging over a small hazel tripod in my Sunset Border, where it blends gently with its encircling neighbours: *Crocosmia* 'Severn Sunrise', *Phygelius* x *rectus* 'Winchester Fanfare' and *Chionochloa rubra*. Flowering late, with them, it replaces the early-summer, brick-pink *Lathyrus rotundifolius* on the tripod, whose colouring should have been echoed by the big speckled-roan bugles of the intended *Codonopsis lanceolata*. As might be guessed, *C. viridiflora* has greenish flowers, although the 'ish' is to be stressed, as it is a primrose-creamy-green, veined delicately on the outside with burnt umber. Unusually, the throat of the bell is unmarked – a pellucid primrose. The bells are small, less than ¾ inch long, and look almost square in outline, as the calyces do not curve back, but hunch over, like adolescent shoulders. The lobes on the hem of each bell, conversely, curl right over, kirby-gripped firmly back to its head, like a Land Army girl's rolled hairdo. Showing the edging of internal primrose against the darkly veined outer bell makes it look as though her roots need doing.

Another creamy bell occurs on *Codonopsis rotundifolia*, this time with a greyish tinge, splashed inside with dim crimson. The outer skin is suffused with lime green at first, that ages to a slatey violet. Subfusc, certainly, but stylish. As must be clear by now, these plants are not for those who do not appreciate subtlety. This one will entwine a host shrub or wigwam support to about 10 feet, and seems to be more vigorous than some, with stronger stems than their usual thread-thin ankles. Doubtless its large, coarse leaves assist with digestion to aid its vigour, but should be borne in mind when choosing a suitable host shrub, ideally not to be engulfed.

Much smaller in habit, and of a clear jade green, with flared trumpet bells, was *Codonopsis* ACE 1626, with violet veins within and black dots in its throat. Was, but is no longer, sadly, as I planted it too dry. I thought the verdigris bells would look wonderful against a clipped column of Irish juniper, whose summer growth has the same turquoise tinge. And they did, the first summer; but it failed to reappear the following year. I should like to try that again.

Not all codonopsis species have bells: some have five-pointed stars, where the lobes have been cut back nearly to the ovary, enabling them to open almost flat, and show off their decorated throats with greater ease. Much of *Codonopsis convolvulacea* has now been swallowed by *C. grey-wilsonii*, as has *C. nepalensis*; *C. vinciflora* and *C. forrestii* are a rhapsody on the same theme. Each is a lovely thing (and all slugs agree with me), but is a Hebe of the slim ankles, so an open jaw can exterminate yards of growth and copious flowers at one bite. If you can guard against that happening, you will be rewarded with stars, facing you at head-height, of a clear, pure lavender blue, flowering from midsummer onwards. Acquire Forrest's form of *C. convolvulacea* (syn.

C. forrestii) and you will be thrilled even more by its ravishing blue stars, centred with a cherry-red disc with a fuzzy outline that bleeds into the veins inside the flower, as if something red has got into the wash, and run. I am fast on the track of a white form, *C. grey-wilsonii* 'Himal Snow', but whether this is entirely white, or a pink-eyed albino, I am as yet unsure.

A further mystery will not be settled this year, as there have been no flowers by which to identify another seed-grown plant. The seeds came labelled as 'Codonopsis, unspecified'. What will be, will be, and I suspect that what it will be is yet more clematidea.

Roses

A UNIVERSAL MOAN RECURS ABOUT the single blooming season of the old roses. The same cry is never heard about any other shrub: forsythia is not expected to be remontant; elder is appreciated for its generous fruit following a single fortnight of flower; we do not require that lilac always in the dooryard blooms. Or viburnum, rubus, ribes, honeysuckle, lavender . . . only roses are criticized. I could understand the lament if it were Hybrid Teas that flowered only once: they are such ungainly sticks without flowers; even with flowers there is plenty to complain about. As long-stemmed, florist-bought blooms in vases they are luxurious, although it is a sad fact that most never open properly, hanging their heads dejectedly instead of stretching petals, and few have any scent. In an informal garden setting, Hybrid Teas can look uncomfortably out of their indoor element, failing their extra-mural studies by a wide margin. Old roses, however, are never at a loss, in whatever society they find themselves: informal, formal, town or country, indoors or out, they have the right clothes and are never self-conscious.

Of course, many old roses do repeat their flowers, particularly those with China blood. But those that bloom in one great impassioned sigh are revered by me for that very reason: the brevity intensifies the pleasure, as does the anticipation. It is the same with asparagus and raspberries, and strawberries too, if one grows one's own and ignores the year-round red blobs available in every supermarket (very like Hybrid Teas, and just as tasteless in many cases). Turn and turn about should be the accepted norm for everything that lives and breathes and has its being. By focusing on constant flowering, rose breeders are becoming cosmetic surgeons, keeping their patient ever-youthfully blooming, no matter how unnatural the result to her painted, tainted phiz.

A rose garden is a charming conceit, but can be a little like a Thackeray novel – full of good characters, but without much in the way of plot. I prefer my roses to be integrated, just like other shrubs, into the borders: to form background blocks, play fountains of arching height, lend support and provide generally well-bred bones beneath the flashy flesh. All this as well as flowering.

Old roses, traditionally, are those that predate 1867, the year of the first Hybrid Tea, 'La France'. Like many gardeners, I use the term somewhat loosely to cover roses that may have been bred and introduced well after that date, such as many of the rewarding Hybrid Perpetuals and Hybrid Musks, but which have the essence of the old rose in their emotional make-up as well as their genes. Many of these, and the wild species, have widely differing styles and colour of foliage, so can make a significant contribution to the border when not in flower, which is more than the charitable can say about Hybrid Teas.

Rosa glauca has moody pewter leaves flushed with crimson and Tyrian purple stems bloomed with chalky-blue. Its habit is naturally big and arching, to 6–7 feet, so it makes a striking background to a solferino phlox, such as 'Starfire', or the magenta *Lobelia* 'Tania', whose pugnacious colours will be challenged by the contemporaneous garnet-red hips hanging in bunches on the rose. All this without even mentioning flowers, so who cares about a single blooming? For the record, they are small but held in plentiful clusters, with twisted petals of a deep rich pink, which is stimulating with the plumbeous foliage.

On the extraordinary *Rosa sericea* subsp. *omeiensis* f. *pteracantha*, it is the young thorns that hold the attention, as they are translucent gore-red, and shaped like a coat hanger, with padded shoulders that extend, through the season, to 2 inches or more along the stem. These thorns are especially fine on the new young growth that appears after the flowers (cream dog-roses, in the teens of June here, but earlier in warmer gardens), so it is worthwhile encouraging more of it by cutting out the older stems, with woody brown thorns that clamour together with the hollow rip of torn silk. It is politic, also, to give some thought to this rose's position: ideally, you need it silhouetted against early morning and late evening sun, so that the blood-red fingernails turn to dripping rubies. For those who have been trying to interrupt with an objection: sustained; yes, I know rose 'thorns' are in fact prickles. This one has bristles, too. But although botanists may shudder, no simple gardener could call these barbaric weapons mere prickles, particularly not when your own blood has emblazoned their gules rampant still further.

Another species with valuable foliage is the Scotch burnet rose, which has jazzy autumn tints of scarlet and coral on its delicate leafy pointillist dabs. This brilliance is sharpened further by association with the almost-black, tuffet-shaped hips — as swart as Keats' blackberries. There are forms of the species with yellow or pink flowers, dwarfs and doubles too, and several varieties and hybrids that have been bred for more spectacular blooms. I grow only the single creamy-flowered native, bought years ago as *Rosa spinosissima*, subsequently known as *R. pimpinellifolia*, and now, once more, *Rosa spinosissima*, in the forward-back, forward-back, of the taxonomy two-step. Its chosen home is on sand dunes, where it runs around making busy thickets and grows only 12 inches high. Gardens with poor, dry soil can expect the same amiable tendency. Here, it shoots up to 5 feet, a slim column dotted with milk-and-honey-scented flowers. It made a dash the first year after it was planted but, growing on its own roots, it was safe to assume that this pup was of the same pedigree as its parent, unlike the cloven-hoof suckers popping out on grafted roses. I dug out the lone runner and gave it to my sister, who gardens with more shelter and lighter soil. Neither rose sibling has demanded further *lebensraum* since then, despite the difference in soil, and in each garden it is the earliest rose to flower, starting, even here, in late May. Mine makes the centre of an appealing group, with lower supporters showing a contrast of foliage: the strap-leaved *Hemerocallis lilioasphodelus*, dexter, with elegant lemon bugles, hauntingly scented, and *Geum aleppicum*, sinister, whose citrus-yellow, typical but small geum flowers sport emerald-green domed centres that ripen to amusing but hair-snagging burrs of rich fox-brown. The leaves, conversely, are typical but large, ripening in turn to bronze and marmalade, and later still, thickly rimed with hoarfrost, inspire one to slip about on the ice with a camera.

The main flush of roses begins to break out here in late June and continues, in gentle summers, until early August. Burning sun sears tender petals that drop early, fainting from heat exhaustion; heavy rain balls them in half-open bud, turning them to a squidge of brown slime. Some roses are better than others at dealing with these irritations, but none of them bask contentedly in such adverse conditions. The thick plastic petals bred into many Hybrid Tea roses will cope better, perhaps, but their kickshaw colours seem, to my eyes, more suited to the intensity of light that favours white adobe walls, savaged by bougainvillea, beneath a sky like a turquoise faience bead.

The dulcet English light that pleased Piers Plowman, as he snoozed on the Malverns 'in a somer seson whan soft was the sonne', agrees with the old roses' Aunt Jobiska tones of lavender water tinged with pink, as well as the sombre voluptuousness of the boodying crimsons. These are particular favourites that can be grown here in full sun without fear of scorching, provided their roots stay cool. Even the sun-shy 'Souvenir du Docteur Jamain' basks with its face to the south; its feet are enjoying an aromatherapy session in what was once an old cess pit. It has long been advised that these prunello-purples need rich soil to succeed, and certainly I lost possibly the darkest of all, the moss 'Nuits de Young', by planting it too dry. 'Tuscany' and 'Tuscany Superb' (Is there any difference? I can detect none) thrive in the same border, although the time-lapse between plantings has seen an improvement in the tariff. Besides, the Tuscan twins, their sumptuous semi-single blooms crammed with a golden flurry of stamens, are Gallicas, the most biddable of all roses in my garden climate, having lusty, self-supporting stems, with relatively benign prickles and healthy, mat foliage. They grow to around 4 feet square and are easily pruned, ideally after flowering, although winter gives readier access. I remove older wood at ground level, which allows air to circulate and new growth plenty of room to develop. Another crimson Gallica, 'Charles de Mills', has the rumpled centre and sliced-off shape of the quintessential old rose. It has more purple in its tone than the Tuscans. All three are lavishly scented and will flower for about six weeks.

Even more than the rich papal colours, I love the old striped roses. One of the earliest in date is the Gallica *Rosa mundi* (syn. *R. gallica* 'Versicolor'), which was named after Henry II's mistress, Rosamund Clifford, who may or may not have been murdered by Eleanor of Aquitaine, in the twelfth century. Its petals are splashed and streaked with a vivacious pink and white over a delicate blush-pink. Sublimely scented, it is the easiest rose to grow. Mine is supported, as it bears the additional weight of the herbaceous *Clematis recta* 'Purpurea', which is certainly as empurpled as its name suggests. (Some forms are not, so buy in spring, when the newly emergent stems are at their beetroot-best, as all of them age to green for summer, unmiraculously turning the wine to water.) It is not, however, as erect as might be expected. Staked on its own, it looks miserably shackled, so plant at the top of a bank and leave it to cascade in a wave of creamy-spindrift flowers, or behind a shrub through and over which it can ooze, like jam from a doughnut.

Whenever a striped rose is featured in a magazine, invariably it will be captioned as *Rosa mundi*. A striped rose is a striped rose is a striped rose. With due respect to Miss Gertrude Stein: it is not. There are many differences between them. Afficionados can tell at a glance, just by the colours and shape of the flower. So it is a pity that many gardeners seem to think that all striped roses are *Rosa mundi*. As perfect as that is, there are several others just as fine. Different in every way is the striped moss 'Oeillet Panaché', whose stance is upright to 6 feet, whose cinnamon-bristled canes are slender and whippy, whose foliage is smaller, more leaden-green than any Gallica, whose moss is a glistening chestnut fur and whose flat double flowers, perfect buttonhole-size, are chalk-white scribbled with light-rose pink. Mine has the restrained *Lathyrus* 'Tubro' entwined in its embrace, with warm rosy-pink pea-flowers, slender, pale green foliage and more cold-tolerance than its brick-pink parent, *L. rotundifolius*.

Another pea, *Lathyrus sylvestris* (more vigorous, but kept in check by pulling out most of its emerging stems in spring), grows into the arms of the Bourbon rose 'Honorine de Brabant', whose stripes are mauve-pink pencillings on white with typically loose Bourbon-cups of translucent petals above light apple-green foliage. It is a strong grower to 5 feet, which does well in the slightly shady situation in which I planted it to support the already growing native pea, whose light-pink flowers are also delicately feathered with rose-pink and green. 'Honorine de Brabant' has a mid-season flush of lemon-scented bloom, then repeats the performance in early autumn if the weather is kind – Bourbons hate the rain in their petals.

The Hybrid Perpetual 'Ferdinand Pichard' barely draws breath between its spells of blooming. It is a robust shrub with athletically vaulting canes to 7 feet and dense, glossy foliage. Its motley is perhaps the most distinctive of all the stripes, being a vibrant cerise flaked and spotted over a ripe rose-pink and sharp white. The peppery scent is equally intense – to my nose, it has a hint of oil of geranium – making a heady blend with the delicious perfume of *Saponaria officinalis* 'Rubra Plena' at its feet. This late-summer soapwort, in faded crimson, flowers arm-in-arm with the repeated blooms of the rose. To partner the first blush, there is *Solanum dulcamara* 'Variegatum', the cream-splashed-foliage form of the native woody nightshade, whose bittersweet lavender flowers with light-lemon beaks (all paler than the type) age to arsenical-green berries, ripening to fiery-red. It is a rather fragile scrambler, needing a shrub to lend a shoulder, and mildly damp feet, to do itself justice. But as not even the tough 'Glasnevin' variety of *S. crispum* will grow here, it is a good compromise between that and the beautiful wilding of the hedgerows.

'Variegata di Bologna' is another Bourbon striped rose, described in the Peter Beales catalogue (whence mine came) as blackcurrant-jam stirred into semolina, which is exactly right, being nearer purple than pink in stripe, on a warm ivory-white background. It has the rounded, wineglass shape of Bourbon flowers, stuffed brimful with petals, and a fruity scent that fits its summer-puddingy colours. Alas for me, it has the Bourbon objection to cold wet heavy soil so does not rejoice in its milieu. It suffers from rust, too (a problem where soil is indigestibly full-bodied) but only as the flowers go over – the new shoots and foliage are completely clean. So it is a temporary affliction that may heal itself, eventually, as the rose starves its own surroundings into pemmican-poverty; it is worth suffering, in the meantime, for the sake of the exquisite flowers. At least, that is how I view it; the rose may think differently.

The ancient *Rosa* x *damascena* var. *versicolor*, known as 'York and Lancaster', needs nourishment aplenty and takes a while to settle into its factious colours. Not exactly a stripe, 'York and Lancaster' will change its mind as often as the balance of Plantagenet power. Sometimes wholly white flowers will bloom alongside entirely pink ones; then an odd petal will be thrown in a Perkin Warbeck way, or a Lambert Simnel stripe will attempt to deceive the eye. Mine, to date, has joined forces firmly with the Lancastrian camp, although its demurely blushing pink is hardly appropriate to the braggadocio-red Tudors.

The dark crimson Hybrid Perpetual 'Baron Girod de l'Ain' might have Calais engraved upon its heart, so bloody is its Tudor red. Its sculptured petals, curved into points, recessed into dimples, are deckle-edged with white. Similar in effect is another Hybrid Perpetual 'Roger Lambelin' – Margery Fish's rose of dreams. She found it temperamental, explaining that the 'Baron' was an easier option for those who suffered from the pique of 'Roger Lambelin'. Here, the 'Baron' is glorious, provided its greed is accommodated. The sulky 'Roger' has just been ordered; I hope it will prove to be the jolly Roger, instead.

These two crimson roses edged with white are mirrored by two more of creamy-white pranked with red. 'Leda' has small, very double flowers, whose rims have been dabbed against wet paint; indeed, it is known as the painted damask. Mine has an ugly-duckling defect, in that the outer petals seem to be too tight for the flower to open properly. I have grown the rose for only two years so I am hoping it is a mere adolescent phase that it will outgrow as it matures to swan's-down splendour. At present it has the tiresome teenage habit of wearing clothes too tight to contain burgeoning puppy fat. None of that on the semi-single-flowered rose 'Hebe's Lip', a damask x sweet briar hybrid, whose large dog-rose petals have been dunked into the tumbling cup-bearer's spilt wine, staining the ivory petals like a flamed tulip. Where 'Leda' has a plump and indolent habit, 'Hebe' shows its teenage temperament with flagrant rambler wands and ferocious thorns. As a result, it has been moved to the Wilderness, where its raggle-taggle air is more appropriate.

Roses of soft yellow and peachy colours are greatly admired, too, so they are well represented in the garden. They need to be kept away from the more carmine of the pink roses, such as 'Duc de Guiche' and the striped 'Camaieux' (both Gallicas) or the melancholic mélange of the centifolia 'Robert le Diable'. But the honeyed tones look delectable with blue flowers, such as *Platycodon grandiflorus*, with huge lavender-blue funnels, or the soft sky-blue helmets of *Aconitum carmichaelii* Wilsonii Group 'Spätlese'. 'Danaë ', a Hybrid Musk rose, has clusters of loosely petalled flowers the colour of clotted cream; blooming until autumn turns them rancid. In the same border is a mystery rose that was here when I came to the garden. It was grown from seed by an elderly neighbour, who could not remember which of her many roses was the seed parent. It seems to have Tea Rose blood somewhere in its ancestry, as it struggled with the weather until I moved it against a cosy-ish wall and, even now, will lose the top half, or more, of every stem each winter. It has typical Tea foliage: large and glossy, plus the equally typical Tea dislike of pruning and, gloriously, the typical Tea scent on its banana-yellow blooms, ageing to a darker tone – also a Tea trait. It will flower well only after an equable winter, so there have been several blind seasons. But in a flowering year, it will go on and on.

Dean Hole claimed that if he were restricted to growing just one rose in his lifetime, it would be 'Gloire de Dijon'. I might agree, if I were forced to be so single-minded. It is truly fabulous, in muddled, apricot fool-coloured flower, but is not, perhaps, as vigorous here as it would have been at warmer Caunton. More pinkly-peach in tone is the Hybrid Musk 'Buff Beauty', whose perfume saturates the air on those still, backwater days of summer, as I rest on idle oars and drift with the garden tide. When the mist-wraiths of dawn hover over the water meadows until midday, held glistening on the tide of spider webs, and cattle appear to float like the Nibelungen as they browse the dew-drench, with swifts screaming and slaloming the skies above, I tie a knot in my mind, to remember the scene, for at such a moment life is truly *couleur-de-rose*.

Sanguisorbas

SANGUISORBA IS AN IGNORED GENUS (undeservedly so, in my opinion) that should be planted more often, particularly if your soil is on the beefy side. The species embrace various shapes and sizes; all have interesting foliage, on some it is really fine, contributing ably both in spring and in favourable autumns by colouring richly; the flowers, though small, are not to be despised. They fall into two groups – bobbles and hairy caterpillars – so a mixture of them brings to mind the gimp trimming on lampshades.

To start with the most useful: *Sanguisorba minor* has cucumber-flavoured leaves, that can be tasty in salads or pretty in Pimms. It makes a dome of delicate blue-green, pinnate foliage with ruffled edges, and sports bobbly, deep pink flowers throughout the summer. It is not the most stunning plant, but it looks well at the front of a border, being 10–12 inches high and deft in habit. Or, if you are potager-inclined, as a low hedge next to the borage (also *de rigueur* for Pimms). Its common name is salad burnet.

The great burnet sounds like a music hall fire-eating act, but is also *Sanguisorba officinalis*, an English native of damp meadows. It is a distinguished plant in a border that is not too dry. Although it reaches 5 feet in height, it can be planted well forward as it flowers late in the summer on fine stems in the airy, *Verbena bonariensis*-see-through style, and its basal rosette of thinly pinnate, bottle-green foliage is quietly pleasing. The flowers are bobbles again, elongated into ovoids of rich burgundy, a bibulous partner to the aforementioned leaf colour. Ideally, these should have a lighter background, perhaps the trendy *Onopordum acanthium*, which is a huge silver thistle, all blotting paper and razor blades. Not in my garden, however, as I have signed the pledge against thorns.

Sanguisorba armena has caterpillar flowers of a blush white, which wriggle in the breeze on their 4-foot stems in midsummer. But it is mainly for the superb foliage that I grow it: if your garden, like mine, is too cold for *Melianthus major*, grow this sanguisorba instead. The foliage is remarkably similar in its glaucous magnificence but bone hardy. It runs a bit, but is easy to control – mostly into pots for friends.

Sanguisorba albiflora has outstanding foliage, too – finely cut, and raspberry pink in spring, and chalk-white furry caterpillars jiggling at 5 feet in early summer. These pupate into a digestive-biscuit colour but keep their shape well until the autumn, so I don't cut them back. The basal foliage, by that time, will be a rich ambrous yellow. Also from the Far East, *S. tenuifolia* can leap up to 8 feet if it gets plenty of gravy with its dinner. It has smallish bobbles for the size of the plant, but in a telling claret, and all the more valuable for flowering so late in autumn. The leaves are a soft greyish green, large and feathery, stained with the spilled claret by flowering time. If the thought of 8 feet is too overwhelming, grow it dry and it will reach only half that height.

Or grow instead *Sanguisorba magnifica alba*, which, for me, stays at about 12 inches, with apple green foliage and fat white hairy caterpillars in midsummer, which are at least 4 inches long. In full flight it is most impressive, despite its lowly stature, and, like its cousin the salad burnet, it is neat enough to plant right on the footlights. Presumably, the type plant will be pink or claret, but I have never seen it. The white form is given the synonym of *S. albiflora* in the *Plantfinder*. Maybe so; but my plants (if they are what they say they are) are entirely different from each other.

Having stated that they all show either bobbles or caterpillars, I am wrong, because *Sanguisorba canadensis* has upstanding white bottlebrushes. Flowering in late summer at 4 feet tall (with damp feet), it is a stately plant with soft pewter-green leaves. It has far more presence in the border than the rather weedy *Veronicastrum virginicum*, whose washed-out colours need vast swathes in order to give any muscle to their narrow, Salisbury Cathedral spires.

All sanguisorbas like full sun and soil that is never desert-dry, and they are all as easy to keep as a plain daughter, as Reginald Farrer so memorably wrote.

Equally easy to keep, and equally seldom seen, are scutellarias. Again there are a couple of natives known as skullcaps, after the curved, gnocchi-shaped seeds. Being shorter than the sanguisorbas, they make convincing front stalls plants, particularly as their flowers are intricate enough – being labiates – to repay close inspection. I'll not deny that some are weedy, and that a few are prodigal of seed; but they take up little room, and grow fast, so you'll not have to wait for years before seeing them in their full mediocrity. It is then but the work of a moment to yank out the surplus.

Scutellaria baicalensis is neither profligate nor weedy; indeed my two plants, although grown from seed originally, seemed never to set any seed, let alone cast it abroad. So when they suffered the same fate as the little princes in the tower, smothered to death by a hunch-backed lathyrus, there were no heirs, alas. I imagine this disinclination to set seed has much to do with its rarity in nursery lists. I managed to buy a plant this year, which is dithering about whether it means to stay or not. If it looks favourably upon me, I shall enjoy, once again, the sturdy 18-inch clump, with its bright cobalt-blue flowers in short spikes.

Scutellaria altissima, from the Caucasus, belies its specific name by growing shorter than many (botany can be a most inexact science). It is a busy seeder, so put it somewhere where the results will be useful, such as at the top of a wall, dry-stone ideally, which it will cover most attractively, making a refreshing change from valerian. It has nettle-like leaves of a lightish green, and bi-coloured snapdragon flowers of violet-blue and white in long, branched spikes, 12–15 inches high. The resulting seedheads are a rich brown, and pleasing enough to leave for a secondary effect in late summer. Prudence suggests otherwise.

Coming from the mountains of Spain, *Scutellaria orientalis* is completely different, having prostrate stems extending to 12 inches or so, with leaves of a shiny yew-green and terminal clusters of large (for a skullcap) citrus-yellow flowers. It is said to be a fast spreader, but mine is as stay-at-home as the plain daughter, and just as chaste. *S. pontica* is another prostrate grower, but with grey-green, velvety foliage and what are said to be bright pink flowers. Those on my plant are a sullen carmine; perhaps it is a poor form. But still it is persuasive at the top of a wall, cushioned in cracked paving or, as I have it, as a gentle foot-muff for old roses. Both of these skullcaps flower from midsummer onwards.

The late-summer blooming *Scutellaria diffusa* is another carpeter, but with a laxness which is infiltrating, in the style of *Viola cornuta*. It has soft, silvery, furry foliage and small, bi-coloured lavender and white snapdragons that hide coyly along the underside of its stems; so the support of neighbours can encourage it to cast its light out from under its bushel. *S. alpina* is a charmer, if you acquire a good colour form. It is available in pink, yellow, purple or a bi-coloured purple and yellow. Mine, from seed, all turned out a dim white, which was dispiriting, as the sheet of silver foliage is sterling. The deep violet-blue *S. scordiifolia*, from Eastern Europe, is a strong grower and makes a rapidly spreading mat, with flowering stems to 6 inches in late summer. With its pervasive habit, it is another useful plant for stitching a dry wall, or terrace, whose mortar has seen either better days or a crowbar.

All scutellarias like sunshine and reasonable drainage, but are not exacting about their accommodation. They are amiable from collected or bought seed in the first instance, but most will not trouble you, henceforth, with their well-practised *accouchement*.

Geraniums Tall

THERE COMES A TIME WHEN one realizes that not only are many gardens seriously over-geraniumed (including one's own, often enough) but that what remains of a gardening life is too short to stake a geranium.

The floppers must go, unless they have any firmly redeeming feature to encourage a reprieve. Many of them could stay for ever and flop for England if one had the space – an open woodland ideally, where *Geranium sylvaticum* and *G. pratense* could carpet the ground over yards of dappled sunshine with refined grace and suitability. In the borders, however, they are congenitally weak-kneed and weedy, and their milk-soppy flowers are too soon spent to compensate for their lollardly habit.

Some of the taller forms of *Geranium endressii* – mostly unnamed, as they interbreed with profligacy – can be beautiful in flower, but at 4 feet tall and spineless, they are impossible to control in my tight borders. Still others are a better shape and size, but scatter seed around even more than incontinent alchemilla. I have found some appealing forms this way; worth moving, as habitually they will sow themselves on the brink of paths or steps, so leg-soakingly in the way.

Seed lists are full of tempting descriptions, but most geraniums over 12 inches tall will need fiddly staking in order to do themselves (and me) justice. Pea sticks won't push deep enough into my stiff soil to support anything securely, so I have to use stout canes, hammered hard to bury a third of their length, and draped with a cat's cradle rigging of string. This works well, except with the style of growth displayed by most tall geraniums: an inverted triangle of spindle-shanked stems. The first gale will blow the whole thing over to one side like a horse's tail, never to recover, having broken large amounts of the plant, and probably most of those surrounding it. Sheltered gardens with pea-stickable soil can grow them all with impunity, but I have reduced my quota steadily over the years to just a few indispensables that need no fussing.

One of the best was among the few plants here on my accession. An old cottage favourite, the early violet *Geranium* x *magnificum*, which makes a hummock of velvety uncut foliage and flowers in one great gulp, before sitting quietly on the back burner for the rest of the summer. In autumn it makes a devastating show as its leaves become diffused with vermilion and amber. It thrives in the meanest soil, in baking sun or gloomy shade. It never needs watering or any other attention beyond cutting off its spent flower stems. It is the perfect plant.

Also early-flowering, *Geranium phaeum* will attain 2 feet easily, but stands resolute whatever the provocation. Its colour range is not appreciated by all gardeners, being, in the type, a reddish-blackberry. Named forms are available in grape-bloom lavender and an unclean white (which didn't like me either, so I have not bothered to replace it). There is also a pink, acquired recently, called 'Rose Madder'; this a nice description, as it is the gentle hue of sun-faded crimson damask. This looks set to become a stalwart of the Beetroot Border, as its parent, the blackberry type, has been for years. They are comfortably ensconced, to the credit of them both, beneath an arching *Rosa glauca*, whose pewter foliage lends further subtlety to the combination. The grape-bloom variety, which came to me simply as 'pale form' but is scarcely a grape-skin away from that listed as 'Lily Lovell', has just the right amount of misty, greyish lavender to be the sought-after contrast to screaming magenta.

Such is the colour of my next indispensable geranium, *Geranium psilostemon*. Like *G. phaeum*, gardeners either loathe the colour or love it – I am one of the latter. It is a true, pure magenta, not the horrid blueish-mauvey-puce that is my personal colour anathema. This is a sensation: a confident, black-eyed beauty, rouged to the hilt, who flaunts in the border, both early and late, burning the candle at both ends of summer. I forgive it for not standing upright after the first flourish of flowers; middle-aged spread sets in by the end of June. It sheds its corsets and elbows its excessive bulk through the borders – popping through there, sneaking into that little gap, threading its way hither and yon like the most determined queue-jumper. Even in heavy rain, it manages to bow only from the waist (a talent it shares with the primrose yellow *Aconitum lycoctonum*) so it never draggles its great exuberance in the mud.

The yellow-leaved hybrid 'Ann Folkard' sounds a little too frenetic perhaps, although never having grown it, I am unsure whether its acid foliage keeps its colour for the flowering period. The deep grey-green leaves of the type are, for me, a much kinder background to the primal scream magenta. And they enhance the surrounding lavender-blue tones that girdle with good taste the rampant *Geranium psilostemon*: *Campanula lactiflora*, the colour of a bluebell milkshake; *Adenophora bulleyana* and *Stokesia laevis*, both a hint darker; *Campanula* 'Burghaltii', in English-sky grey.

The native meadow cranesbill is as cross-legged as a crusader knight, but its offspring, *Geranium pratense* 'Striatum' contrives a less wobbly stance with just a touch of judicious propping by the adjacent rose 'Mrs Oakley Fisher'. An unlikely Hybrid Tea, with large single flowers of a delicate apricot, it lends a gentle counterpoise to those of the geranium – clusters of bi-coloured blooms, white splashed haphazardly with lavender. If deadheaded after the first flush, it will produce yet more strong flowering shoots (as, indeed, will the rose) to coincide with its other neighbour, the late-flowering shrub *Caryopteris* x *clandonensis*, which has fluffy panicles of soft blue.

In stronger tones of blue and white – especially when the early autumn temperatures begin to chill the air – is the splendid *Geranium wallichianum* 'Buxton's Variety'. This might start off with a dry run in late July, when its flowers will look a little morning-after-the-night-beforeish: pale and wan and, frankly, dull. But it will be better directly the sun's ardour has cooled and will be fully into its stride by the time the Japanese anemones are into theirs. It is an affable plant, accommodating itself to any position, whether in sun or shade (provided it is not too dry) by threading its wide-spreading arms through, between, over and under its neighbours, the ideal weft to the cut back warp of lupins and oriental poppies. The banded blue flowers with their wide-eyed white centres are reminiscent of the annual nemophila – known as baby blue eyes – which can give the same woven, if impermanent, structure to the border. *G.w.* 'Syabru' has this ability too, but with a quiet rose-pink flower, produced much earlier in the summer than its brother 'Buxton's Variety'. They both disappear completely for the winter, so markers may be necessary, as their large growth emanates from disproportionately small crowns.

Geranium pyrenaicum – the hedgerow cranesbill – is an English native that deserves and earns its place in the garden. It is short-lived, but seeds itself around fortuitously, settling its large tap root into corners, or in rooty soil beneath trees, where planting from a pot would be impossible. Here, on a regime of hard tack, it spreads to cover the soil prettily, but puts on little weight. In the Michelin-starred borders it can grow very big indeed, but it is never ungainly as, once again, it threads its way delicately amongst its compeers, giving a gauzy purple underglaze to old striped roses – which it was born to partner. The species itself is a rich purple but the effect is not heavy, despite the vast number of flowers throughout the season, as individually they are small – a mere shilling size. There is a named form, 'Bill Wallis', which is a mite larger and darker in flower, and a superlative white, *G. pyrenaicum* f. *albiflorum*, which is probably one of the ten best plants in the garden (of which, so wrote Clarence Eliot, there are at least a hundred).

Alliums, as well as roses, benefit from the companionship of *Geranium pyrenaicum*. Planted snugly over the bulbs, it will uphold encephalous flowerheads, such as *Allium christophii*, and disguise oniony ankles and disreputable leaf remains. Indeed there is no end to the genius of this geranium. After flowering its socks off from May to the middle of July, it begins to look a little jaded, and I feel that, like Mary Bennet, it has delighted us long enough. It is sheared over, yards of top hamper are removed (a timely chance for a midsummer tidy and feed of the now visible soil beneath) and then away it goes again, flowering until the frosts. A short life, but energy-packed for every minute. Its final aid to busy gardeners is to show an evergreen rosette of leaves throughout the winter to tell you where it has died out, and also where the self-sown seedlings are not vital to your scheme.

Another native, *Geranium sanguineum*, largely deserves its epithet of bloody cranesbill, as it not only flops like a wig displaying its canvas parting, but also attracts mildew like a magnet. It is a good long shriek of magenta, but its habit is unpardonable. I was delighted therefore, when my clump sported a short, neat form that has all the aplomb and none of the problems of its parent.

The white form, *G. sanguineum* 'Album' could be a completely different species, exemplary in behaviour, deportment and colouring – a pristine white, on airy, well balanced and self-supporting stems that lock together to form a 2-foot dome. I have never found any seedlings, but it has a slightly rhizomatous root system that aids removal of bits for friends. Both this and the short magenta form have blazing autumn leaves. Each suffers from moss growing thickly on its woody crown, candidly apparent in wet winters. Clearly this would not be a consideration for those on well drained, rather than my lazy, soil. I used to fret about it, but soon found that the plants were not deterred by their green shawl. When it becomes very obvious, I dig out the whole lot, and replace just the cleaner outriders. With so much else to enjoy about geraniums, I'll not let a little moss concern me.

Geraniums Small

THE SMALLER GERANIUMS ARE A DELIGHT where they can stitch themselves through dry-stone walls or around unmortared paving. Some of them, like the ubiquitous 'Johnson's Blue', are rather too efficient at embroidery, so need careful placing if your fancy is to grow them. Personally, I should carefully place nine-tenths of them on the compost heap each year. Others won't spread fast enough for my taste: the wide bells of *Geranium clarkei* 'Kashmir White' are more like an oenothera than a geranium (if you don't look at the leaves). It flowers once, and early, but is still worth its place, which in my garden is not expansive; clearly the hills of Shropshire are not as free-draining as those of Srinagar.

Geranium renardii is another white-flowered variety, but its blooms are neither beautiful nor beguiling, being an over-washed underwear grey-white, accentuated by heavy dark veins. Large but dim, in fact. That this description covers many of one's best-loved friends should be reason enough to grow it; the leaves provide still further impetus. These are dimpled velvet, almost circular in outline, with scalloped pie-crust edges. They are the colour and, from non-touching distance, the texture of shagreen. I find this plant needs the best possible drainage, at the top of a dry-stone wall. For company it has *Pulsatilla vulgaris* – the native anemone in a pashmina, so soft and furred and snuggly a plant. When its Strüwwelpeter seedheads hold the late summer dew next to the moist, besprinkled sharkskin of the geranium, it needs Reginald Farrer's purplest ink to do it justice.

Geranium dalmaticum is a chalky pink with long *retroussé* stamens of a darker shade. The small leaves are pinkish too, turning fiery red by autumn. Being of prostrate habit, it hugs the wall edge on which it grows. It is much favoured by mice or voles, who sit in comfort upon the supporting stone, and nibble away from beneath, leaving an unattached toupée of fibrous, and now dying, growth, as an umbrella above their dining table.

For some reason, the white form is not so tasty. Stronger in growth, perhaps it is also too strident in flavour, being powerfully scented. Once I had *Geranium dalmaticum* 'Album' growing next to some shallow steps that were feather-stitched with *Cymbalaria muralis*. The tiny creeping, purple and white snapdragon flowers mingled most daintily with the white geranium. It was a charming effect, until 'Johnson's Blue' marched through it, like Hitler in Sudetenland.

I wish *Geranium macrorrhizum* 'Album' had more of the stormtrooper in its blood. It is the best of a good species, although I simply cannot bear the peevish puce of 'Ingwersen's Variety'. The blush-pink of the type is an easy mixer, as are some of the colour forms in between. The white, however, beats them all in my book, with its rich red calyces and curling-tongued red stamens; by autumn, its foliage will be red too. The variegated form has splattered cream and grey-green leaves, like a Jackson Pollock painting (albeit quieter in tone). It really struggles here, even with the best of bad drainage. It is just too cold. I might pot up the last scraps and keep them inside for the winter. It does well in a pot, and one can more easily pounce upon the puce, to remove the foul flowers. This gives the added joy of leaving the deliciously pungent oil of geranium on one's hands.

The short form of *Geranium sanguineum* has been expounded upon already, but there is another, completely prostrate variety that I grew from seed, called *G.s.* 'John Elsley'. It has sugar-mouse pink flowers and the pretty, small-fingered leaves of the species. How similar it is to *G.s.* var. *striatum*, I know not, although that is also described as prostrate and pink.

Some years ago I bought a plant labelled *Geranium cinereum* 'Ballerina', which should have had enchanting mauvish-pink streaked flowers, with a beady black eye, and a lowly growth habit. Instead it turned out to be *G. subcaulescens*, which, roughly speaking, is *Geranium psilostemon* in little – blaring magenta flowers, with great belladonna-enhanced black pupils. It was a triumph for several years on the edge of a dry wall, flowering on and off all summer, until a mouse found that one too. Gardening is as full of mice as life is full of flies.

Deadheading

As June ripens into July, I view with dismay the battalions of thistles in the meadow beyond the stream, armed to their spiky teeth with Molotov cocktails of botanical warfare. Weeds are ordained, inescapably so in rural gardens, where the air is a minestrone soup of mixed weed seed, and where every creature passing through outdoes Darwin's partridge with the seed-encrusted mud on its feet.

But there are more good gardens marred by negligent deadheading than by weeds. Weeds point to a lack of time; deadheads seem to denote a lack of care. Certain weeds can look picturesque, even though they are thieving bandits — stealing food, air and water from more valued plants. I mind weeds very little in friends' gardens, although I am less tolerant of them in my own. I do object to paying for the privilege of viewing them, however. Just as half of all plants that are bred should be scrapped as unworthy; a similar amount of open gardens might be shut for the same reason.

Where weeds can be overlooked by a generous eye, deadheads interrupt the flow as surely as the person from Porlock, and will themselves mutate into weeds faster than the surge of sacred Alph, as all those geraniums spill their seeds, measureless to man, over the paths. Happily, deadheads increase in proportion to available daylight, so an after-dinner trug may be employed to aid digestion. After lunch is safer for the crimson scabious, *Knautia macedonica*, as in my garden it attracts small wasps that arrange themselves for bed, in the early evening, as the spokes of a wheel behind each flowerhead, nose-in, sting-out, fizzing with outraged hysteria when disturbed by grasping fingers.

Embryo weeds they may be; worse still, deadheads can look so frowzy — especially when heavy rain has turned them to brown ooze. Bearded irises are notorious for frowze and ooze, but snap off the finished flower and your hand will be stained with thin violet dye, like Victorian love-letter ink, seraphically scented. Some plants manage the transition from flower to seed with panache, however, continuing to make a gainful contribution throughout each phase. Many alliums form fine skeletons; species roses turn to jolly fruiting heps; *Robinia hispida*'s pea-pods are furred with crimson bristles. So plants must be judged individually, with consideration for effect – height may still be required to lead the eye onward, or to sustain bulk in proportion to the rest of the border. Colour should be studied, as toasted biscuit is not the only colour for seedheads: *Paeonia mlokosewitschii* flaunts clotted-cream petals briefly, then blares crimson-lined pods crammed with Stendhalian scarlet and black seeds; the umbelliferous *Peucedanum ostruthium* 'Daphnis' has deeply chined leaves splashed with cream and pink, and variegated seedheads as flecked as a peckled trout. Next in consideration is shape, which may alter in seed, giving a secondary season of interest: clematis stars whirl into sparkling pirouettes of furry seed-tails, like a nest of lemurs; *Lathyrus niger*'s ebony pods spiral into paired antelope horns as they ripen. Nuisance-value to border-neighbours must be weighed – surrounding plants should be given their chance to shine unhampered by tawdry has-beens, but still be cushioned where necessary. Cutting back might be accomplished in two stages of cosmetic surgery, giving progressively more elbow-room to the next act, rather than either quelling it with a sudden agoraphobic gap or leaving it to drown under shrouds of neighbourly excess.

Most important of all is to consider the future: by removing each finished head you may prolong blooming for weeks instead of days; or where flowering occurs in one great early gulp you may encourage a repeat performance later in the season by removing all the exhausted stems. *Viola cornuta* and *Phuopsis stylosa* will repay you well after this treatment. They need a pit-stop by midsummer anyway, as paths disappear beneath their eagerness. When early-flowering shrubs go over – *Lonicera tartarica* 'Rosea', with perky pink flowers in clusters along wand-like stems, or *Buddleja alternifolia*, whose tiny, sickly-sweet, lavender flowers coil around pendant branches – you must plan for next year's blooms by cutting out this year's played-out stems. Deadheading is simply pruning.

Unless bulbs are very vigorous, or indeed, where they are too enthusiastic and need curtailing, it is always better to deadhead them by removing simply the head itself, thereby leaving all of the stem to continue feeding the bulb. An encouraging thought is that the unenticing foliage will die-off all the sooner, once the urge to ripen seed has been suppressed. Individual deadheading is all very well where the bulbs are in small groups in the borders, but what about orchards full of daffodils or meadows awash with camassias? Victorian gardeners would cut hazel switches from the hedgerow and walk among the bulbs whisking the cane from side to side, decapitating the daffs as surely as Boadicea's bladed chariot wheels. Margery Fish used an old cavalry sabre. Deadheading is simply swash-buckling.

Conversely, future plans may require plants to seed around; many small bulbs can be left to colonize with self-sown abandon: no one ever has too many cyclamen, or *Scilla bifolia*, or the tuberous *Anemone blanda*. As deadheading such early tinies would be an irksome task, it is just as well that the garden's appetite for these generous carpeters need not be quenched. Larger voracious seeders are not sufficiently housetrained for the average garden, requiring a firm hand if you are not to be inundated. The worst offenders, foxgloves, sweet rocket, Spanish bluebells, can be picked in full bloom. Deadheading is simply flower arranging.

The campanula family are fervidly fertile, of imagination too: their varying styles of deadheading could illustrate a manual on the subject. My favourite is the rampant spreader *Campanula poscharskyana*. It is a truly sporting gentleman. Knowing that its roots are ungovernable, it has no need to take too much advantage by having flagrant seeding arrangements as well, so makes deadheading as simple as possible: as the flowers recede, one snatches the stems, gives a mild tug, and the whole lot breaks neatly at the base, leaving tidy leafy growth to continue as useful, evergreen, ground-cover. Several good colour forms are now available, alongside the usual light lavender-blue, including the appropriately icy-blue-white 'E.H. Frost', and a deliciously muted pink 'Lisduggan Variety', so yards of awkward terrain could be pastel-painted in this way, with a mere half-hour's work per annum to tidy up the finished flowers. Those gardeners chary of introducing such a renowned hooligan should recall the social workers' mantra that thugs become thugs only when their background and surroundings are all wrong.

Another lowly grower is *Campanula cochlearifolia*, which displays another style of deadheading: when the powder-blue thimbles finish in late summer, snip off the thread-like, 3-inch stems with shears, to leave a clean hassock of ripe avocado green. The double forms, such as 'Elizabeth Oliver', give a longer, showier, flowering season. All of them make a cosy blanket over the smaller spring bulbs, such as *Crocus chrysanthus*, or the early summer flowering *Scilla litardierei*, like tiny blue pipe cleaners. In either instance the faded foliage will be out of the way before the campanula begins to flower.

From a ground-hugging spreader to the giant of the family – *Campanula lactiflora* can grow 6 feet tall, with plumey turrets of milky bells covering a foot or more of stem in early summer. As these go over (in violently wet weather it will be sooner than later), cut back to the leaves beneath the flowerhead, where new shoots will be developing, to bloom all over again, but on a lower storey. Favourable summers could encourage a further reduction, with a third, *piano nobile*, set of blooms. The lime-washed pink form 'Loddon Anna' is particularly long-winded; the silvery-blue type form less so. I have not yet tried a white variety, as I suspect that in wet summers (and this is England) it would require constant housemaiding in the removal of individual bells within the head, to keep it more white than brown – an exasperating design failure of many white flowers. *Campanula lactiflora* needs thoughtful placing as it will become a mighty clump whose vast starchy roots dislike disturbance. A back-bencher's seat would suit as to height, and keep the unappetizing scent, redolent of disinfectant, beyond wafting-distance; but a cross-bencher's berth might show more of the descending-escalator style of flowering. The rich violet 'Prichard's Variety' can be still more perplexing as it demands a light background to do itself justice. Before an aluminium curtain of *Eleagnus* 'Quicksilver', I have seen it give a virtuoso performance. But as the eleagnus dislikes my conditions, I leave them both for someone else to grow. The weeping silver-leaved pear might do, if I were not weary of seeing its baked-alaska beehive dome dumped on every lawn.

Much easier to accommodate is the elegant *Campanula* 'Burghaltii', a cross between *C. latifolia* and *C. punctata*, with all the amiability of the former, and none of the slug-temptation of the latter. Its drooping bells are slender, almost 3 inches long, with deeply pennoned lobes. They are a delicate whey-grey, opening from bruise-purple buds. It is an immensely stylish plant. At 2 feet tall it sits comfortably in the border, playing a polished accompaniment to old roses, and bridging the subtle sea-mist shades of *Iris* 'Florentina' with ferocious phlox – it is miraculous partnering the bold magenta 'Starfire'. Deadheading will ensure the timing, as more and more smoky bells will chime forth if you nip out the single spent blooms with a nimble thumbnail. The native bats in the belfry, *Campanula trachelium*, needs the same handling.

Campanula latifolia is treated differently again: you cut back the whole flowering stem, whose narrow, swallow-tailed bells open like a foxglove, from the basement to the penthouse, and do not repay individual tinkering by sprouting further flowers. The hazardous *C. rapunculoides* behaves similarly; its pinky-purple spikes of bells are worth risking if you have an acre of land to disguise within a week, but the wantoness of its roots would not make contented bedfellows in a border. Equally awkward is *C. ochroleuca:* not because of rampant roots (it is a sedate clump-former), but because its stems lean at an angle that becomes steadily more obtuse as the weight of the cream flowers increases. It looks hideous staked, but splendid lurching out from the top of a wall. But a 4-foot diagonal wave-crest would overshadow a larger space beneath the wall than I could spare. The same idea, but in miniature, is shown by *C. makaschvilii*, whose creamy bells age from a blushing pink youth. As it grows to only 18 inches, its sloping habit is less ungainly. As before, the whole spike can be left to flower, then cut back.

Campanula latiloba 'Hidcote Amethyst' is dealt with in the same way, even though it would look better if dead flowers were nipped out singly, and would doubtless bloom longer too; but its sessile bells sit so tightly against the stem that my blundering fingers knock off buds or break the stem, so I leave them, and am never very satisfied with its appearance. It is begrudging of flower stems anyway, unless it is split and replanted every other year: it would be happier in lighter soil than mine. But I persevere, as it is such an appealing colour – not the rich deep purple of the finest Siberian amethysts, perhaps; it is more like the watery, Blue John-mauve of the quartz pebbles one can find sometimes on British beaches that split to reveal the quilted lining of amethyst crystals within.

Other bellflowers within the family display their originality too: adenophoras vary from species to species, some flowering on branched stems to be lopped bit-by-bit, others making a contemporaneous jangle of bells on single spikes – to be cut back to base. Platycodons favour the removal of individual flowers starting with the central keystone bell and working through the flowerhead in a fishbone sequence. These are worth daily fussing, as the hot-air-balloon buds should be given a clear field to show their paces: splitting and splaying out the pointed lobes from the curious flanged buttress at the balloon's shoulder, into enormous, outward-facing bells of deep mazarine-blue, a delectable shell-pink or a blued white. The double forms are good, but not so large in flower. All of them have petals of vellum-smooth, magnolia density, and late-appearing shoots in spring that look like sapphire asparagus.

Codonopsis, another campanula cousin, not only varies from species to species in its deadheading requirements, but from plant to plant within the same species. Here, one clump of *C. clematidea* is efficient and disciplined, opening the flower at the extreme end of each stem first, then working steadily backwards, so that one is reducing the size of the plant repeatedly, and keeping it tidy throughout its flowering season. Another clump is scatty and unhelpful, opening bells haphazardly, and springing tiny secondary buds in inconvenient junctions of gangling stem. To keep this one neat I must sacrifice many of these buds, or the path over which it cascades.

But the campanula whose deadheading I least enjoy is *C. persicifolia*, which is sad, as the plant itself is splendid, or would be if the conditions were kinder: peach-leaved heaven would be warmer than my garden, so it does not flourish its blue and white bells in the profusion I should like. The crisp white cup-in-cup 'Hetty' (syn 'Hampstead White') is made still more chalky by having white petioles and ovaries behind each flower; 'George Chiswell' (syn 'Chettle Charm') has white bells deckled with faint lilac; 'Pride of Exmouth' has a double ruffle of bells in rich lavender-blue. Ideally, all should be attended daily, taking out blooms individually as they are ravaged by bees, the weather and slugs (who shin up the staking canes and tightrope-walk along the fillis to reach them). The flowers themselves are somewhat sticky, and will cling together, tearing easily. This is made worse by the milky plasma that seeps from each nipped stem, coating my fingers and turning to black glue within moments, tenacious enough to bind the collection of spent heads to my hand so that it is necessary to peel them from my palm rather than simply dropping them into the bucket. Dealing with them every day keeps numbers down (and yes, I always count as I deadhead) so the glue does not reach merciless levels nor the black stain on my thumbnail become too obstinate. Using scissors or secateurs is no help as the glue gums them up so that every adhesive, finished flower will stick and rip each bud as the scissors reach among them. Gardening gloves are too fumbly, for me, at least, and rubber or latex gloves drag against the tacky bells, bruising them (which means more deadheading). E.A. Bowles used ivory glove stretchers to weed in between his collection of spiny opuntias. Perhaps I should try a pair.

Worst of all, the first day of the open season for deadheading *Campanula persicifolia* is Midsummer Day, and then it is downhill all the way to winter.

——————

LATE SUMMER

——————

THE GARDEN HUMS IN DEEP SUMMER. The colours are curdled with the heat. One's thoughts are accompanied by the continuous chorus of bees, mumbling over the marjoram and thrumming in the poppies. They clatter against the petals, sounding as though they are talking as they eat, the noise ebbing as they swallow. Butterflies flicker in and out of one's vision, then settle and work their way, meticulously, over each helenium and scabious, watch-spring tongues sipping greedily at the nectar. As I push through the path-engulfing lavender, they rise in clouds, dragging the scent with them. A painted lady brushes my hand with the softest furred wings of tortoiseshell-cat colours, before settling once again in a feeding frenzy, as urgent as it is gentle. For the days are shrinking, and the nights are cooling rapidly – already there have been slight frosts – and the swallow-chicks are strengthening their wings with longer flights each time, in readiness for the day when all the wires are suddenly empty, and the air no longer echoes to their swooping screams.

It has been an uncharacteristically harsh summer, of blistering heat and scorching winds. With no rain at all for weeks, and none of the damp coolth of a normal English summer, the soil is bleached and parched to dust in areas where it has been disturbed or left bare for any reason. It is concrete elsewhere: any water poured on to it simply rolls off like quicksilver. The worms have sunk like stones to the bowels of the earth, so their relentless work of soil-laundering is left undone, as they strike, and roll themselves into torpid coils like barristers' knotted silk cufflinks. How long can the soil wait, in abeyance, I wonder, for its linen to be washed, dried and ironed by the washerwomen worms? Is it dying by inches yet? Will next year's garden be affected by this year's intense struggle?

It is affected now; leaves hang like limp rags, flowers last for probably half their usual span, spalled by the heat, as they rush into seed to safeguard their species in the next generation. There is no egotism in the garden, no 'darling me' about plants. Just as the female spider will feed her hatching babies with her own dying body, so will plants spend their last ounce of energy in producing viable seed and die in the attempt. There have been no plant deaths yet: I am luckier than many to have the oft-cursed clay soil. As tenacious as a terrier, it just will not let go of one drop of moisture from within, so deep-rooted plants are still being wined and dined, at the moment, at least. Shallow roots, such as those of monarda, are discomforted, particularly as they are in full flight of flower, which saps their strength still further. The coming winter will be the real testing time, however; a hard one will tip the balance for many over-stressed plants. That is when the deaths will occur, here, when Atropos will cut the thread of life.

Unlike the worms, moles are busy at the surface. Always before, they have kept to one area of the garden, in and around the Dawn Border, with occasional forays along the inside of the ha-ha wall, at the back of the Beetroot Border. Now, suddenly, they are everywhere. Tumps explode overnight, where in the past there would be only superficial tunnels. These were quite bad enough, as the mole would encircle each plant, particularly if newly planted, so that the poor thing would either be thrown up and out of bed, or else would sink below the covers. This is a particular problem for small bulbs, whose natural home is within the top 3 inches of soil. Suddenly catapulted into cavernous tunnels several inches lower, and rolling around like marbles, they will either give up in disgust at their treatment, or else mice, who quickly become tunnel-squatters, will pounce upon such easy bounty. Either way, I cannot know their fate until it is too late to do anything – the following spring, when they don't show up, will be the first sign, to me, of their demise.

Often plants will begin to wilt for no apparent reason, and I will find them hanging by their eyelashes above a yawning chasm, drowning in air. Now, with mole-hills as well, the damage is greater, as not only are the fox-holes and craters there, beneath their dangling roots, but the poor plants have also been buried with the spoil of the heaving sapper, above their crowns. It requires daily inspection of the trenches, on my part, at least. Often, as I stand at the kitchen window another hillock appears, immediately beneath the feet of feeding birds, who might jump a bit the first time, but take very little notice, henceforth. I wait to see if Moldywarp himself will stand on the fire step, and show his nose above the parapet. He hasn't yet; sappers always learn to keep their heads down.

This has never been the sort of herbaceous border garden of intense and, let's be frank, often coarse colour only in high summer. My aim is to have something of interest, (ideally, something in flower) in each border or area, every month of the year. So I expect July and August to be colourful, yes, but not at the expense of the other seasons. Here, those months are simply a continuation of June's irises, poppies, roses, *et al.*, and a forerunner of September's asters and anemones. They should, and usually do, run into one another seamlessly like clouds in wet watercolour. This year's unconventional summer has spoilt the colour wash; everything seemed to bloom in one lump at midsummer. Earlier flowers were held back by the dry spring, and then hurried after a wet June. Later ones were delayed in their bud-preparation, so flowered anyway, at half cock. The subsequent, and far worse drought, has stopped any more buds forming. June's flowering total was much in excess of last year's figure; July's, still more so, seeing 150 more plants (different species and varieties, I mean) in flower, than in the same month last year. August, by comparison, is more than 100 down on last year's total.

Nor, I believe, are the colours so intense, this sun-bleached summer. So, with many fewer flowers, and those paler, the garden is looking and feeling rather subdued. Perhaps this is no bad thing, once in a while, for the sake of re-evaluating performance: give a good plant a bad year, and it will still show its worth. As for the others . . . well, their space will be useful. And we don't always want even the August garden to be Brazil at Mardi Gras – at least, I don't. I like a little restraint and asceticism to creep in, even when the light levels are at their strongest: Boston austerity with a few Miami flounces. Or, as this is England, the Yorkshire Dales with a touch of Torquay.

Torquay, this year, has been suggested by zinnias, which a friend grew from seed of a mixed cactus-flowered variety, and the old faithful, 'Envy'. This has been a success in a large pot with *Nicotiana langsdorfii* (also grown by my green-flower-fingered friend) I had an unexpected gap in the Beetroot Border, when a vast plant that should have been *Echium russicum* mutated into *E. vulgare* – the native viper's bugloss. It gives a splendid effect, with its sword and halberd foliage and its unrolling croziers of cobalt blue flowers. Bees love it as much as I do, and we can't both be wrong. Indeed it would probably have been better value than the intended *E. russicum*, as these have been a disappointingly poor form, with washed out elastoplast-pink flowers at 9 inches, rather than rich *sang-de-boeuf* at 2 feet. But the viper's bugloss, left to itself, would have put out of bounds too much of the central path down the garden. At the time of removal, I noticed that a *Potentilla recta* var. *sulphurea* that had seeded itself into the embrace of the sultry rose 'Tuscany' was beginning to bloom in the fresh, pale greenish-primrose which exactly matches *Zinnia* 'Envy'. So it was the work of a moment to place the pot in the bugloss gap. Thus are stars born. The envious green, mixed with the prevailing crimson of the Beetroot Border, and most particularly 'Tuscany' and its neighbouring *Lysimachia atropurpurea*, has been a triumph. Strangely, at the same time, *Clematis viticella* 'Purpurea Plena Elegans' (but don't let its name put you off – it is worth every syllable) has strayed from its usual billet on the front of the house, round the corner to see what was going on in the Blue Border, and has draped itself alluringly among the 7-foot stems of the hollyhock called 'Lemon Light': the same partnership again – crimson (although greyer and moodier, this time) and sulphurous greenish-yellow. It is tempting to leave the serendipitous potentilla and to plant more of that colour in the Beetroot Border; but that would mean moving out a lot of the pink, which, to my eyes, would not mix to mutual advantage with light yellow.

It would not be so unappetizing as that hard dense pink one sees so often in phlox combined with the all-pervading sunflower-yellow at this time of year. Each can be an obliging colour if used with a little thought for the nerves of onlookers. But so often they are lumped together just because they flower together. No wonder so many people are attracted to cannas and other exotics, instead of the classic herbaceous plants of the late summer border. One can't help a subconscious blending of that pink and yellow on the palette of one's mind: it can be stomach-churning in the unforgiving light of an August afternoon.

Phlox paniculata, in all their shades, are wonderful plants if you can accommodate their thirsty souls. A dehydrated phlox is a sorry sight, whereas well-tapped plants are the glory of the summer garden. Most of mine came from friends, so their names are unknown, except when the friend had recently acquired the plant, so could still remember it. Thus, I have 'Blue Paradise' and 'Mount Fuji' – the latter being a tall, late white, which runs; the former, an awkward customer, whose ultra-violet neon glare is difficult to place. In warmer gardens, with dulcet light, it would mix well, I've no doubt; here, with the normally wet-blanket light reflected on all the dull grey stone, it is much trickier to get right. With it, pinks are putrid, purples worse, yellow – even the much-lauded sulphur – looks horrid, blue is vile. White is all right, provided it is a warm, ivory-white, not the ice-white of phlox, which, being chill, makes the 'blue' phlox look gun-metal gaunt. With all unwieldy colours, their saviour, and mine, is lavender-blue – the universal adaptor. So 'Blue Paradise' is surrounded by safer, earlier-blooming plants in pink and purple. Companionship at flowering time comes from the lavender *Adenophora campanulata*, a 4-foot bellflower from the Himalayas, and the warm-white fluffy plates, at 3 feet, of the North American *Eupatorium aromaticum*. That, at least, was the name by which I acquired it, but to me, it seems indistinguishable from *E. rugosum* and, perversely, has no scent.

All the eupatoriums are good, but there is a lot of repetition in their ranks so you probably don't need them all, even if you do have a collector's temperament. I don't, so I am content with my four: the white, above; a taller light pink, also in a flattish, fluffy corymb, which is the sweet joe-pye weed, *E. purpureum*; another tall one (these are both 6 feet or more, but never need staking), *E.p.* subsp. *maculatum* 'Atropurpureum', with a more pointed dome to its pruinose-plum flowerhead, which is botanically described as a cymose panicle, if you care about such rarified information; finally, my favourite, the English native hemp agrimony, *E. cannabinum*, which is very similar to the American version, joe-pye weed, but somewhat smaller, at 5 feet, with a darker rose-pink colouring to its fluffiness and a much stronger scent of vanilla sugar. Butterflies, bees and hoverflies dote upon it. All the eupatoriums like rich soil – they are sound trenchermen and come from swampy ditch edges so they do not appreciate temperance with their liquid diet.

The muted pink tones of the eupatoriums provide a perfect background to phlox and the kaffir lily, *Schizostylis coccinea*, in polished coral-red, fleshy-pink and chalk-white. Equally good together are the tawny shades of kniphofia and crocosmia, with the ubiquitous yellow daisy of late summer, whether it be rudbeckia, helenium, helianthus or the less-encountered ratibida – the Mexican hat (which can ring the changes with red daisies, too). I prefer to keep my pinks away from the yellows, but only the confines of a small garden stop me from growing more of both disparate colours.

Rudbeckias are great favourites, although some are better than many, and more are too little different from countless others, to justify space in all but the emptiest gardens. I am particularly fond of the variety of *R. hirta*, sold in seed lists as 'Nutmeg'. It is a short-lived perennial, which will flower profusely in its first year from seed sown in March, so it is treated invariably as an annual. The large daisy flowers, on 2-foot branched stems, are in sumptuous spice colours: ginger, cinnamon, mace, turmeric, paprika. To the uninitiated eye, they are brown and damned with contempt. I am a sucker for brown flowers, which used to be a bit of a battle – trying to convince myself, as well as others, that my taste was not flawed. Since reading in Harold Nicolson's letters, that 'Vita will now only grow plants which are difficult, or which have brown flowers,' I and my errant taste have been justified. Young gardeners need that kind of absolution. One of the compensations of increasing age is the confidence to stand four-square by your own vagaries of taste, without feeling the need to excuse or explain them or to have someone pat you on the back for holding them. But it is still good to know that one marches in tandem with such a talisman of taste in the garden as Miss V. Sackville-West.

Of the yellow-flowered species of rudbeckia, I grow only one and a half at present: the half being *R. maxima*, which was planted just as the drought ensued and, despite copious and frequent douches, it is still sulking at the poor accommodation and may spite me by dying. The coming winter will decide matters, as it is a mite tender for this garden anyway, and its position is a little exposed. But if all goes well, (and if one can't live in hope, one can't be a gardener) I shall expect to see large paddle-shaped leaves of glaucous blue beneath the bright yellow daisies. This is why its position is exposed: to show off that steely basal foliage.

Leaves, after all, are not usually what a rudbeckia is about. It is, first, last and in-between, the quintessential yellow daisy *par excellence*, which, in its various forms, will flower for months with no fuss about staking and manage very well without any deadheading at all, although naturally it will be all the better for this small service. It is not an entirely labour-free plant, however. If I remind you that Linnaeus named the genus after his friend Olof Rudbeck, who was the father of twenty-four children by three wives, you may get an idea of the fecundity of these plants and the rampant proclivities of their fast-spreading roots. They need frequent division, not only to rid your border of the excess but also because they quickly exhaust the soil in which they grow and, if left too long, will starve themselves into dying off in their original placement and irritate you by springing strongly from right in the middle of the crown of your best peony.

Rudbeckia fulgida var. *speciosa* seems not so rampant here. It has made a tight mat, about 2 feet in diameter, which is kept in control by the moisture-leeching yew hedge immediately behind it and also by the scratchings of the various large mammals which tend my garden so assiduously with their stamping and chewing and digging and rolling. This yellow daisy grows to only 2–3 feet and has a gibbous eye of bitter chocolate. Its petals are the rich egg-yolk colour that one sees only in organic eggs, whose mammas have been fed on equally organic corn, muesli, potted prawns, champagne or, best of all, hellebore flowers – which nine out of ten hens seemed to prefer to anything else they could get their teeth into on foraging raids into my garden. Please don't try this at home, children, as hellebores are meant to be poisonous. Hens, of course, know better.

Another late-summer plant that needs frequent division in order to flower well is crocosmia, in all its glorious cultivars of fiery orange and chrome yellow. I was given a clump of the intense scarlet *C.* 'Lucifer', shortly after I began the garden, and on the strength of its commanding presence, which is not inconsiderable, I began to acquire others. These, sadly, have been variable in their degree of success, for some are much less hardy than others. 'Emily McKenzie', for example, was splendid the first year; I cheated, as I bought it in flower, but at least that means I have seen those large tawny, henna-rimmed eyes, just once – but never again. It is still alive, just, but that is all that can be said for it.

The common orange montbretia, *C.* x *crocosmiiflora*, was here when I came, naturally, and still does well if I remember to divide and reset it now and then. I did so last year, so this is a floriferous year. 'Coleton Fishacre' (whose passport has been issued, previously, under the names 'Golden Fleece' and 'Citronella') has the same, rather thinly textured, grassy foliage and romps lustily, but it doesn't flower much. 'Severn Sunrise' is better, flowering abundantly each year with its apricot-jam trumpets that fit so aptly into my Sunset Border. This year, the second flowering of the bronzy-green pansy, *Viola* 'Irish Molly', is surging around the crocosmia's feet in a rich harmony of tertiary colours. Also in that border is *Crocosmia pottsii* 'Culzean Pink', which is the singed rose colour of Tudor bricks and exactly matches the old-style day lily, *Hemerocallis* 'Pink Charm', not far away.

A singular failure, though, is with a crocosmia I bought as *C.* 'Amberglow', which is self-explanatory as to colour, but turned out to be 'Emberglow' – did the breeders of these not anticipate that mistakes would be inevitable? – which is equally self-explanatory: the hardest aniline-vermilion it has been my misfortune to encounter in a garden. How mortifying that it should be mine. I am not in the least against red in the garden, indeed it is a favourite colour generally and I have included many plants with strong red flowers. But some reds, and 'Emberglow' is one of them, have a taint of harsh purple, which begrimes the purity of the red, and this makes me clench my teeth at the aggression it throws in my face. Clear reds, such as the excellent 'Lucifer', or *Lychnis chalcedonica* (especially in the double form, which holds the colour longer) are an asset, with their strength and exuberance. But *Crocosmia* 'Emberglow' has none of these riches. It is a bully. Out it shall go.

Too much pink in the late-summer garden can be cloying, as the autumn tints make a tentative beginning in the tree canopy, and frosts hone the lowered light. Equally, too much yellow can be strident. One needs blues and purples to brace one and tone down the other. It is now that I long to be able to suit ceratostigma, with its tropical-sky blue, phlox-shaped flowers and astonishing autumn-frosted, crimson foliage. The best species for colour is *C. willmottianum*; it is also more tender. It died. I compromised on colour a little for the sake of toughness, with *C. plumbaginoides*. This grows shorter, at 12 inches or so, and has a running root that would be perfect for pointing my dry-stone walls. It died. In fact, three times it died. So I shan't try again. Gloom.

This year I have bought *Strobilanthes violacea*, an unlikely cousin to the acanthus, but which looks more like a salvia. It has soft, ashen-green, rather sticky foliage and hooded flowers which are a marriage of Roman-nosed acanthus with Hapsburg-lipped sage. They are also the most intense Imperial Purple (so magnificent that it demands capital letters). As yet, mine is still in its pot, as are many more plants this summer – they are less onerous to water as a block of pots, than scattered in their planting positions in the borders – so it is a mere 14 inches tall. Opinion seems to be divided as to whether it will stay at 2 feet, or swarm up to 5 feet. Likewise is opinion divided as to hardiness; so we shall see next year, or not, as the case may be.

Late summer is an unexciting time, as maintenance takes over, relentlessly, from sowing seeds and planting. All my time is taken up by grass, hedges, deadheading, watering and the repairs which result from the various mammalian visitors to the garden. Leave the lawn a day too long, and the time taken to cut it doubles. Rough grass is worse, as the pause between not really needing attention and being too tough for the nylon line of the strimmer is a millisecond. I miss it time and again, and have to spend an afternoon at the job instead of an hour. Most of the afternoon being spent winkling out the rank stems from the bowels of the machine, where they have twisted themselves so fast they seem melted to the metal.

Hedges and deadheading need essays all to themselves, as their ways are as legion as their arts are precise. Watering, too, is no job for a fool, if the pots you are drenching contain plants from diverse habitats with dissimilar requirements. It helps, naturally, if one can keep such disparates well apart, but neither greenhouses nor cold frames are ever that large. Crammed together to maximize space, it is almost impossible to lift an individual pot to judge its parched and weightless state, or else its logged and spongy heaviness. A pressing fingertip can seldom appreciate the condition below the surface compost. Well watered roots can still show wilting top-growth if the sun is hot and the air stagnant: it is shade that will help, in this instance, not adding more water, which will simply encourage mould spores and rot. Dampness, whether hot or cold, explains why England was popularly known as Blighty.

Running repairs become a daily task in a garden that is on the visiting list of many of this country's larger mammals: pots to be righted, pushed over in play or flight; broken and chewed stems to be cut off; dug-out soil to be pressed back over exposed roots; divots to be returned in the lawn – it can be heart-breaking as well as plant-breaking. Boisterousness is to blame, largely, and boredom with juveniles who don't yet know their own strength. Their hunting for grubs and slugs makes some of the damage worthwhile, although the neat burial of peanuts by squirrels tempts clumsier, four-legged gardeners to dig a hole just to see what is at the bottom of it. This is also the case where I have been planting, and gives the impression that my every movement is being checked out. Has she planted that thing properly? No, I thought not; try once more . . . and I do, as, time and again, I find the newly buried plant disinterred and tossed on to the path. Bulbs are particularly tantalizing. First, the recently disturbed soil might provide a tasty grub or worm, and then the bulb itself makes a rather jolly football that can be dribbled and kicked yards from its original home. Potatoes are good for this game too, and Jerusalem artichokes, if there is nothing better. I loathe planting bulbs, so having to do it twice or thrice with the same bulb does not improve my attitude – or my language, when I find that the already-shooting bulb has been broken. Yesterday I planted *Colchicum cilicicum* and *Sternbergia lutea.* Today I planted them again. One of the colchicums, thankfully not yet shooting, was several feet away, beyond an 18-inch-high box hedge, so it must have been tossed rather than dribbled. No damage, as far as I could judge, but lying out all night would not do anyone any good, still less a naked lady, particularly as the temperature was below freezing, and the dew penetrating. The sternbergia was lying above ground only inches away from its cosy new home of yesterday, but it can't have enjoyed the light frost, especially as its flowering shoot is already 3 inches long. I am taking no chances on tonight's soccer game or incipient frost so, having replaced the bulbs, I have scattered chopped fruit-peelings – banana, lemon, pineapple – over the surface above them. Sometimes their pungent smell masks that of any tempting bugs in the soil, or the disturbed soil itself, so may stop the digging for a while – ideally until after the ravishing mauve goblets and startling yellow quasi-crocuses have completed their recital. Sometimes, however, it does not work and I suspect this may be one of those times: the colchicums are planted beneath the spreading foliage of *Crambe cordifolia*, whose firework display of frothing white stars at 6 feet or so is early and soon spent. Ever after, it is a damp squib that needs further enlivenment to justify its colossal ground space – hence the colchicums, whose leafless autumn flowers should do just that, and whose capacious spring foliage (which can be difficult to ignore in its unconscionably long time a'dying) should be quickly covered by the unfurling crambe. Immediately beside the newly planted bulbs is the greenish-white bracted form of *Salvia sclarea* – a pretty thing to look at but definitely not to touch or even approach too closely. Not for nothing has it been known as hot housemaid; its stench of stale sweat stays on your hands or clothes for hours. Sir Cedric Morris went further, and claimed it was redolent of 'a whore sucking a bullseye'. I am not familiar with that particular scent (indeed, I am surprised that Sir Cedric was) but my local foxes must like it, for it not to have deterred their initial digging. I fear lemon zest may not be able to compete, to my advantage, and that my itinerant colchicums will be out on the path again, tomorrow.

But then disaster is the natural state of affairs for a gardener, according to Henry Mitchell; it is how you cope with it that proves your worth. 'Defiance,' he said, 'is what makes gardeners.' At present, I am deaf to defiance, so worth very little.

Porridge

I AM EATING PORRIDGE, sitting at an old gateleg table facing the window. Not very gentlemanly, perhaps, but I am four years old, and such tender years are not invariably compatible with simultaneous walking and eating.

The window looks to the east, so the early morning light dimples through the hollyhocks crowding straight across it, turning the snowy tablecloth to a limpid, submarine green, and my mesmerized gaze to that of a sea otter glimpsing sunlight through the waving kelp forest.

I try not to scrape my spoon in the silence, listening for the bees' intermittent bumble and hum from within the flaring trumpets. The light from beyond is keen enough now to show which flower holds a shadowy, murmuring bee. The spilled pollen snowflakes down as it emerges. The flowers sparkle with phosphorescent cells among their Neapolitan icecream colours. Even the sturdy stems – thicker than the peeling, white-painted mullions – trap prisms of light within their bristles.

All is framed by checked blue and white cretonne curtains.

It was an old garden, bound by high stone walls to offset the salt-laden Atlantic gales. For me, at least, it exists no more, as the family connection has lapsed. But it remains fast in my memory.

How fascinating it would be to walk its paths again, to listen to its history, to talk to the crusty old Head Gardener, long since dead. To us as children, he was a captious Mr MacGregor, thwarting all our cherished but wayward schemes. But he was kind too, for once he picked a great bunch of pelargoniums and presented it to me, the serious child, with a courtly bow. Long-stemmed vibrant globes of glamorous, lipstick colours – cerise, coral, scarlet and magenta – they grew in a lean-to glasshouse and were trained up against the high back wall and on across the rafters like an ancient vine, covered from ground to roof-tree with gorgeous colour and warm, spicy scent. In my mind's nose that greenhouse smell – acrid, stagnant, damp – is with me still. As is the plink of water echoing flatly into the sun-warmed, leaden tanks.

A curved, linking walkway to a pavilion sitting room made a more formal glasshouse in the garden. The back wall was painted with a mural (or was it an old Chinese paper?) of riotous plants, exotic butterflies and mad-eyed tropical birds. There were large tubs of lilies, plumbago and jasmine; and let into the flagstone path were tiny pools – just the merest slice cut from the rim of a sphere, and only an inch or so deep – lined with minute tessellations of turquoise and gold. Doubtless they were designed to keep the air lambent, but I thought (and still like to believe) they were for the birds.

Outside this glass arcade, and held within its curve, was a flagged terrace dotted with Spanish daisies, miraculously changing from white to pink. A small sunken pool, whose lilies seemed never to flower, but where frogs could be seen if one kept still long enough, boasted a portly putto blowing into a conch shell for a fountain. The spray, on windy days, caused relentless hilarity; children having much in common with Holy Roman Emperors concerning a delight in unexpected cold water and other gems of *schadenfreude*.

Beyond the pool was a monumental pergola, whose rusticated columns were of Ramesesian girth. Above, the silvery hammerbeams of split chestnut were warped and cracked by time and the Atlantic (which sounds like a J.B. Priestley play). Then, as a child, I probably wished it to be wreathed in 'Dorothy Perkins' roses. Now, looking back, I realize it was exactly right as it stood, proudly naked. Any planting would have been as crass as clothing the Apollo Belvedere.

From the strict architectural austerity of the pergola, one plunged forthwith into the Tissotesque frou-frous of hortensia hydrangeas massed along the drive. Ceruleanly blue, certainly, but somehow I couldn't love their smug, aldermanic embonpoint then, and I can't now.

Another small area was open to the sea on one side and called the Wind Garden. All I remember of it is a slight, lead figure of a boy with panpipes. Was this just a shepherd boy, or was it the capricious god himself? I don't recall hoof or horn or curly goat legs; to me he was Dickon from *The Secret*

Garden, especially when rabbits from the downs nibbled around his feet, the setting sun glowing pinkly through their soft ears.

Of perennial interest was the ruined temple: in reality a circular summerhouse with a thatched rondel roof. This was drowning slowly in sand, disappearing inch by inch, its progress marked by tallies, as the neap-tide of the dunes slipped ever closer.

The cliff steps dropped down to the bay amidst tumbling Hottentot daisies and thrift; gale-stunted tamarisks and wind-clipped hedges of hebe and escallonia. I remember the fustian foliage of the self-sown gawks of tree mallows; the silken swirl of montbretia leaves through my fingers and the eye-aching brilliance of naturalized *Gladiolus byzantinus* – jumping jacks, as we called them.

I remember the dense blackness of the granite flags and walls in rainy summers, the harsh, refracted light crisping through the raindrops boiling on the surface of the pool. But also the languorous, heat-drenched days, with an idle surf teasing the sand and crickets creaking in the long paddock grass.

Most of all, it is the hollyhocks that I remember, their stems barring the window, and framed by checked blue and white cretonne curtains.

Oh! And the porridge was made with the true catholicity of Sassenach flavours. Cooked like a risotto, and stirred, if necessary, throughout the night. As my grandmother used to say: always choose a cook with the highest boredom threshold.

Hostas

HOSTAS ARE A BORE. Shrieks of horror from the urban garden fashionistas; cries of 'Philistine!' from the tasteful brigade. But there it is: the few hostas that I grow do not inspire me with breathless wonder, nor do I itch to acquire any more out of the remaining ten thousand or so. There is precious little difference between most of them: the odd white splash, a yellow edge, a few more, or less, wrinkles and puckers. We've seen them all before a hundred times and, as always, familiarity breeds if not exactly contempt, then certainly a lack of attention. Like conifers, hostas have become horticultural wallpaper: unexceptionable as a background to more exciting garden paintings. But so often there are no further ornamental extras to catch the eye, only the bare conifer/hosta wallpaper – embossed Lincrusta in shades of green, safe but dull, overdone and, largely, overbred.

Breeders are concerned, quite rightly, with colour, but often at the expense of elegance and deportment. All too many hosta hybrids lack an air – they are squat and solid, with no movement to the coarse, rubbery leaves, whose substance is thick and nasty, like something left over from the oil industry, extruded over a mould, then coloured garishly with acrylic paint.

And the names! The *Plantfinder* lists almost ten pages of them, in all their absurdity, beginning with 'Abba Dabba Do' (no rock garden should be without one) and finishing with 'Zounds', which is old enough to know better, but still compares favourably with most. There is a whole family: 'Big Daddy', 'Big Mama' (why not 'Momma'? So even hosta breeders shy away from the *totus porcus*), 'Big Boy' and the baby of the family, 'Little Fatty'. There is also a menu of cholesterol-happy food: 'Fried Bananas', 'Fried Green Tomatoes', 'Crepe Suzette', 'Sweet Tater Pie' and 'Tea & Crumpets'. Then the squirmingly trite: 'Cheatin' Heart', 'Elvis Lives',

'Munchkin', 'Shining Tot' and 'Striptease'. And the downright unseasonal: 'Night Before Christmas', 'Christmas Tree' and 'White Christmas'. Let me remind you that these are hostas.

Before I became a half-hearted hosta-phobe, I grew many from seed collected from an old *H. sieboldiana* hybrid growing contentedly in a tight and bone-dry pocket on an old rock garden. It was the bluest, most seersucker-crumpled and most floriferous hosta I have ever seen – doubtless as a consequence of its anorexic regime. The resulting seedlings were more plentiful than good, varying greatly in blueness and in dimple-quality. But I gave away a large number to seemingly satisfied donees. I hope they grow them still. There lies the temptation: the ease with which hostas will grow from seed. Had I been a fraught nurseryman, beset by banks and Brussels, with expensive children, mountainous mortgage and rapacious ex-wife, it would have been simple to label those seedlings as *Hosta sieboldiana* and to forget that, at best, they were forms too poor to justify the name; at worst, mere by-blows on the wrong side of the mulch.

Although notorious for being fast food for slugs, hostas struggle more with the cold here than with the resident gastropods. Frequently frosted as they emerge in spring, either they battle on, displaying their wounds for the rest of the campaign, or go to ground again, to try afresh. Whichever manoeuvre they choose, they will not reach their full potential before early frosts turn them to beige slime. I have never yet seen any (let alone vivid) autumn colour on my hostas. This shortened season brings further problems: as the soil above their crowns is exposed for all but two or three months of the year, weed seeds lodge themselves with rapidity like squatters in an empty house. Dandelions and docks are almost impossible to remove by the time they are big enough to see, without carving the poor hosta like a shoulder of lamb: first this way, then that, as one attempts to extricate the ruthless roots, leaving the sacrificial plant more hostia than hosta.

Slugs are controlled (not eradicated, naturally, this is a wildlife-friendly garden and the slug-eaters must have safe food in order to encourage them to stay and multiply) by planting my few hostas close to the stream bank (a pool would do the job even better) so that frogs and toads can snack between dips. Were I to plant the hosta called 'Guacamole', they could dip between dips. So far, it is working well and, after a poor showing elsewhere in the garden, the hostas now look (in the dusk, with the light behind them) quite presentable enough for me.

Even so, I can't love them. *Hosta undulata* var. *albomarginata* looks light and pretty, with movement added by the wavy leaf edges. *H. sieboldiana* is possibly in too much sun as its foliage has a slightly glazed look, as though the varnished coating has been scratched and made opaque. The third one is an unknown with jade-green pointed leaves and deep (for a hosta) lilac flowers. This has begun to show a slight, but uncalled-for, variegated blotch of unattractive gamboge. All of them flower profusely, but the flowers do little to improve their appearance, or my opinion of them, being the usual meagre mauve and dirty white.

But there are hostas, and then there are hostas, as Raymond Chandler almost wrote. The one hosta I do like is *H. plantaginea* var. *japonica*, whose long leaf stems give it the presence and *élan* that other hostas can only dream about. The foliage is thin to the point of semi-translucency, with a glinting phosphorescence in the low-backing sun. The flowers are unusually beautiful, being a clean white trumpet, like a miniature regale lily, and well spaced along a fine stem. The scent is sublime but (there had to be a but) they flower so late, and require so much warmth to encourage growth that I have achieved only buds here before frost wipes them out. I have grown them in pots to warm the roots; I have stood the pots in the warmest, sunniest place in the garden; I have even brought them inside the house for the summer – standing on either side of the sitting room fireplace, in terracotta urns. Their leaves were sumptuous, but no flower buds appeared at all.

I have done probably all I can for *Hosta plantaginea* var. *japonica* except, perhaps, to give it to a warmer garden and cultivate a liking instead for 'Munchkin' and 'Little Fatty'.

Olde Vege

THERE ARE TWO GOOD PLANTS growing in my kitchen garden, that would more than pay their ground rent grown in the border. Both are perennial vegetables; both are grown for their edible roots; and both have the form, foliage, and flower to satisfy the ponciest of potagers (where, it seems, the vegetables are never picked, for fear of spoiling the design, so taste is immaterial).

Skirret is an olde Englishe foode stuffe of the umbelliferous tribe. Like its cousins, carrot and parsnip, the root is eaten, but unlike them, skirret has never achieved the school dinner status of universal (un)popularity. *Sium sisarum* is of unknown origin, according to the gospel of the RHS Index, but of the amphibious family of the water parsnip, frequenting wet hollows in the Northern Hemisphere. This makes it sound anything but tantalizing, indeed more like something to be attacked with a spud at first glance, to save its taproot descending to Hades and beyond and its seeds from girdling the globe. But this is an umbellifer with manners: it behaves itself in a neat, almost prim way, with its delicate Queen Anne's lace flowers and gently colouring autumn foliage. So far, I have not been troubled by self-sown infants. Angelica and hemlock can be difficult to germinate purposely but are all too willing to take over the world when left to their own devices. Skirret seems to have reversed the family tendency, which makes it a still more welcome resident.

Neither does it have the encephalous waggon-wheel flowerheads of hemlock or its virulent poison, nor the vinous colouring of the suddenly fashionable *Angelica gigas* or its short life. Skirret has 4–6-inch-wide umbels and masses of them, in a stark chalky white, held at 4–5 feet on strong and well-branched stems that need no staking. The leaves are shiny, grass green, aging to butter yellow, and are, quite candidly, parsnip-pinnate; but then, I never promised you a rose garden. Had it the distinguished feathery foliage of *Meum athamanticum* or *Selinum wallichianum*, skirret would be a dress-circle plant; but no, this is firmly rear-stalls. Worthy of its place, though, as it flowers all summer, unlike the fizzing white froth of *Crambe cordifolia*, which has three weeks of interest in a good year but whose rancid foliage attracts cabbage root flies much more than it does me. And skirret can be picked with safety, too, with none of the family irritants or the foul-smelling flowers of the otherwise lovely cow parsley.

The second vegetable delight is *Scorzonera hispanica* – another root to eat, another flower to enchant – this time in clear citrus-yellow. Not quite a daisy, not quite a thistle, it makes a zingy show, starting in May and, after a drawn breath in July or August, goes on again until the frosts. This means that, wisely, it misses out on the competition of the late-summer chrome-yellow daisies, with which all our gardens overflow. Again, this is not a front-of-the-border plant: this one does need staking, and you will only achieve the second flush of flowers if you deadhead betimes. So plant it in an accessible position and enjoy the pleasurable pastime of deadheading, as this is one of the easiest plants to manicure, having long individual stems (yes, it is good for cutting, too) within the branched system. By cutting straight back above the next stem junction, you will keep the plant tidy and viable for months.

So often one sees that the deadheader has simply nipped off the spent flower and left inches of headless stem, which will put unnecessary strain on the plant, as it will try to keep that stem alive, instead of putting all its energies into producing more flowers. Naturally the plant will eventually decide that its resources are being stretched too thinly, and will shut down production in the cul-de-sac stems. These will then die back, leaving a forest of brittle brown ends that look slovenly and can damage the plant still further if they are hollow, by letting rain and rot do their worst. Dahlias suffer in this respect from both hollow stems and shag-pile deadheading; chrysanthemums, too – especially in bunches bought from a florist, where the leading bud has been removed to encourage secondary side buds. There it is again, the little decapitated stem in the centre, rapidly becoming brown and smelly.

After my deadheading diatribe, let's return to the scorzonera, whose buds are most attractive, like unripe pinecones or simplified pineapple gatepost finials. Salsify, *Tragopogon porrifolius*, is similar, but with lilac flowers, although it is not perennial. It comes from the Mediterranean, whereas scorzonera is from Siberia. Both are related to the English native goat's beard, *T. pratensis*, but don't be put off by their rather weedy cousin. I am fond of that, too; a meadow of goat's beard and moon daisies takes some beating. Just remember that lemon daisies, on 5-foot stems starting in early summer, are not exactly numerous and should be welcomed.

And for those who feel with William Morris that all things should be both beautiful and useful, the roots can still be eaten. Skirret doesn't taste of a great deal – just that rather pleasant, slightly earthy, green taste that is interesting without being exhilarating. Scorzonera and salsify have been dubbed 'vegetable oyster', but neither taste nor texture is remotely similar. It tastes of slightly bitter water or, I suppose, if you like your vegetables boiled to death, of watery bitters. Frankly, I prefer the flowers.

Nicotianas

WHEN CORTEZ MET MONTEZUMA (which sounds like a film title) and saw tobacco being smoked for the first time, the pipe is said to have been made from liquidamber wood. Perhaps the Aztecs used an adapted form of the Doctrine of Signatures and, having noticed the fiery autumn foliage of the liquidamber tree, appropriated the wood for a different type of blaze.

Smoking was encouraged in gardens until recently, as exhaling the fumes over pest-prone plants was meant to help. 'I always take my garden walk with a cigar,' said Dean Hole, 'in case I should meet an aphid.' Nicotine was used in glasshouses as a fumigant of perhaps the most potent force. The fastest sprinter among garden boys was given the task of lighting the touch paper, dashing out of the greenhouse and closing the door tightly, before he could be overcome by the toxic vapour.

According to Wilfrid Blunt, humans share the same number of chromosomes with the tobacco plant – which may explain why some find it so hard to desist from smoking: we are sisters under the skin to nicotiana.

Of course, whether one smokes or not is irrelevant to the cultivation of this fascinating family. From the bedding tobacco plants in lime green, crimson and white, to the giants of the various species, they exude style from every stomata. There is even a tobacco tree, *N. glauca*, that can grow to 12 feet or so, provided your garden can approximate the Bolivian jungle over winter. Grown in a conservatory, it can make a statuesque shrub, with waxy blue foliage, quite unlike any other tobacco plant, and small yellow flowers in dangling clusters – a telling contrast.

Nicotiana sylvestris can grow almost as tall in favourable conditions: the sun-dappled edge of a well-fed bosky coppice for choice – the sort of place that would suit cardiocrinums. These giant lilies will make congenial bedfellows, but will appreciate, indeed demand, Rabelaisian catering arrangements. Vita Sackville-West claimed that it was necessary to bury the equivalent of a dead horse beneath each vast bulb if one expected truly titanic cardiocrinums. *Nicotiana sylvestris* is not so insistent but will benefit, nonetheless, from the largesse, and will grow apace with the cardiocrinum, making an impressive Pantagruel to the lily's Gargantua. And like Pantagruel's tongue, this tobacco plant's huge leaves could cover an army (of ants, perhaps); they are sticky with the powerful essence of nicotine and show the giant's great thirst by flagging wearily in heat and drought. The white flowers, with slender, hautboy-necks, have a rich, heady perfume, redolent of steamy, tropical nights.

Nicotiana knightiana is of similar size, but is constructed from jade and malachite velvet. The leaves are large but silky-soft, with silvery down covering the deep nephrite green. The flowers are green too, but of a misty viridian rather than the more usual lemon-lime green. Another all-green tobacco plant is *N. paniculata* – of Granny Smith apple-green, this time. The small flowers are held in large, airy, branching panicles at 3 feet, giving the effect of a frothing green gypsophila.

Less refined, indeed, rather bumptious in style, is the brighter green *Nicotiana rustica*. With stout growth, and rounded flowers that bulge like a pantomime dame's mob-cap, this is rustic in attitude as well as looks, being naturalized in parts of the country, including Shropshire. There is no sweet scent to these flowers, only the mundungus odour of cheap tobacco. E.C. Brewer maintained that not only was green the imperial colour of the Aztecs, appropriately enough, but also that there are 106 different shades of green. Perhaps fortunately, he does not list them. But it will come as no surprise to find that there are yet more green tobacco plants: *Nicotiana langsdorffii* has become highly fashionable, but is still worth growing despite that stigma. Its green is that of pea soup. There is a form with variegated foliage (splashed with creamed pea soup) that causes the flowers to look anaemic, and the whole plant, frankly, bilious. Away with it.

The tobacco plants sold as bedding in every garden centre are hybrids of *Nicotiana affinis* and *N. alata*. Plant breeders have been busy trying to 'improve' them by reducing their height to the usual squat dumpling for which they imagine gardeners are yearning and by persuading the tobacco plant to flower all day instead of just in the evening. Naturally this has been achieved at the expense of the scent so the whole process has turned the formerly delicious tobacco plant into just another blob of colour. And no doubt this colour range will continue to be expanded into yet more filthy pastels and art shades that no one wants. Such is progress.

The 3-foot-tall, ambrosially scented, old-fashioned tobacco plant is quite good enough for me. I am particularly fond of the crimson form, although the imperial Aztec green and the white are magical too. Some are more scented than others, so buy with your nose as well as your eyes, bearing in mind that late-night opening will give you a better chance of detecting scent than lunch-hour shopping.

All are ease itself to grow, and most will seed themselves around in sheltered gardens, largely coming true to parental colours. Presumably due to the poison they contain, they are not greatly susceptible to pests, so there is no need to take a cigar for a walk around them, except in the interests of genealogy.

Composers

GARDENS ARE FULL OF MUSIC: bird song, the wind wuthering through the leaves, the burble of the stream, the slurp of mud-laden boots lifted from the soil. . . . But there are symphonic undertones elsewhere that can clearly be heard by an imaginative ear, when considering the essence of a plant. I think of cherry blossom and the music that comes to my mind is not Butterfly humming and waiting for the fickle Pinkerton but a swooping waltz by Franz Lehár: a merry widow's picture hat adorned with swags of 'Kanzan'. Lilacs are Ivor Novello. Noel Coward (so said Constance Spry) is Nelson's Column entirely wreathed in pink hortensia hydrangeas. Cole Porter scarcely fits the great outdoors so would more suitably be represented by a hothouse plant – something bright, brittle and geometric, like a waxy scarlet anthurium. Rogers and Hammerstein would be comfortably old-fashioned and a little garish, like 'Masquerade' roses or hybrid yakushimanum rhodos.

Gilbert and Sullivan should be greenery-yallery euphorbias: very jolly from a distance, even more enchanting close to. Wagner is a pine forest, so fits no more contentedly in a garden than he does within the confines of a personal stereo, magnificent but gloomy and verging on the endless. Puccini is a regale lily, sumptuous, intoxicating, pure romance. Mozart is a laced pink of delicate form and exquisite precision. Purcell would be lavender, meticulous and astringent. Billowy old musk roses represent Tchaikovsky, luscious and wearily immoral. Vaughan Williams is wild honeysuckle, sweet but heady, pensive and poignant, in soft, sad colours. Elgar is box: very English, sometimes clipped and intricate, often lax and free, with a powerfully emotive scent. Handel is yew: very formal, very grand, rich and deep with sparkling jewel-like fruits. Beethoven would be a sturdy, wine-purple cabbage: crisp but succulent, heavy and important, a monumental presence in the garden.

A water lily would symbolize Ravel, with its illusion of floating freedom belying its rigidity of flower – a water lily painted by Seurat rather than by Monet. Leonard Bernstein is a 'Queen of Night' tulip, dark, elegant, mysterious, urban. Chopin is a fern, finely cut and crimped and besprinkled with dew. Bach would be a gold-laced polyanthus of flawless perfection. Debussy is a wisteria, drooping, mauve and world-weary.

One could go on and on, with more musicians, or with painters: Michaelangelo would have to be a garrya, firmly dioecious, monumental but sometimes out of proportion. Uccello would be a fine stand of miscanthus, each stem with its own isometric perspective, lance-straight, whether upright or fallen. Renoir could be a bed of buxom snapdragons in fleshy pinks and streaked golden-apricot; Hockney a tubful of stark zantedeschias beside a shimmering swimming pool.

Or poets: Byron a striped parrot tulip, exotic, flamboyant but rather obvious. Wordsworth would be a crown imperial, majestic but staid, and countrified too. Shakespeare is a crimson damask rose of velvet depth and strong personality. Betjeman is a daisy: prosaic but delicious in detail, traditionally English and recognized by all. Emily Brontë would have to be moor grass, resilient and tenacious, but fugacious of flower. Louis MacNeice could be convolvulus, twisting and turning, with no end and no beginning. Hardy is old man's beard, profoundly rural. Tennyson would be sweetbriar, romantic, endearing, somewhat cloying. Blake is woody nightshade, mysterious, complicated, sombre; John Clare a buttercup, simple and shining. I see Chaucer as a dandelion, robust, joyful, heraldic; Milton a nettle, dictatorial, biting, puritanical. Gerard Manley Hopkins would be a passionflower, all repression, religion and stricture, and Dylan Thomas is a Welsh onion – useful but not entirely beautiful.

There used to be a parlour game known as Botticelli, where one defined those taking part as a type of dog, or an article of clothing, or as a style of architecture, or as food, or, indeed, as a plant. We might all have known clinging ivies and shrinking violets, sedate wallflowers and English roses. Equally, friends may be as profligate as opium poppies, as raffish as scarlet salvia or as ascetic as astelia. The more one studies plants (and people), the more their individualities and quirks of character shine forth. It doesn't do to generalize: red-flowered plants, like red-haired people, are not all as brash as Barbarossa. Think of the scarlet pimpernel, or the feathery pheasant's eye – they may be seed-flinging annuals of waste ground, but they are as delicate in form as any Victorian shell-flower beneath a glass dome. Nor are all blue flowers the epitome of innocence and freedom: most gentians are as cross-grained in temper as a gouty Henry VIII. The formidably toxic aconitum family are all gentle tones of winsome white and blameless blues; and imagine the courage it must have taken to be the first person to eat an aubergine, whose lurid colour and solid flesh accord more with deadly dwale and henbane – rat bait, rather than ratatouille.

We all see people and plants in different lights: where I see Holbein as a scarlet ranunculus, or Nijinsky as a striped zinnia, others may see only the need for a straightjacket.

Lawn

FOR THOSE WITH THE QUESTIONABLE JOY of retentive soil, the grass will always be smaragdinus-greenest on your own side of the fence. Admittedly, the winter-green will be mostly moss, but it is still pleasantly springy to walk upon, except after prolonged rain; but then the same can be said about the finest bents, so, unless your aim is to play championship bowls, I can't see the need to worry unduly. I doubt that Plymouth Hoe was any better than of the turf, turfy, but the pre-Armada game was completed anyway.

Here, not only is the winter lawn mossy, but the summer lawn is mostly clover. I am encouraging it to spread where it listeth, as it looks spruce at all times (better, indeed, than the grass, which, owing to sleepy drainage, will never be more than adequate). It requires much less cutting; it beefs up the feeble grass, too, with its nitrogen-fixing abilities; it makes bumble bees happy; and it squeezes out the moss. Recently I have read that 'Capability' Brown mixed bushels of clover seed with hayseed for all his parkland grass-sowing, so history is on my side too. Patches of clover in a large lawn of fine grasses can look terrible, there's no denying. They stand up and yell for attention from afar. But my lawn is tiny – just two hollyhocks by three, as A.A. Milne nearly said – so the patches have joined up and almost spread to the skirting boards, and the complete block of green is gently soothing.

As the blessing of a daughter was deniged me (and Mrs Gamp, too), I do not need a marquee-supportable lawn. Yes, large expanses of grass are very restful to the eye, but only if the whole garden is large in proportion. Too often, one sees vast acres of lawn (and usually badly cut, which negates the restful quality immediately) with meagre little borders clinging to the edges. There is no cohesion between the two. The garden becomes wall-eyed. Unable to look at both elements at once, one stops looking at either – and a good thing too.

Proportion is of paramount importance in the garden. If your garden is small, keep the lawn in proportion: a large lawn will not make your garden look any larger; it is enclosure, rather than expanse, which will do that, particularly if your boundaries are visible. But do keep your small lawn whole: it is the interruptions that make it look squashed (as well as adding to mowing difficulties), so resist the temptation to plant too many specimen shrubs with circles cut round them in the turf, or complicate your lawn, like the eighteenth-century Lady Luxborough, with plats the shape of Lord Mayor's Custards. Instead, plant your shrubs or trees to one side and incorporate them within the nearby border. Whether you like formal straight lines, so that you slice around your tree with a set square, or Sharawadgiesque curves, so you swoop round it with a hose-pipe to guide your half-moon, is a matter of personal taste. Either way, a more interesting effect will be achieved than the spotty specimen.

Larger gardens often have enormous lawns by default, as their owners don't know what else to do with all that land. In skilled hands, miles of lawn can be exciting, with vast areas of planting to keep it company: forest trees aplenty and swathes of ground-covering plants wherever possible beneath. This is all to cut down on work, naturally, but also to add to the picture, to calm the eye as well as excite it. Rides and pathways, clipped tight through swaying meadow grasses, are enticing: not just to see what is at the other end of them, but because of the abrupt change of levels in the grasses, making it possible to walk amongst them – the hare's-eye view. The less skilled hands rarely get so far; for them, grass is grass. But when there is a disproportionately large amount of it, the grass becomes a partridge: *perdrix, toujours perdrix*. A lot is not the same thing as enough.

It was all very well for Bacon to claim that 'foure acres of ground be assigned to greene'. He never had the mowing to do. Being an unrepentant Luddite, when it comes to so-called power tools, I think longingly of Gracie Fields, the booted pony who mowed the hallowed turf at Sissinghurst Castle until the 1940s. I should adore to have a pony in boots to mow my grass, just as I should cherish Miss Jekyll's panniered donkeys instead of wheelbarrows, which are impossible over the numerous steps here. But my lawn is so small, it would have to be a muntjac deer, or better still, a hedgehog in boots – or a puss.

The more normal lawnmower is not so attractive, nor, in many cases, so biddable. Most of them must be humoured *and* drove (to misquote Dickens), leaving me a panting Sisyphus. My personal preference is for a flat block of green – no stripes, which I think look too busy in a restricted area, and weirdly mechanical in parkland. I like my lawn to be a quiet background to the garden, to enhance, by its very monoculture, the variety of plants that surround it, rather than to compete with them. Stripes on a lawn can give the same fidgety feeling as a patterned carpet among gaily coloured furnishings. Given this preference and the small space which is to be mown, I am happy with my lightweight, cylinder-bladed, electric machine. It is quieter than many and I cope willingly with the power cable rather than suffer the noise and stinking fumes of a petrol-driven mower. I also own a Pushmi-Pullyu powerless machine. I love it. But on heavy soil it is not always practicable (even if I always had the energy) as it can turn into a plough unless the ground is completely dry.

Having mown, I always trim the edges with long-handled shears. It is part of the cutting exercise, not a separate operation at all. If there is no time to do the two, then neither is done. I dislike seeing untrimmed edges, like a badly shaven chin, or an immaculately dressed woman with a frayed hem hanging down. So many people give lack of time as their reason for the neglect; perhaps they should consider whether their whole lawn is too big, not just that the edges are endless. Some gardeners border their lawns with paving, 'so the edges never need doing'. This works only when the grass is well-behaved enough to grow only vertically, so that the mower slices it off, edges and all. I have never seen this sort of grass, and doubt that it exists. Once it begins to grow horizontally over the paving (which it will, all too soon), cutting it becomes very tricky, as shears will not squeeze between the edge of the turf and the rim of the paving-stone. A half-moon will have the same problem, until it has been winkled in several times, so that a gap ensues; nail scissors would work well, and more than use up all the time you have saved by not edging in the first place.

An obsession some gardeners display, is against worms. Theatrical worms, with their casts of thousands. They poison them, and then wonder why their grass won't grow. Without worms, there is no aeration of the soil; without aeration, there is no drainage; without drainage, there is no grass

— just moss, and they poison that too. If worm casts are so obnoxious to you, then sweep them off with a besom: it is very good exercise. As is raking moss — indeed there's nothing quite like it for flattening flabby tummies. There are machines to do the raking for you, and no doubt, by now, machines to sweep worm casts too. All kinder, one hopes, to the humble and hardworking worm, than odious poisons, which lambs could not forget, nor worms forgive.

Tomatoes

THE FINEST TOMATOES EVER TASTED were grown by old Billy Briscoe in a curlicued Victorian glasshouse close to a conveniently threadbare hedge. Pushing through it was simple indeed, whenever the urge for a luscious tomato was upon us, my sister and I, and we would help ourselves with abandon and thoughtless frequency. Mrs Briscoe's kitchen window overlooked the path to the greenhouse, but the dear soul never shopped us to our parents. Perhaps she didn't like tomatoes.

Entering the old glasshouse was almost as exciting as the tomatoes themselves: the heavy heat, the ecclesiastical silence, which was complemented by the nave-like central path between the columns of the monumental tomato stems, their branches fan-vaulting above my head and arching across the path like a carved Tudor rood screen. Squeezing through them was parting the Red Sea of fruits, the pungent scent as strong as ozone, which clung to my hands and hair. Even now I have only to snap off the side shoots of my own tomato plants to relive that moment, or, indeed, to deadhead petunias – the scent is the same (both being of the Solanaceae family), as is the subsequent green stain on my fingers.

Inevitably, with plants remembered from childhood, I have no idea what variety of tomato they were. As has been said of the elephant, it is impossible to define, but you'll know one when you see one; I shall know the tomato again instantly, when I taste it. So I am working my way through all those of suitable vintage whose seeds are still available: 'Moneymaker', 'Gardener's Delight', 'Ailsa Craig', 'First in the Field', 'Harbinger', even some of the more *recherché* tomatoes offered by membership distribution from The Heritage Seed Library, such as 'Carter's Fruit' which was bred in 1928, and 'Sutton's Everyday', a Dig for Victory favourite. So far I have drawn a blank, although 'Ailsa Craig' has something that is mildly reminiscent, a diluted essence of Mr Briscoe's perfect tomato.

But then science must rear its head and proclaim that conditions here would not even vaguely approximate those in which his tomatoes were grown: my shed – for all its clear perspex roof – is scarcely in the same league as that magnificent old glasshouse. If I were a tomato, I know which I should prefer to call *chez moi*. The soil borders there had been cultivated and nurtured over decades, whereas my tomatoes are grown in large pots of standard John Innes mix, with a flirtation of added chicken muck, and given occasional liquid feeds when I remember. So my basic bed-and-breakfast tariff compares rather poorly with old Mr Briscoe's Le Manoir aux Quat'Saisons voluptuary splendour. Of course I could add that the summers, then, were always long and hot and gloriously berry-ripening, but this is a scientific paragraph.

David Hatchett writes that tomatoes grown from modern seed of old-fashioned varieties are disappointing, compared to the same varieties grown twenty-five years previously (he writes in the 1980s). He believes that this is due to the lack of rigorous control over selection of seed, so that the strains are weakened. So perhaps that is what is happening to my tasting-test tomatoes. Maybe the diluted essence of the modern 'Ailsa Craig' is all there is left to taste.

Interestingly, Mr Hatchett also comments that whereas greenback and virus diseases were virtually unknown in these older varieties back in the 1950s, they are now prevalent. Is this due to weakening of the strain, or is it more to do with environmental pollution, which, even though we may grow our tomatoes organically, is unavoidable in its insidious presence? Certainly the 1950s had their share of chemical horrors: wall-to-wall spraying of DDT was practised nationwide, and heavy industry was then still a potent force, blackening the skies above the satanic steel mills, and causing sulphurous pea-soup fogs of blanketing blindness, before the Clean Air Acts attempted to redress the balance. Modern air may be relatively clear of these poisons, but other pesticides have more than filled the vacuum, and traffic, of thousand-fold increase since then, pales the pestilential effects of the old industries into insignificance. Rose gardeners regret the lack of sulphur that manifests itself as black spot covering the leaves. But not even Long John Silver's roses would die from this black spot, and besides, one rarely eats rose leaves, unless in the archaic sense of rose leaf jelly, where leaf translates as petal.

One wonders if supermarkets expect their customers actually to eat the travesties they offer in the name of tomato, or simply to marvel at their uniformity of packable size and unshockable thick skins. Still more do I wonder why seed catalogues aimed at gardeners and allotment holders, who are growing produce for their own use, should offer varieties of tomatoes advertised as having 'excellent keeping quality', which is market-garden speak for 'long shelf-life' and means that the skins will be impenetrable. Equally, they offer tomatoes where the whole truss ripens together – again, these are for market-gardeners to harvest in one fell swoop. If we are feeding ourselves and families, we want tomatoes that ripen a few at a time, not a one-off glut; and we do not require a long-keeping skin where we are picking our daily requirements straight on to the plate.

This year I failed to sow any tomatoes at all. A friend came to the rescue with some plants she had bought at a village fête, nice sturdy fellows, but with no name. Potted up as usual, they grew strongly, but the flower trusses, although of decent dimensions individually, were set wide apart along the stem. Being late in the season, I stopped each of them at three trusses, and was glad to see the fruits building up to an impressive size. And there they sat, getting bigger and bigger, but staying green, green, green. The trusses became so gravid with fruit, they had to be propped like ancient plum trees, liable to burst asunder with the weight of their own fecundity. But still they would not ripen. When frosts began in earnest, I knew the writing was on the wall, so they were all picked and spread out inside plastic boxes, each with a ripe banana, sealed tight and kept warm. Do you know this trick? It never fails, as the ripe fruit – an apple will do just as well – gives off ethylene gas, which ripens the tomatoes. Supermarkets know it well: their suppliers ship fruit from abroad that has been picked and packed green in containers which are then impregnated with ethylene to ripen as it travels; hence the appalling stench as the shelf-stockers in the green-grocery section unseal the cases of wringing-wet bananas.

Checking the progress of my own green tomatoes, I realized that they were all ripening together, regardless of size, or situation when picked.

When finally I ate one, I solved the riddle. No doubt you are ahead of me, and have guessed: these were the quintessential supermarket tomato – rhinoceros-skinned tasteless balls of water, with not an atom of citric acid or vitamin C. The plants had the long stems between trusses to aid mechanical stripping of all the fruits on all the plants in one operation. And they were bred to be grown in a warm polytunnel, probably with overhead lights to quicken the ripening process, not in a home-grower's cold greenhouse or, as in my case, an even colder shed.

Tomatoes such as these are an abomination. Not fit to be eaten, not fit to have all the care of growing lavished upon them. In the Middle Ages, saffron dealers who vitiated their stock and were caught by the draconian inspectors were burned to death on a pyre of their own adulterated saffron. The breeders of these tomatoes should be treated similarly, in my humble, but vengeful, opinion – except that they would have to be drowned in them instead, in a butt of purée, as the watery blobs would never burn.

Height

DRIVING RECENTLY THROUGH AN EXPANDING market town on the other side of the county, two thoughts occurred. Firstly, the rash of conservatories (one of my Dr Fells) provides ground-cover *ne plus ultra* for those whose 'gardening' inside these plastic temples consists of an acetate phalaenopsis on top of the telly and a dried 'arrangement' standing on the fitted carpet. Secondly, the tallest thing in any garden is the fence; all the plants are dwarf blobs. People do seem to be intimidated by height in the garden.

'Well, I have a small garden, so I need small plants.' This is nonsense. I am not suggesting that all small gardens should be planted to look like a 'Douanier' Rousseau jungle (although there are city gardens where meeting Livingstone would come as no surprise), but limiting yourself to miniatures ensures that your garden will look cramped and fussy and even smaller than it is. At a time when people move house, on average, every seven years, there could be an argument in favour of small plants, in that one will never see them grow up anyway, so why go to the additional expense of big ones. But an established garden can raise the value of a house substantially, so borders holding only coveys of tiny tuffets surrounded by bare soil will have 'just planted' written all over them, even if they have been there for the full seven years.

If the estate agents' creed is 'location' cubed, the gardener's should be 'proportion' to the nth. Nothing is so important, in design or planting, and nothing is so ignored. For most of us, the classical precept of echoing the height of the building with the depth of the terrace beneath is unlikely to be feasible. Nor is it expedient to match a soaring imagination with the sowing of acorns. Many straight drives are bounded by a row of Lombardy poplars – an inspiration, perhaps, after trips to France, where they were planted in profusion during the revolution, because of their populist botanical name. Corotesque avenues may have a stately air, but a bungalow on the tail of a queue of poplars looks like a full stop at the end of a sentence in capital letters. Not far from here, there is a tiny Victorian estate-worker's cottage with a grandiose Victorian wellingtonia planted ten feet away. The cottage looks like a windfall apple. *Folie de grandeur* perhaps, but in neither instance was proportion considered before planting.

Of course it is easy to underestimate eventual size. Even when height and spread are documented, it is impossible for some to envisage cubic content – like imagining a ball dress from a 1-inch swatch of silk. We can all plant too closely. But where well grown trees and shrubs may require spacings equivalent to their destined height, there are tall herbaceous plants whose columnar or arching habits fit easily into even small borders, allowing close planting around them. I should not advise that their contribution be confined to the back row, standing on forms, of the school-photograph style of border of carefully graduated heights; in a small garden this could lead to a claustrophobic wall of colour, or worse, if there are double borders: a corridor. Many tall plants have poor knees and ankles, so are ideal for back row planting, where their defects will be hidden among the ruck of the crowd; some varieties of aster, helianthus, and rudbeckia have legs that could never be described as poems. But others are sleek from top-to-toe, and should be given the chance to show their full acclivity by more isolated planting, such as species of rheum, macleaya and some of the big grasses.

This trick of solitary planting has further advantages in a small garden by creating a barrier, which not only prevents you from seeing too much (or indeed the full extent) at one glance, but also encourages you to wonder what it is hiding – an air of mystery and discovery makes every garden more interesting, no matter how small. Like a blind bend, one knows not what to expect on the other side, which settles the foreground into gentle security, and increases the anticipation of the unknown. Intriguingly, height can give the effect of space. The isolated giant may be surrounded by lower plants, or grass, or gravel, emphasizing both its height and the emptiness around it. A carefully sited giant can draw the footsteps towards it; denoting a progression to something new. A pair of tall sentinels flanking a path may be all that is necessary to show that a different area of the garden has been reached, even though there is no dividing hedge, trellis, or whatever, to separate this new 'room' from the last. We know instinctively that the points have been changed and we are off on a divergent track.

A tall plant placed in the middle distance can lead the eye onwards to a good view, or to the one patch of sky visible between encroaching buildings, or to borrowed landmarks outside the garden – a clump of trees or a church spire. Alexander Pope referred to this as 'calling in the country'. It pushes the boundaries of the garden out towards the landmark. The same middle-distance plant can so concentrate the eye that less attractive sights on either side – the neighbour's washing, or a vast road-sign – disappear from the picture held on the view-finder of one's mind. 'All gardening is landscape painting.' Pope again.

We are told always to plant in threes, or greater odd numbers, for a more natural appearance, but troikas of tall plants are not always necessary, even where there may be room on the broad Nevsky Prospekt borders of your garden. A pair of carriage horses looks right, whatever their height, beside forthright steps or formal paths. But there is always parking space for hansoms in every style of garden: many single plants have sufficient consequence to be outstanding without the support of a consort.

Such an eminence is *Macleaya cordata*, whose stems will surge to 8 feet, the lower two-thirds being clothed with graduated leaves of a dense, opium poppy-squeakiness, combining grey-green and buff, veined with apricot and reversed with silvery felt. In shape they resemble a cross-section drawing of a carved stone capital, with deeply pot-bellied lobes interrupted by crimps and curls. The stems themselves are a roasted-apricot bloomed with waxy-white; after frost scarifies them, they look like polished bone. The upper third is an apotheosis of bloom that would thrill even St Teresa, so ecstatic is the frenzy of dripping creamy stamens that form the flowers. They're soon spent, there's no denying. But clusters of tawny seeds will form (coral-red on the variety 'Spetchley Ruby') to continue the interest until autumn gales clatter the sere foliage to the ground. For all its ebullience, macleaya is abjured: it runs. In mitigation, let me plead that it takes several years to build up a head of steam sufficient to propel itself. Once moving, it is a simple matter to pull out excess stems as they arise in spring, or to spade around it and lift the stragglers – not too early, here, as the young cabbagey shoots are blackened by frost almost every year, requiring extra effort by the plant to hoist itself once, often thrice, more. Probably this, and stiff soil, help to keep it within bounds. I have planted my macleaya on a raised border, adding another 2 feet to its stature. It makes an impenetrable palisade viewed across the lawn from the entrance to the garden, preventing the visitor from seeing any more until he has been enticed by its come-hitherness around the curve in the lawn on to the central path, drawn on, in turn, by Irish junipers that mount guard at the head of some shallow steps, then on again towards an archway through the yew hedge. A classic enfilade of successive eye-catchers to tempt the feet to follow where the eye beckons.

Yew's depth of green makes an ideal background for tall see-through plants: not yet more *Verbena bonariensis*, I beg. All gardens should be emancipated from the surfeit of its suffragette purple-and-green. The tone of neither colour is remarkable; the plant itself is a gawk; its one redeeming trait is that it provides late food for butterflies, so worth planting for that reason, but not as a major feature and certainly not as a recurring one. We should remember that a feature can be classed as such only by its exclusivity. Apropos: repeated clumps of the same plant (whatever it may be) along the length of a border are said to give continuity; but they can also give the impression that the gardener simply has no friends upon whom to offload the excess. If a plant is exciting, its impact may not be doubled, but halved, by repetition. If a plant is dull, repeated clumps littered about will look like vapid couples at a Moonie wedding.

The popular *Crambe cordifolia* looks its bubbling best in front of a dark background, like yew, to show off the effulgent white froth of flowers that explode in early summer at 6–8 feet tall. Given perfect drainage and no cabbage white caterpillars, its bold brassica foliage could make an impressively masterful clump at the hedge-base. Here, I have a slowly expanding swirl of grassy fingers at my yew-foot: *Calamagrostis brachytricha* has suffle-soft plumes at 5 feet in late summer, starting smoky-purple and ageing to a pinkish buff. It is much gentler, more feminine, than the dazzling *Stipa gigantea* and seems to absorb light into its snuggly warmth, rather than reflecting every drop of sunlight like the fountaining giant oat.

My calamagrostis works, therefore, against the yew, whereas the stipa needs all the light it can get, from all angles, so must be planted in isolation. This need made it impossible in my windy garden, where heavy soil encouraged it to be sulkily sensitive, so that it rowed into the wind upon a bow-wave of its own feeble culms. A more determined giant for slow-draining soils is *Stipa splendens*, with young plumes that glitter in the sunlight, ageing to parchment ostrich feathers: its slender fountain looks like a pampas grass that has foresworn anabolic steroids.

Achillea grandifolia is another huge plant that carries interesting foliage from floor to ceiling, so need not be hidden away at the back of a border. On sharper drainage than mine it should not require staking. Its sturdy stems launch themselves to 6 feet or more, well clothed with leaves, spliced and fretted into deep fjords of fir-green. The flowerheads are oval dinner-plate corymbs of tiny ivory daisies with biscuit-coloured centres, blooming from early summer, when mine coincides to perfection with the custard powder-tinted rambler rose 'Goldfinch' above its head. By late summer the achillea's corymbs have aged to toffee and its foliage is beginning its annual bleaching trick as, starting at the top, the colour fades through lime, to primrose, to cream, as though the ravenous roots were slowly sucking all the colour, draining the life-blood from the stems, leaf by leaf. By autumn all is umber-drab, the ragged leaves flapping limply. I cut it back about halfway to reduce the smack of gales on still-tough stems. By early spring the fresh new foliage is uncurling like young acanthus.

Still more exciting in late-spring are the raspberry-pink leaves of *Rheum palmatum* 'Atrosanguineum' as they peel away from the rugby-ball bud, which has been bursting through its papery collar for some weeks. Once started, the procedure is remarkably fast, from polished porphyry bud to crinoline of basal foliage ruffling enticing pink petticoats, then 8-foot flowering stems with barbarous crimson plumes. All this by midsummer. I leave the finished stems, as they, and the seething seeds, turn to vivid chestnut, and stand firm till autumn gales throw them down. Keep or cut the finished stems, the leaves continue in glorious amplitude. Some gardeners grow the titan *Gunnera manicata* in a pot, where their soil is too dry or too cold for the gigantic beast. To me this smacks of keeping an elephant in a hatbox. Plant rheum instead; it is tough, and will grow satisfyingly vast on a diet of ordinary garden soil, without the sultry bog requirements of the voluminous gunnera.

Colossal height and cartwheel flowerheads are displayed on the notorious *noli me tangere* giant hemlock, *Heracleum mantegazzianum*. Shrieks of terror and anxious grabbing for straying children occur whenever the plant is mentioned, as though its venom might be transmitted from great distances, and kill anything in its path, like some intergalactic monster. Do let us keep things in proportion. It is a wonderful plant, and is considerably less dangerous to responsible mankind than a motorcar. So there is no reason why, with due care, every home should not have one of each. But is it just the hemlock's virulence that is so feared, or is virility a worry too? A plant reaching 15 feet is certainly impressive, so there may not be room for this as well as an umbelliferous washing line in every garden.

Ghettos

I HAVE NEVER FELT PARTICULARLY DRAWN towards herb gardens. Many of the plants traditionally grown therein are not worth a candle anywhere other than an official physic garden, and I feel no need to grow a weed simply because it was used for mad-dog bites or the gravel. Parkinson's earthiness was not restricted to his muddy boots, and he can be both amusing and exceedingly tiresome to read. Either way, simple by name or by inclination, herbs will not be grown here simply for their fey association. I do grow many herbs, both of the culinary and medicinal mad-dog varieties, but they are integrated within the borders or kitchen garden, depending on their virtues, rather than exiled to a separate area – ghettos never work.

With native wildflowers too, the ghetto-effect is frequently adopted. Meadow gardening, at its best, can be heartbreakingly potent, but is encountered more often at its worst, which is simply as an excuse not to mow the lawn. Admittedly, I am luckier than many, as rural life is still accompanied by wildflowers, although both quality and quantity are reducing yearly. Once again, I feel no need to keep all my natives in one compound, but to plant the worthy ones within the garden and exclude the feeble ones altogether.

Even on my Wilderness area, where many English natives are planted, I include species from other countries equally. I have no wish for large-flowered hybrids on there – they would look as out of place as would a wildflower growing within the municipal scheme of blazing bedding on a seaside esplanade. But all species are wild somewhere in the world, so provided they have the look of the unglamorous wilding about them, I am willing to plant them there, even though they may speak Croatian, or Russian or Chinese, when they are at home. I may call it the Wilderness, but it is still my garden, after all.

One reads increasingly of American gardeners being coerced into planting only American natives in their gardens, in a Thoreau-esque attempt to live the wilderness. But even Thoreau wanted to make the earth say beans – a genus not native to his home state of Massachusetts – and to follow his bean-field crop with a sowing of truth, sincerity and faith. These may have been indigenous, but nothing came up. I don't want to *make* the earth say, or do, anything. Such control should be both undesirable and unachievable.

Purism in planting is as subjective as any other notion in gardening. My own feeling is that almost anything fits almost anywhere, with one proviso: that the style of building – house, outbuildings, etc. – must be considered within the context of its surroundings. I should not be so didactic as to insist that architecture must command the style of planting, but a prehistoric tree-fern planted in the south-facing front garden of a suburban bungalow is not doing justice to either, any more than would agaves in aluminium crates outside Anne Hathaway's cottage.

Sensitivity does not always march hand-in-hand with suitability: Coleridge wanted to mass-plant laburnums all over the Lake District, and was apoplectic with fury when he was prevented from doing so by the hard-nosed team of Harriet Martineau and John Ruskin. One can see the attraction, even now, when laburnums carry more bourgeois connotations than in Coleridge's day: they can be sensational trees. I shouldn't mind one or two reflected in a Westmoreland lake. I shouldn't mind many more than that if the breeders could develop a white form – what a stunner that would be! And that is the point: white-flowered trees are welcome anywhere; they look right, whatever the surroundings, whatever the architecture.

Here I plant trees with white flowers, as I feel they are not too assertive in these rural surroundings, even if the expanse of white is large, such as the bracts of the handkerchief tree, *Davidia involucrata*, or the blossoms of magnolias or some of the cherries. I would not plant a 'Kanzan' cherry here because, apart from the fact that it is the essential suburban, Sir Leicester Kroesig-tree, it has flowers that are so obviously man-made, with those enormous double pompons of blueish-mauve pink. They can look splendid against tarmac and concrete, but less inspiring amidst water meadows.

That's not to say that I should refuse to plant *Embothrium coccineum*, in all its sizzling, scarlet glory, had I the acid soil to make it, and a sensitive eye, happy. For while peaty soil is black, mine is lime-washed grey; the mild, damp air that suits the Chilean firebush has a softer light than the frost-bound air of limestone hill-country. Each condition suits different colours. Swap them around and they look all wrong. Brilliant scarlet on something as large as a tree would look tawdry in limey light, whereas the gentle colours of limestone wildflowers would look insignificant under the acid conditions that show off azaleas to such fine effect. This is not so much purism as physics and chemistry.

So I have planted native silver birches and a gean in the main part of the garden, where their quiet elegance dovetails happily with plants from more exotic climes, just as the Canadian *Amelanchier lamarckii* and *Cornus alba* from Siberia look very much at home on the Wilderness. Alongside these are the native *Salix alba* in its red-stemmed variety, 'Britzensis', and two Americans – *Rubus spectabilis*, the salmonberry, with brilliant magenta flowers in spring, and the weary-pink, autumn-flowering *R. odoratus*. They look right together, even though they can never have grown together in one native land. It doesn't matter: this is a garden. I am not recreating wild wilderness; I am not Thoreau.

The shrieking purist, who would never allow a horse chestnut to be planted in an English parkland, because it was not introduced until the seventeenth century, is missing the point. They may come from Greece, but they have become as quintessentially English as the Elgin Marbles. And they have white flowers, so they fit anywhere. I only wish I could fit one in here.

Some English natives are surprisingly sophisticated in colouring: the rest-harrow, for example. Visitors always ask what it is, so I give them the botanical name first – *Ononis spinosa* – before jumping in with its native status and its archaic nickname, cammock. It has large pea flowers of a rich raspberry-ice pink, scattered along the 2-foot spiny wands of shrubby, sprawling growth. I hack mine back each spring to within an inch or two of the crown, which keeps it bushy and does not deter flowering. Growing naturally on dry, calcareous soils, where its presence either arrested the harrow's progress with its tough roots, or else caused the ploughman to stop in order to admire it all the more; it is a consolation for those gardeners whose soil is too alkaline to keep hybrid brooms happy.

Another example is soapwort, *Saponaria officinalis*, with its rose-pink, phlox-like flowers. Better still are the double forms, in the same pink, a clean white, or the matchless *S.o.* 'Rubra Plena', which starts off sugary pink and ages to a deep, rich faded crimson, the colour echoed in its 4-foot, branched stems. And the scent – of very expensive soap – is exquisite. It wafts on the air for yards around the plant and has no flavour of the wilding about it. Certainly its habit is vigorous and romping, so it needs plenty of room to run about. But that is no reason to exclude it from the garden, particularly as it flowers so late and so willingly.

It holds its scent well when picked too. I have just picked a small bunch of late-summer flowering natives, which could compete successfully with any shop-bought exotics: the double red soapwort; long purples – *Lythrum salicaria*; hemp agrimony – *Eupatorium cannabinum*; and old man's beard – *Clematis vitalba*. This last plant also features in my Christmas arrangements in its hirsute stage of bearded seed awns, which, if you can catch before the autumn rains glue them together, will open properly inside forming fluffs of shining silvery-cream. At the moment, in my present assortment, the greenish-cream flowers are just opening, so the sprays consist of these mixed liberally with egg-shaped buds. There is a slight vanilla scent.

Much stronger, and more spicy, as though a grating of nutmeg has been added to a jar of vanilla sugar, is the hemp agrimony. Again, the sweet scent pervades the room, particularly in the evenings, which makes me wonder if moths dote upon its charms as much as do butterflies by day. The nutmeg-brown has been grated into the flesh-pink of the flossy flowers too, giving a warmth that matches the late-summer sunshine.

Lythrum salicaria has no scent, but makes up for the lack by the sheer pzazz of its vibrant pink flowers. These are individually quite small, but are displayed on long spikes atop 5-foot stems, so are emphatic, both from a vase and from a distance – which is often how they will be seen, as it grows naturally in boggy ground. It doesn't want to be too dry in the garden, but it by no means demands a swamp. Hilda Murrell noticed that the lythrum's pollen was emerald-green, but as briefly as the green flash on a sunset at sea.

All of these English native wildflowers are strongly growing, inexacting plants, which would grace your smartest border. So don't be tempted to file them away in a wild garden – grow them anywhere. Ditto herbs: I'm not suggesting you should plant spearmint or chives in the border as, after a season or two, there would be no border – just a snarled web of mint roots and self-sown seedling chives. There are more interesting varieties of both that are just as useful in the kitchen. Apple mint, *Mentha suaveolens*, has a superlative taste, and velvety leaves and stems. For those who are not worried about disturbing the nightingales (unlike A.T. Johnson), there is a variegated form, which will frequently start off its new growth entirely ivory-white. This will not affect the flavour of your mint sauce, and will look fresh too, both in the garden and in a posy. Having so little chlorophyll, the whole plant is considerably less rampant than the green form, so is a safe bet for the border. I have mine as a white flannel petticoat beneath the crinoline skirts of *Rheum palmatum rubrum*; possibly unknown to the rheum, which, like the Discontented Sugar Broker, has everything in life except a waist, so cannot see its own feet. The mint is tough enough to compete, unnoticed, when the rhubarb-leaves display their early-summer opulence, and then grows tall enough to steal the show from autumn's dwindling of the rheum's expanse. On the principle of keeping all my thugs in one basket, I added the running roots of *Euphorbia cyparissias* 'Fen's Ruby', which fill any gaps left by the others. It starts into growth early in spring; its greyish-green cheeks brushed with rouge, so its crimson tones match the contemporaneous new growth of the rheum.

Why bother at all with the insignificant flowers of the ordinary chive, when you can grow the giant form, *Allium schoenoprasum* var. *sibiricum*? This has stronger, longer foliage, to 18 inches or more, that tastes exactly the same as the punier version, and has much larger flowers, making far more impact. Even more of a statement, both in the border or on the plate, are the bright rose-pink flowered variety, *A.s.* 'Forescate', and the tiny 'Scottish White', which has grass-green narrow foliage to 6 inches or so. A pale, opalescent form turned up here; I have it next to the equally nacreous *Papaver orientale* 'Graue Witwe' – all moonstones and mother-of-pearl. A colour-break turning up in the midst of these co-operative chives is easy to deal with, as the whole clump can be dug up, pulled apart, and replanted, without turning a hair — even when in full flower. Indeed, for more and better flowers, the clumps should be divided fairly frequently, as they build up such a conglomeration of bulbs that they will starve themselves to death, unless you reduce the queue for the refectory.

Lemon balm is another useful herb — it makes sublime ice-cream, or sauces for fish — but the species, *Melissa officinalis*, looks like a green blob and reproduces itself quicker, and more plentifully than a greenfly. The scent as you brush past it is utterly delicious, but it is equally mouthwatering on the less promiscuous form *M.o.* 'All Gold', that makes a loose tuffet of light, bright, lemon-yellow. It will burn in strong sunshine if its roots are too dry, but will not be so radiant if you place it in shade. If that little planting conundrum is too abstruse to reconcile, try the variegated form, *M.o.* 'Aurea', which has broad, irregular splashes of sun-proof yellow amongst the green. I am told that this will still seed around if grown on light soils, but on my cold clay I have never found one seedling. The moral of this is to grow lemon balm on heavier soils, and try lemon verbena, *Aloysia triphylla* instead on the light, warm soils that it prefers. Again, your ice-cream churn will see recurrent use.

The ordinary marjoram — both a native and a herb — would be worth growing for the sake of pleasing bees and butterflies, even if you dislike the taste. But once again, there are dozens of varieties to choose from, with different coloured flowers, bracts and leaves. *Origanum vulgare* var. *album* 'Aureum Album' has sharp citrus-yellow foliage, impervious to the sun, and white flowers that are as much beloved by bees and butterflies as the usual mauvey-pink type. Mine was planted at the top of a dry-stone wall and is busy infiltrating every crevice with its fresh foliage. The new spring growth looks like chenille, looping through the wall, zingy lemon against the grey. By midsummer it is a cumulous-cloud of billowy growth covering the wall, with a second cloud over it of appreciative insects.

Parsley (*Petroselinum crispum*) makes such a dense dome of strong green, when well suited, that it can be used as the ultimate foliage plant, to deserved applause, either as part of an annual bedding scheme, where the intense heat of some of the colours will benefit greatly from the cooling and solidifying effect of the rich green pillows of parsley, or as a temporary green background to herbaceous plants or bulbs. My aim is to partner parsley with the great mauve goblets of colchicums. These tend to be spineless, so appreciate a firm, but gentle backboard to improve their posture. Parsley, I believe, would be perfect, closely planted in summer as a supporting act for the colchicums' autumn flowering period, then eaten, to keep the spring stage clear for the prima-donna leaves. These are too large and lush to be trusted with any permanent underplanting, unless it is very tough, which would not necessarily be so attractive as a partner to the delicate flowers. It all sounds so simple; to you, perhaps, it will be. For me, it appears to be impossible, as I am a complete duffer when I try to grow parsley from seed: either it won't germinate or it won't grow. Yes, I know about the boiling water trick – pouring it along the seed trench immediately prior to sowing; it doesn't work for me. I also know the old chestnut about parsley never growing where the woman rules the household: that does work for me. As I seem to have been adopted, lately, by a little feral cat – a tom – my years of parsley-failure should be over. My colchicums can look forward to their perfect partnership next year.

AUTUMN

'BLISTER MY KIDNEYS, THE DAHLIAS ARE DEAD!' Jorrocks would have waited a long time between the death of my dahlias and the start of the hunting season. There are frosts in every month here. July sometimes escapes with nights of just zero degrees, but no frost (which sounds like a yellowhammer in full song). The extensive growth of summer will surround and cushion the more susceptible plants, so damage, beyond a brrr of crisped leaf and petal edges, will be circumvented. But a star-chilled night of crystal clarity will cause the temperatures to plummet well below freezing point. Even then the minor damage that results is negligible when compared to the heart-stopping grandeur of such a night sky: the Milky Way curdling the blackness with a gauze of smoky light; shooting stars arching like fragmented rainbows; the whole fathomless depth alight with rose-cut, billion-carat diamonds, even bigger than the Ritz. If the timing is right for a giant harvest moon to sail forth as well, the effect is breathtaking in its magnificence. More jaded palates than mine have declared it to be pure Disneyland, and have also been surprised to find stars, as was Wilde's Gwendolen that there were flowers, in the country.

But any time after the beginning of September, when the days are noticeably shorter, one begins to think that it is time to trim back the jasmine that has grown in through the bedroom windows, and entwined the hinges, sealing them open. There is a nip in the air, most evenings, and it becomes a matter of determination not to light the fire before October begins. The field mice start to perform clog dances in the loft and hunting spiders lurch across the floors, and appear in the bath each morning. The village shows are done, hedging takes over from combining, the church doors are set wide for the Harvest Festival. The swallows have flown. It is autumn.

There are years when the process from summer to winter is so gradual as to be scarcely noticeable – usually when a poor, dreary summer slides into a mild, wet winter. Autumn barely happens at all. How disappointed we feel when the seasons don't respond to popular demand: we like our autumns to be crisp and colourful, full of warm sunshine and blazing foliage. We want to feel ploughed and scattered, in a season of mists and mellow fruitfulness – no matter that we buy our potatoes and plums and that our Harvest Festival altars are decorated with tins of baked beans and grapefruits.

Thankfully, here, closer to the soil, and bound more firmly to the vicissitudes of the weather, we are perhaps more aware than urban dwellers of the gently dying year and its timely tasks. The often deluging autumn rains can wreak havoc, as can the attendant gales, so preparations are vital in areas where overhead wires cause frequent powercuts: alternative sources of heat, light and water (bore holes and piped springs require power for their pumps where there is no access to the mains) must be accumulated and stored. There is little point in expecting to be able to shop for all that is necessary only when it becomes necessary, as the lanes are often blocked by fallen trees or flailing power cables, and, frankly, it is best not to add to the blockage yourself.

I've known snowfalls in early November to be sufficient to cut us off from the world for several days, until snowploughs break through, but nothing like the snow in 1947, when a gang of twelve men with pickaxes and shovels took thirteen weeks to cut through the icebound lanes to outlying hill farms. Perhaps global warming is happening after all. There is not much sign of it in this valley. Weather reports are notoriously unreliable, countrywide, let alone here, for more than twenty-four hours in advance, so I don't take a lot of notice of them, especially when they trill about 'overnight lows of ten degrees' when our midday temperature didn't even reach that and the frost is already visible. Far more irritating is the terror of rain that grips them in summer: in the midst of a killing nationwide drought, they will forecast 'a risk' of rain. Clearly the thought of crops ripening means nothing in comparison with having fun in the sun. 'Leisure activities' being as paramount as urban youth in the scheme of life as we are forced to know it, there is no room for seasonal weather in the media world of virtual reality, nor for the traditional reasons for welcoming rain with regard to food production. But then, when supermarkets here sell asparagus in May from Peru rather than from the Vale of Evesham, which is less than sixty miles away and then in the full flow of the English asparagus season, or strawberries from Spain in June, reality becomes less than virtual, it becomes negative.

Many people move to the country imagining it will be just like a Thomas Hardy novel. Naturally they find it inconvenient on the occasions that it is. But they are often the sensible ones, who admit their mistake and go back to town. Sometimes, those who stay are not so sensitive, apparently believing that their lives shall not be changed or adapted one jot by the alien surroundings in which they now live. They hold fast to their suburban values and habits, perhaps not even noticing that there is any difference. But they use too much water and more power than the system can accommodate; they drive cars too wide for the lanes; they feel unsafe without white lines in the road and street lamps, so they demand them and, sadly, they get them. Most irritating of all: they are terrified of the quiet and dark, so they pollute the night skies with tungsten lights and our ears with blaring alarms. They are throwaway people, out of kilter with the recyclable area in which they now live, and too arrogant to notice. The countryside is not a peaceful place to live any more. I think with longing of the quiet that pervaded life in Jane Austen's time: she may never have known the sound of a machine. I would willingly trade a little convenience for the sky to be free of shrieking jets, the lanes to echo only to the sound of hoof and harness and for combustion only to be spontaneous for the likes of Mr Krook. In the autumn, the air pressure acts like a cider press on all the vehicle fumes and bonfire smells. This valley collects and holds on to these stinks; long after their perpetrators have disappeared over the hills and far away, we are still choking on them.

A friend has a theory that those of us who were born in the autumn love this season more than any other with symbiotic empathy. I am less convinced, feeling perhaps an inexorable battening-down of hatches and a woeful foreboding of the months ahead of Strindbergian gloom and moaning gales. I like the promise of spring: what could be more uplifting than a balmy May morning of bluebell and primrose, and a lark ascending?

But of course autumn has its sublime moments too, such as the morning I travelled into my local market town in glorious rich sunshine beneath the canopy of a deciduous wood, which should have been the original spice road to Zanzibar, so meltingly caramel were the colours: ash turned to turmeric, silver birch to cinnamon, willow to paprika and ginger. The road was carpeted with the fallen splendour – a Bokhara rug of aspen and oak leaves, and larch needles like filaments of saffron; the brilliant sunshine hollowing the tunnel, and leaching through the trees to enrich the colour of the shadows to mace and nutmeg.

Autumn colour cannot be guaranteed as the high water table encourages the trees to stay green until gales pick clean the bones. But we are far enough north and west for ash trees to turn to buttercup yellow – a conjuring trick they don't always manage in the warmer south. Aspens rattle their lemon-zest leaves to the ground in the slightest breeze. Picking one up, I found it was like polished kid, malleable and lively, unlike the frail silver birch leaves, which are almost translucent, tissue-thin and wasted. I have never tried aspen leaf-mould. Would it work, I wonder, or would those leathery leaves stay long-unrotted, like holly and some magnolias? This is not natural beech country: our most common natives are oak, ash, willow, alder and hawthorn. This list would once have been headed by elm but, alas, no longer. These all make good leaf-mould, although perhaps not so ambrosial as that made with to-the-manna-born beech. I never have sufficient quantities to make a separate brew, so the few leaves which stay in my garden (it is upwind from the main stands of local forest trees) are included in the compost heaps. Not that I collect even these few in any purposeful manner – where they flock among plants in the borders, they are welcome to stay, and rot down where they lie. I'm not about to make work for myself by first gathering them up and then, later, spreading them back in the same places. Once again the worms will do the work for me, hauling each leaf down under the surface. I am told that they always pull them down stem-end first, which is easier work, but also shows a certain level of intelligence – both working this problem out, and recognizing the stalk end. Compared with ants, who blunder about in their automaton way and, indeed, with many humans, who behave similarly, the humble worm is a model of intellect.

Invariably I will spread some compost in the autumn: just enough, usually, to empty one of the bins ready for winter filling. It is awkward at this time of year, as the borders are still so full. But where an area has earlier been overhauled – large plants split and reseated – a thick mulch can be spread over the now-visible surface, after the soil has been well watered. This is particularly important after a dry summer, as any autumn rain will not penetrate with ease through the blanket of mulch; so this will turn to slime, the soil beneath will remain bone dry and the worms will still be too deep and dormant to know that there is work to be done on the surface. If the weather is unseasonably hot after you have well-buttered the bread of the border, the butter will overheat and burn, shrivelling to cinders, and your work will have been wasted. More likely, here, is that frost will get under a newly-laid mulch, and be sealed inside, like damp within double glazing, and doing just as costly damage. Mulching, then, is better done in the spring, when the ground is likely to be plentifully soaked and beginning to warm up, and when new growth is starting to show itself, to guide your clumsy fork but usually not your clumsy boot, as your heel crunches tulip noses just pushing through. It is the newly planted bulbs that are most at risk. The picture of them in full growth and flower has not yet imprinted itself on my memory, so in their first winter's residence they are still simply buried brown bulbs in my mind and easily overlooked.

Bulb planting is a chore and a bore. It has been helped enormously, this year, by a recent present of some hand-forged tools, including a slender bulb trowel. As it sliced its way through the drought-dust, I realized how pleasurable the exercise must be for those with light soil. Normally, by bulb-planting time, my soil is leaden with rain, requiring ten times the effort. I try to minimize this by practising severe discipline at bulb-ordering time. Neither my borders nor my back are accommodating enough to allow large numbers. Not for me the hosts of golden daffodils – at least, not all at once. The nurseries that supply in small quantities of ten, five, three, even individual bulbs, are the ones I prefer. It may be a more expensive way of doing it, but it suits my planting capabilities. After years of trying one nursery or another, I have also found that these small quantity purveyors will usually supply the exact bulb that they say they are offering, and of good quality too. Neither of these factors can be taken for granted with many of the larger concerns, which keep down their prices only at the expense of accuracy. It is galling enough to find your white tulips turning out to be red, even more so when just one is wrong, standing sore-thumbingly obvious for what seems an eternity. Still more provoking is when a rare bulb is offered, for which you have long been searching; you pay an inflated price but it turns out to be a standard variety available in every garden centre. Yes, of course you can have your money refunded, but that is not the point. It does not refund you for the years of growth wasted, for your disappointment, or for the fact that you turned down an opportunity to acquire the real thing, believing that you had it already. Mistakes are more likely to happen where bulbs are shovelled up with a JCB than where individuals are selected by hand, preferably by someone who can tell the difference between an allium and a tulip. The smaller nurseries are more likely to grow their own stock on site, so control is greater than where a large warehouse packs bulbs delivered from a middle-man depot who has shipped them from abroad. And the smaller nurseries will care if they do make a mistake, which is more than can be said for some of the larger ones.

I like to have the bulbs planted as soon as possible after they arrive. They may be dormant, but they are not improving by being out of their natural element. And field mice find bulbs irresistible. Bagged up and lying about in the cool larder, the bulbs must appear like a Christmas stocking full of gift-wrapped delights to the hungry mouse. Here, where winter soil freezes solid to great depths and animation can be suspended for weeks, there is no danger in planting tulips at the same time as daffodils. They'll not be tempted to push noses above the covers too early, as the covers themselves will still be icebound. My one favourite, the acid-drop *Tulipa turkestanica*, will be the first to flower, towards the end of March; my other favourite, *Tulipa sprengeri*, as red and polished as a baby's coral, brings up the rear in early June.

'The Toolip,' according to Thomas Fullar, 'a well-complexion'd stink, an ill favour wrapt up in pleasant colours,' cannot be relied upon here to be more than annual. Neither the sun nor the soil is warm enough to bake the bulbs in their summer dormancy, to encourage flowers to be formed, and the small bulblets which develop rarely grow large enough to produce more than one floppy leaf each. Some perform better than others: the aforementioned species are soundly perennial (I am touching the table as I write, so as not to tempt fate) as is the delicate *Tulipa batalinii* 'Apricot Jewel', which the *Plantfinder* now groups with *T. linifolia*, another good one, whose startlingly scarlet flowers stand at 3 inches tall above Marcel-waved leaves that lie on the ground like a beached starfish. Of the larger hybrids I grow, only two can be expected to reappear each spring: 'Purissima', an enormous white of the Fosteriana persuasion, and the dazzling lipstick-pink 'Elizabeth Arden', which is a Darwin. Other varieties of these two groups are tried repeatedly, but with little success after the first year. Many are thwarted in their attempt by squirrels nipping off the flower heads. Frequently I find a row of heads laid out on the top of a nearby wall, like traitors on Temple Bar.

Having an ongoing love affair with striped roses, I thought that adding some striped tulips to the borders would provide a trumpeting herald of the joys to come. Last autumn's planting of the lily-flowered 'Marilyn' and the lusciously double 'Carnaval de Nice' was a triumph in spring, but will they reappear? Who knows? Of course you can order more each year, if you don't mind the expense, to keep the display constant. Or you can look on the resulting gap as an invitation to try others, for a different display. I fall between the two stools, wanting the show to go on but also willing to experiment with a change to the cast. The dark chocolate 'Queen of Night' does poorly here, but is a firm favourite nonetheless, so is planted often. But this year, for a change, I am trying 'Couleur Cardinal', a more obvious crimson, and with a reddish tinge to the leaves too.

Autumn is a time for reappraisal. What has worked should be consolidated; what has failed must be obliterated. I hope there won't be too much of the latter, but there is always room for improvement. Every year, at this time, my aim is simplification, which means moving out the excess, in order to see both wood and trees. I prowl the borders, my mind's eye stretching to accommodate the necessary changes, talking to myself as I go: gardening *à seule* needs the encouragement and criticism of someone, even if it is only the horticultural equivalent of John Doe and Richard Roe. It is a good time for decisions, as the borders are stuffed to the gunwales and one's eye is sated with summer. Come the spring, the feeling is different, as one is longing for growth by then and weary of seeing the winter soil. So all those spaces look vast, when one's eye is accustomed to the modest flow of springtime, rather than the swollen spate of summer. It requires more fortitude than I can always summon not to pop a couple of plants in here, one more there, especially when those waiting to be planted are outgrowing both their pots and their standing space. A way of avoiding this is to fill those gaps with bulbs – then you know that there is something there, not just a tempting gap. But bulbs are not always suitable companions. Herbaceous plants that spread rapidly and need frequent division do not make congenial stablemates for bulbs, which prefer stay-at-home neighbours like peonies, oriental poppies (although some of these have rhizomatous roots, so would not be so complaisant), or shrubs. I do plant pink bluebells – *Hyacinthoides hispanica* 'Rosea' – among the running roots of Japanese anemones. They are tough enough to compete; indeed, each may have a little excess energy rubbed out by the other – no bad thing.

Moving out plants that are surplus to requirement is one thing, dividing and replanting quite another. This is not a job for the autumn in such cold heavy soil as mine: there is no time for the damaged roots to re-settle themselves and repair sufficiently to feed the plant prior to the long winter. So they will tarry, unattached to their new surroundings (like people waiting too long at a bus-stop, chary of sitting down and making themselves temporarily at home for fear of missing the bus), starving and freezing by turns, in a slough of despondency. By spring they will be moribund; desperate growth will be weak, so prey to both frost and pest. You will have wasted your time as well as the plant's life. May is the month for division here. June would be better, with warmer soil, but too much top growth would be knocked back then. Obviously I am preaching the doctrine of perfection here, whereas, in reality, dividing and replanting goes on, as necessary and when I can get away with it, throughout the summer. Top growth will be sacrificed for the ultimate good of the plant – *il faut souffrir pour être belle* – so that it can put all its effort into roots rather than flowers. The watering will be onerous, but will be outweighed by the ease with which the plant grows apace, with warm summer soil rather than a cold sump around its feet.

Even in warmer gardens, some plants prefer to be split in spring rather than autumn. One might suppose that late-summer-flowering plants, like asters, echinaceas and Japanese anemones, would benefit by division immediately their flowers have faded, to allow the maximum of time to build up for next year's growth. Not so; all of these strong, hardy plants may die with such treatment and will certainly not flower so well as those divided in the spring. Here there is no question of division after these flowers fade. They don't. They are pulped by frost long before that, often just as they are opening their first buds. The spent heads are removed but the stems are left standing over winter – I think it helps to protect the crowns a little.

This year, although the echinaceas and anemones were badly frosted in their prime, the asters, being a little later, survived in tight bud and went on to flower profusely. Usually, autumn rains will brown what colour the frost misses, but they have escaped that attention too. They have been, indeed, still are magnificent. Michaelmas daisies, even the newer varieties, have an Edwardian sumptuousness that I find compelling. All those parma-violet mauves and greyish-purples are the mourning colours for the Great War and the gentle world which preceded it. I feel the lack of a train and parasol as I walk among them. Correctly, only *Aster novi-belgii* varieties are Michaelmas daisies; *A. novae-angliae* in all its many cultivars, is the New England daisy. No doubt I am not alone in thinking of them all as Michaelmas daisies. Luckily for me, this is not a mildewy garden, so I can grow the prone *A. novi-belgii* daisies with impunity and much pleasure. For those on drier soil, the *A. novae-angliae* varieties may give better value, or the *A. amellus* hybrids or the species. I am unwilling to give houseroom to many of the species, which can grow vast and invariably have squinny little weedy daisies in dishwater tints of whey-mauve-white. Worst of all, to my eyes, are the varieties with *A. lateriflorus* blood, whose colouring reminds me of chilblained feet. Nor do I care for the much-lauded *A.* x *frikartii* 'Mönch', whose wiry stems look strong enough to stand up for themselves, but which clearly carry a lazy gene: unstaked, they will swamp everything for a yard around; staked, they look as out of their element as Dickens' dolphin in a sentry box. I grow *Aster thomsonii* 'Nanus' instead, which is similar in effect, but short on height and long on discipline.

Another flopper is *Aster laevis* 'Calliope'. I love its great trusses of lavender daisies, later than most, and its blue-stocking stems. But at 6–8 feet tall, with weak ankles, it must be staked as firmly as a large dahlia if one is not to be playing spillikins in the border. I find it a problem because, being so late in flower, its neighbours have usually been blitzed by frost by then, so do not provide an adequate supporting act to hide the aster's props. It came to me from a warm garden in Dorset, where it was chopped back in early summer to curb its height. 'Calliope' would then flower on shorter, more manageable stems, but even later in the season. This is a good wheeze for mild gardens, but not here, where it is a gamble, even on regular timing, whether it will contrive to beat the onset of hard frosts and flower at all. This year the dry spring held it back in growth, and the warm dry summer egged it on to bloom earlier than usual, so its navy stems had reached only 4 feet, which was better. Originally I had it planted at two o'clock behind a variegated elder, *Sambucus nigra* 'Albovariegata', by which it was supported and with which it mingled deliciously, along with the earlier-flowering *Clematis viticella* 'Etoile Violette'. But despite annual stooling, the elder outgrew its meagre space, as it always will, and the replacement cutting (grown on betimes, so the size difference is not too startling for the clematis) was chewed to the ground by something. So I replaced it instead with *Viburnum sargentii* 'Onondaga' – a lovely thing with an apricot blush to its creamy flowers in early summer and a peachy glow to its foliage in autumn. Irritatingly, this had not made itself at home sufficiently to brazen out the drought over summer. With copious watering, it is alive, and will no doubt romp ahead next year, but its leaves were crisp, curled melba-toast by late summer, so did nothing towards hiding the aster's stakes. My poor 'Calliope' would not inspire any epic poetry or eloquence this year. But next year will always be better.

Those with a nervous disposition should look away – now. One of my favourite groupings for this time of year is centred around the native spindle, *Euonymus europaeus*, whose autumn colouring is most exciting: Schiaparelli-pink cushioned pods, which split open to reveal squashy orange seeds within, like a Dali sofa with the stuffing coming out. The frosted foliage flares equally shocking pink. Beneath it I have planted *Clematis texensis* 'Gravetye Beauty' to entwine its branches with dangling, cherry-red bugles. On one side, *Aster* 'Alma Pötschke' (as it is known by its many admirers, but *Aster novae-angliae* 'Andenken an Alma Pötschke', if you want to order one), whose outrageously cerise-pink daisies are not for the faint-hearted, and on the other side of the spindle, the darkest form of valerian, *Centranthus ruber* 'Atrococcineus', whose second flowering echoes the vibrant crimson of the clematis. The total effect is that of a conclave of cardinals dancing a cachucha, fandango, bolero, with the spindle as the Duke of Plaza Toro.

Still more astounding colour is provided by *Aronia arbutifolia* 'Erecta', a small shrub that clearly loves to shock. It is as easily overlooked as a

Victorian governess for fifty weeks of the year, then suddenly she breaks out and dresses herself in Jezebel-scarlet to frolic for a brief fortnight. More subtle colouring can be seen on forms of cotoneaster. These can be difficult to name, as they interbreed with the freedom advocated in the sixties – swinging from bee to bee and from berry to bird with unrepressed profligacy. I have two of these hippy children, collected as seedlings beneath a contented bird roost. One has *C. bullatus* blood, with great clusters of crimson berries and large leaves which turn to the exactly matching crimson, most autumns; the other is a mystery. Its berries have a pubescent white down overlying their tomato red and are high-shouldered and rather clumpy in shape and held in small bunches. Its habit is that of a sparse *C. horizontalis*, plastering itself against a wall. Its leaves are sharply pointed and about an inch long, and are a pale silvery-green, with a white downy reverse. Now, in autumn, they are a mat, lustreless tangerine, which is outstanding against the grey stone, intermingled with the tiny palmate filigree of *Tropaeolum speciosum* foliage. It was too dry for the flame flowers this summer, but the unravelled threads of grass-green still look attractive. *Cotoneaster atropurpureus* 'Variegatus' needs neither flowers nor berries, as its ashen-green and white circular leaves streak themselves, in autumn, with drops of spilled claret and rosé; then hoar frost rims the leaves like a salted Margarita glass (to muddle the boozy metaphor). Newly grown from seed this year is *Cotoneaster zabelii*; already, though still small, it is showing a shambles of liver and ox-blood on its large, lustrous leaves.

And the few dahlias I do grow are invariably of these sanguineous colours too, which glow like jewels in the lowering, softened light. Frost-free does not necessarily mean mouse-free, so I have problems with successful overwintering of dormant tubers and find that spring-purchased tubers will not have a long enough season ahead of them to get into full-stride of effective flowering, before frosts knock them back. Without flowers, there is no point to a dahlia, as the plants themselves – grown here, where it is too cold for them to flourish and wax fat – are tawdry beasts. Even the empurpled foliage of the magnificent 'Bishop of Llandaff' is a mess when August frosts prank the diocesan purple with brown. This year I have grown one called 'Dark Desire', which is lusciously rich in its percentage content of cocoa solids, and abstemiously slight as to flower size. This is not a dahlia for those who like cactus dinner plates, as it looks to be a cross between the delicate *Dahlia merckii*, for size and shape, and *Cosmos atrosanguineus* (which is School of Dahlia), for colour.

I am always on the lookout for my favourite dahlia of all; remembered from childhood but, sadly, without the benefit of a name. It was a maroon pompon with a fine white edging to each petal and the engine-turned precision of form, which, to my eyes, only the pompons achieve. It was grown by a much-loved aunt in a garden of Edwardian splendour, with cutting borders of dahlia upon dahlia, all with their upturned pots of straw for earwig nurseries, which a gardener visited each morning with a collecting bucket of water. Foolishly, I never asked the name of the dahlia, nor of the propeller-flowered scarlet pelargonium that I still grow from her original cutting. From dahlias to aunts is an easy Wodehousian step, which reminds me that I think of Bertie Wooster's Aunt Dahlia as darlia, not daylia – it sounds more euphonious. Anders Dahl, for whom Linnaeus named the dahlia, is also pronounced 'darl'. Perhaps it is time for both aunts and plants to have a long A.

I'm told that effective earwig nurseries can also be made with empty cartridge cases upturned on canes. Autumn days are punctuated by volleys of shot echoing around the hills; nights too, for that matter, as 'lampers' wreak their unsporting havoc, roaring over fields in 4 x 4s, or simply along main roads, shining their searchlights over field or garden hedges and blasting off at anything that moves into the beam. If the victim is a protected species or a pet it is left in the path of oncoming traffic, to be disguised as a road casualty. Frequently, of course, the lamper's shooting skills are as negligible as his morals and the wounded crawl away to a miserable death, often in the comparative peace of a garden.

Perhaps it is only an old gardeners' tale that a dead fox is beneficial to the roots of fruit – especially peach – trees. Perhaps, in the same way that the relics of saints are said to exude the scent of violets, there are particular salts, extracts or attars, given off in the process of vulpine decomposition, that make a peach particularly peachy. Never one to miss an opportunity to feed my soil, nor to spurn ancient wisdom; when I found a fox cub in my garden one morning, dead from a shot gun wound, I thought of my newly planted 'Crimson Queening' apple tree. Reader, I buried him.

Gentians

I AM A LATE RECRUIT to the regiment of gentians. They have such a sniff of the rocks and valleys about them that, even here at 800 feet, I felt sure to disappoint their romantic souls. With limestone rocks to poison their soil and vaporized fuel from all the jets tainting their air, how could they thrive? But the opportunity to bark my visual shins on those swimming-pool blues would brook no denial.

Despite that, the first gentian I acquired was cream. Curiosity was piqued into ordering such an incongruity. *Gentiana tibetica* is an odd fish, to be sure, with lush cabbagey foliage, deeply tramlined with veins and clusters of urn-shaped flowers in midsummer, set in toby-ruffs of pointed leaves, that wobble and crash-land when collected rain becomes too heavy for their 14-inch stems. The flowers are easily missed, being a greyish-cream, muddied still further by a faint violet blush to the outside of the bells. Looked at closely, they are quietly stylish; the plant has a dispassionate air that keeps it a little aloof from its neighbours. As I knew not what to expect, mine was badly sited, visually at least, on the edge of a crowded border, which does nothing to display its discreet charms. But the situation seems to suit its diet, so I am loth to move it.

Some of these big gentians have vast roots that demand as little disturbance as possible. Having once tasted the liqueur made from the roots of *Gentiana lutea*, they need never be disturbed again on my account. This is another surprising gentian for those more accustomed to the carpeting blues, as it grows to a spire of bright yellow flowers in early summer, set in whorls scaling 4-foot stems. The basal rosette makes a hosta-like mound but with longitudinal vein-ridges scored gravely into the metallic-green leaf – a wholly unhosta-like colour. *G. lutea* grows in wet alpine meadows so needs plenty of both sun and moisture. Dry springs, which seem to be the norm lately, will stop it producing any flowering stems, although the weather is less of a culprit, here, than mice, who gnaw the fat, pointed buds that push above ground in hungry late winter.

A hot spell in late spring was doom to another gentian, whose seedlings frazzled in the shed while my neglectful back was turned. *Gentiana purpurea* adds the third primary colour to the gentian spectrum, being a reddish-purple version of *G. lutea*, but of slighter stature. *Gentiana*, therefore, joins the small number of genera (including, *inter alia*, delphinium and meconopsis) with red, blue, and yellow flowers represented in their species. Farrer calls *G. purpurea* brown, and claims it is an evil, weird thing, but handsome. As I have failed to repeat that germination success with subsequent seeds, I can say no more about it: *de mortuis nil nisi bonum*.

White is another gentian colour, seen here in the albino form of the willow gentian, *G. asclepiadea* var. *alba*, which flowers in October – much later than the type blue, or the low-pitched-pink variety 'Pink Swallow', both of which kick off in August. Drought is the only enemy of these superb gentians. Given adequate supplies of water, they will stand full sun as happily as the dappled shade of their chosen woodland glades. They will grow to a gracefully curved 2 feet, the weight of the large flowers held in the leaf axils arching the stems in a far from modest bow. There are several blues to choose or collect, from white-throated turquoise to deepest ultramarine.

And once you start, it is easy to wallow in the sheer magnificence of the blueness of gentians. They are never just blue: there are always dots and dazzles of green or black or violet, streaks and feathers of light or dark, glistening hairs, reflective cells like mirror-beads. Blue becomes so much more than just a colour. *Gentiana paradoxa* has 2-inch-long bells in late summer on thread-leaved 8-inch stems that flop around in a leisurely way, draping themselves across their neighbours' shoulders in a matey fashion. It would be helpful to plant this gentian (most gentians, indeed) in a raised bed or trough, or you will need to spend some time lying on the ground in order to look at the detail within the trumpet's throat. The mouth, where the petal-edges point outwards and a ring of blue hairs point inwards like sharks' teeth, is the blue of a tropical sky in late afternoon, when the sharpest glare of the sun has melted, leaving the essence of deep-blueness.

The throat is pure white, delicately veined with black, but minutely so — the colour has been applied with a one-hair brush and the lightest of hands. As the white meets the blue, they merge like the dots on a Warhol silk-screen print, fading down to blue on white, and out to white on blue.

On the Himalayan *Gentiana decumbens*, the midsummer whorls of small flowers along lax 10-inch stems have the cloudy haze of a Gainsborough sky. The late-summer blooming *G. triflora*, from Japan, has clusters of tight-lipped urns of the royalist blue on 2-foot spires here, but with a less alkaline soil it would top 3 feet. This is the only 'unsuitable' gentian I attempt to grow. The others shrug their shoulders at the lime, although I make sure they never dry out: most gentians like plenty of moisture around their roots, and drainage as sharp as you can manage.

One plant out of my three clumps of the spring-flowering *Gentiana acaulis* will stay on circuit for an autumn session too. They have huge bells, more than 2 inches long and splayed wide at the mouth to an inch or more, of an intense sapphire-blue, streaked and flamed inside like a treacle tulip, but with emerald-green and white. They make tight cushions of shiny, laurel-green basal leaves, from which the flowers radiate on short stems.

Its gratuitous later blooms are most welcome, as I prefer my gentians to abide by Trinity and Michaelmas terms, rather than Hilary. There are so many other blue flowers in spring whose tones are lighter, less ardent, than gentian-blues. Springtime light is fresher, more silvery, than the bleared, golden heaviness of late summer and autumn, which suits the peacock-enamel tones of the gentians. A black-winged, neon-green damselfly once rested on a flowerless, summer clump of *Gentiana acaulis*, looking like a flower itself. Clearly it settled there *pour encourager les autres*, as this is the plant that has sung a reprise each autumn ever since.

Recently I have acquired a small plant of *Gentiana farreri*; still too small to display its Cambridge-blue and kingfisher bells of such luminous loveliness, as Farrer described them at first sight on a Tibetan hillside. His enthusiastic outpourings and vitriolic opinions are not appreciated by all, even though the plants he introduced are still among the best for all gardens. Not long ago, I was reading his book *My Rock Garden*, when the cut pages came to an abrupt stop. Had the reader become bored, or left it on the Clapham omnibus by mistake? Or, as my copy is the 1913 reprint, was it abandoned in the dugout when the reader went over the top, never to return? Vain to speculate, but exciting to continue cutting and reading these particular pages that have never before been seen.

Frequently, in the garden, stones will split in two, or shale into *millefeuilles* layers, as they are prised from deep in the soil, revealing tiny fossilized shells. Four hundred million years ago, this area of Silurian limestone was a shallow sea around a reef that is now Wenlock Edge. When these little cockleshells were alive there were no eyes to see them – neither fish, flesh nor good red herring. A brief life in the sun-warmed sea, perhaps, then countless aeons of entombment in clay-stone darkness, until my probing fork cleaves the blind rock and shows the shell to the sun once more. And to my eyes – the first ever to gaze upon it. When something is so tiny and so perfectly preserved in its petrified state that not only are the delicate flutes and flanges of its shell miraculously precise but sometimes even its colour has remained different from the surrounding stone, it beggars belief that it can be so incredibly ancient. Uncut pages in an old book are scarcely in the same class of wonderment, but still they confer, like the fossil shell, the sense of a secret revealed only to me.

Perhaps it feels a little like that when you find a spectacular plant that no one else has ever discovered. When you behold a hillside splashed with peacocking gentians. The experience awed Reginald Farrer to silence, which must have been a rare occurrence. Just a couple of years later, in 1920, Farrer was dead, aged only forty. His grave is on a lonely hillside in Upper Burma, spread, I hope, with a pall of turquoise-blue gentians, and not vanished from sight like a fossil within a stone.

Crimson

THREE PLANTS ARE STEALING THE LIMELIGHT now, in autumn, having been building their crescendo since the summer. When early frosts have put roses in their cheeks, they will begin the gentle fade to diminuendo. But at present all is loud and clear.

Their joint biography began about seven years ago when I attempted to grow *Phytolacca clavigera* (now renamed *P. polyandra*) from seed. This is the Chinese version of the American pokeweed, *P. americana*, which had also been sown, with a plan to test Thoreau's remark that the juice from the purple-black berries made a better ink than he could buy. One of these germinated, then damped-off; nothing came up in the Chinese pot. Having kept the pots, just in case, for two more years, I abandoned hope, and tipped out the compost on to a border recently cleared, whose soil had been starved under a row of leylandii. These had been planted too close together by my predecessor, who then lopped the scrappy, middle-aged trees too heavily, which inevitably killed them. When I arrived, death row was still there, gaunt and nettle-swamped, and stayed that way for much too long, until the cadavers were removed for scaffolding access when the house was re-roofed. I call it the Moat Border, as a shallow channel runs to one side taking storm-water to the stream. It is planted with shrubs – viburnums mostly – and the soil is improving slowly, with frequent top-dressings of spent potting compost.

Out of the blue, then, appeared a stout seedling, which I left, on the principle of not weeding out anything I cannot identify until it has proved itself sufficiently to survive the pending tray. The first early-autumn frost dissolved it to slime. That was that, I thought; dead, for a ducat, dead. Not so. Next spring up it jumped again, with long fleshy leaves, flushed with red. Was it a pokeweed, I wondered? Frost again; goodbye mystery.

This year it decided to introduce itself, by flowering in pink. Mystery solved: *Phytolacca clavigera* (*P. americana* is white, with smaller, drooping heads in fruit).

The phytolacca is not a refined plant; it grows coarsely, with thick stems and large oval leaves. Worse – it dies egregiously in these conditions of early frosts, its 4-foot stems explode, leaves become flapping beige rags, berries shrivel like sucked-in, toothless cheeks; this is not a plant for a formal border. Indeed, had it not flowered, it would have been evicted without mercy. But now it stays; its decay is worth ignoring for the sake of its confectionery.

In tight bud, its flowerhead looks like a bright green corn on the cob or a slender pinecone, tapering to a sharp point, 4 inches long at this stage but rapidly lengthening to over a foot as the flowers open. These start at the bottom, working their way upwards, turning from green niblets to rose-pink chenille truncheons, 2 inches in diameter on rosily blushing stems. By the time the upper flowers have opened, the lowest will be turning into apple-green berries, puckered and buttoned like an over-stuffed chesterfield, and with a curious construction of bright-pink, byssus-like fibres attaching each large round berry to the pink central stem. As the green fruits climb to the top, the lower fruits will turn cyclamen-pink, darkening to crimson, then violet and finally gleaming black. This virtuoso performance begins in early June and continues until frost brings down the curtain.

By late summer, the overture for the second act is tuning up: *Lobelia cardinalis* times its rich crimson flowers to coincide with the phytolacca's two-tone scheme of cyclamen and crimson, both in berry and stem. The lobelia is planted in damp soil on the opposite side of the moat but, as the pokeweed stretches towards it, they are close enough for a harmonious duet. *Lobelia cardinalis* forms often have beetroot leaves, but on mine they are dark green, which I prefer, as the flowers are outstanding against green but can be swallowed by identical crimson. It grows to about 3 feet, the top 12 inches or so forming a spike of flowers with fan-shaped lower petals and white-streaked throats.

The trio has been completed by another Chinese plant, *Primula wilsonii* var. *anisodora*, planted next to the lobelia. Of the candelabra persuasion, and flowering normally at midsummer, my plant has been delayed for some reason this year, so has begun its blooming season in early autumn, sharing the crimson of the others in its buds, darkening to a winey purple in its whorls of pendant flowers. Like the lobelia, it needs damp, well-fed soil to reach its full potential of four to six whorls around 3-foot stems. The whole plant is pungently aromatic, especially the glabrous strappy leaves, a scent which, to me, is redolent of suntan oil rather than aniseed.

None of these plants is rare or difficult to grow, nor was the effect planned: the primula should have bloomed earlier, the phytolacca should not have been there at all. Gardening is full of these serendipitous events, often working far better than any intended grouping over which we have toil'd, moil'd, fuss'd, and scurried.

Hedges

STRAWBERRY HILL, ACCORDING TO Horace Walpole, was set in enamelled meadows, with filigree hedges. If one may be allowed to define 'filigree' as a thin tracery of twiggy tangle, interspersed with large gaps, then I too have a filigree hedge, its tangle and gaps most evident in winter. Even so, that is a kinder season for the hedge than autumn, when the voice of the flail is heard in our land. Arise, my love, my fair one, and come away. Would that one could, without risking a brace of punctures from every lane. When technology can land upon Mars, it seems unjust that a mere terrestrial machine cannot clear up after itself, so that the hedge trimmings no longer rip tyres to shreds. 'Trimmings' sound so soft and benign, when the reality – in hawthorn country – is as treacherous as the rowel on a spur for readiness to prick from any angle. Which is presumably what John Gerard meant by 'spoky rundles'; I wish these spokies were less spiky.

According to Hooper's Rule on dating hedges (where each different species within a given length approximates one hundred years of age, not counting various 'weeds' such as dog rose, brambles, and ivy), my boundary hedge could be up to 500 years old. It contains (as well as the above weeds) snowberry, quick thorn, midland thorn, elder, and hazel. It is more likely to be 300 years old or so, with a basis of the two thorns and hazel. This would be an appropriate date fitting the history of the house, and also the heyday of Enclosure Act hedges. The extras, bird-sown elder and snowberry, would establish themselves and squeeze out slower growth, much faster than the hundred years each allowed by Hooper. In some instances the rule doesn't work, where hedges have been made by transplanting seedlings of mixed species from nearby coppices, rather than making the hedge from just one type of plant, and allowing time, wildlife and the weather to cause further diversity. However, in these

Marcher uplands, it was traditional to make hedges from hawthorn, particularly the midland thorn, *Crataegus laevigata*, which grows well in cold, heavy soil, so it is possible that all the other species in my hedge are of natural colonization.

The very earliest hedges were made from hawthorn, *Crataegus monogyna*, a trustworthy stockade against marauding man or beast. The Anglo-Saxon village boundary was called the haga, but did that take its name from the fruit – the haw – or lend it? Which came first, I wonder, the fruit-chicken or the boundary-egg? Later, hawthorn was known as quick, not to describe its growth rate, which is slow but sure, but to differentiate it from the dead wood of fences. It has had a chequered career: hawthorn was said to have been made into Christ's crown of thorns, so is meant to groan on Good Friday. It represented the badge of the Tudors, after Richard III's crown was found hanging in a thorn tree on Bosworth field. In ancient Athens brides would wear crowns made from the blossom, even though its scent shares a chemical with rotting fish (the flowers are pollinated by blow-flies) and has been likened to the reek of the plague pits in seventeenth-century London.

Long known as may, the flowers rarely bloom for May Day as we now know it, but will usually be evident by the second week of the month, still setting their flowering clock by the old-style calendar, before Pope Gregory's eleven-day hiatus was adopted by Great Britain in 1752. Slow growing and conservative in habit, may has relied upon day-length for countless aeons to tell it when to display its bread and cheese, without bothering its head about upstart Julian or parvenu Gregorian calendars.

Snowberry, *Symphoricarpos albus*, would not be my first choice for a hedging shrub; indeed, I should have to work my way through several dozen others before turning to it, either in total desperation, or else because I wanted to keep contented bees. A late-summer hedge of snowberry is alive with burbling bees, tippling voraciously from the tiny rose-pink tubular flowers. This seems to me to be a good reason to keep it, if you find yourself in unwitting possession, but not necessarily to plant one in the first instance; plenty of other shrubs would do the hedging better as well as keeping the bees in full employment.

If I were planting a brake for pheasant cover, *Symphoricarpos albus* and *Leycesteria formosa* would be all I should need, the one suckering to form a thicket, the other to fill up any gaps with self-sown zeal. They would look rather striking, too, both in extravagant fruit, and in bare winter stem – warm brown, whippy canes on the snowberry and jade-green bamboo pretenders on the leycesteria, which is also known as the pheasant berry, although the pheasants here ignore it. I have read descriptions of leycesteria berries, set in their inverted pagoda racemes, comparing them to carved jet mourning jewellery. This has the root of the matter in it, but overlooks their absurdity: one can't help but smile at those ludicrous stripper's tassels. Snowberry fruits are equally ridiculous. Being too weighty for the slender stems, they plunge down and joggle about like a bungee jumper. Birds disregard them here, and rain turns them quickly to brown squidge that drips on to anyone passing. More sheltered gardens should have a longer and more spectacular display, the arching stems alight with polished white marbles for most of the winter. There are varieties with a grideline tinge to the berries, which a friend likened to gallstones, and a form with variegated foliage, said not to sucker. If so, it would be a blessing, but still it would not convince me that the snowberry is any better than a second-rate shrub.

For hedging, it is worse than that. It grows about 3 feet every year and is too springy for any machine, whether hand-held or tractor-driven, to cut with precision; it dies out in rotting hanks in the centre and suckers all the more readily for its constant tip-pruning, so the hedge becomes wider still and wider, 4 feet athwart and more, but ever less dense. Even at its best, most animals with the determination of a gnat could push through it, so as a stock fence it is laughable, particularly as large animals like to lean on hedges, as well as eat them. As the cutter, I appreciate its defencelessness, unlike the ancient thorns, whose weapons are like the quills upon a fretful porpentine (if one may quote a ghost).

Hazel, *Corylus avellana*, is as gentle as it is venerable. Would that the whole length of the hedge were hazel. It is dense and springs freely from old wood, so can be renewed in perpetuity; it will grow lusty stems each year, but is ease itself to cut; and it has attractive silvery bark to delight the winter eye, when autumn's gilt, from spring's fresh green, has fallen. If you encourage wildlife in your garden, hazel is essential; if you merely tolerate our furred and feathered brethren, hazel will give them plenty to concentrate on, leaving other, more precious plants alone. A mixed planting of hazel and wild honeysuckle may entice dormice, if you live in an already favoured area: I study every gnawed nutshell that I find, hoping to see a gadrooned edge to the extraction hole. Invariably it will state the obvious fact that I have field mice, as if I didn't know.

Plague years occur now and then, when numbers of mice explode. I set no traps in the garden, only in the house and, occasionally, in the shed, when there is evidence of overwintering lily bulbs being disinterred from their pots and chewed. These are the box type, live traps that catch the infuriating but entrancing creatures without harming them with a bait of peanut butter. This allows me to study them briefly – sometimes they are rare yellow-necked wood mice – before relocating them. This must be somewhere quiet, with reasonable cover, away from houses (or you are simply saving them for someone else to kill), and at least half a mile away from your own house, or they'll be back home before you are. Usually the haul will be half a dozen or so between October and January, when they disappear back to the garden and fields. One year I caught thirteen, which was the record until this time, when the total (so far; who knows if they are yet in retreat) is 275 spread over sixteen months, as for some reason they chose to prolong the visitation throughout the spring and summer months too.

I love to see great stands of elder, *Sambucus nigra*, bursting from old hedgerows, particularly in autumn, when its foliage glows with vinous purples and fruity flames among the red twiggy stems of polished berries. I have neither flowers nor berries nor autumn colour on the elder in my hedge. A vast sprawl of elder growing from beneath an old henhouse fares better, with a froth of creamy champagne in early summer, pursued by a bounty of ruby port berries by September. The annual *vendange* is supervised by blackbirds and thrushes, who gorge and squabble alternately until every fruit has disappeared, leaving only a crimson residue staining the ground beneath each roost. But even this large elder is small on autumn colour, managing only a tepid lemon tinge or two before the leaves are picked by gales or pulped by frost.

Elder is never a tidy grower, so needs equally rough companions in a hedge. Nor does it rejuvenate itself from old wood with much ease or any grace; it's an ungainly beast. But its thick corky stems are simple to cut and it stands rigid against the flail, so it earns its keep, here, where looks are not everything. *J'y suis, j'y reste.*

I used to cut the hedge with secateurs. It would take me three days, but was the only way as the snowberry stems were too thick for shears. It looked superb, although I say it myself, as sharp and straight as such a mixture ever could look. Then I bought an electric trimmer. This reduced the time spent to two hours, but at a price: wrenched shoulders, naturally, but twice every year rather than just once, as the snowberry simply swayed with the trimmer, like dancers cheek to cheek, unless it was caught very young. My problems were made worse by the fact that the lane outside the hedge rises to crest a bank, whereas the garden inside the hedge does not. Which means that to keep the laneside level at chest height, the inside will be nearly 10 feet tall at the end of the garden. Clearly the laneside cannot be reduced to shin height to compensate – cattle, sheep and the occasional unattended horse frequent the lane and there is the ever-present threat of deer to consider (not that even chest-height would give a peckish roe deer pause, and an unpeckish one has yet to be born).

I had no wish to resort to scaffolding – the hazards of a stepladder are sufficient where ground is uneven; but was reluctant to reduce the hedge height too much. Like Jane Austen, I am not fond of the idea of my shrubberies being always approachable. But to balance that there is the theory of katabatics, which sounds like the maniacal frolics of a kitten with the wind in its tail, but is, in fact, the sober study of air drainage: cold air, being heavy, will roll down to whatever barrier stops it, and settle to form a frost pocket. The height (or depth) of the barrier will increase the pocket within its arc. This suggests that a reduction in hedge height might enable the frost to keep on rolling away and allow my garden to carry mere ticket pockets, rather than its usual over-packed cabin trunks, of frost. Miss Austen: 1, Kitten acrobatics: 2. With bow-saw and axe, the height was curtailed. I can't say that it has made much difference.

It is a sad fact that as opportunity and time increase, energy and strength diminish. A kind neighbouring farmer now cuts the hedge. With a flail. The warrior king Chaka of the Zulus could use the lane afterwards for training his barefoot crack troops. So I drop everything and rush out with a broom and shovel as soon as the tractor departs and before the punctures begin. There will be chunks of hawthorn on upstairs windowsills too, down chimneys and on the bedroom floors if I have forgotten to close the windows. The lawn must be cleared before the mower can be used – brushing with a stiff broom is the best way. Paths and borders for 20 feet or more inside the hedge will be carpeted with debris. Some of it will be flung with such force that it will slash leaves and break flowering stems. I've even found pieces of hedge lodged in the canopy of the alders beyond the stream. The clearing up will continue for days.

And that's not all. There are iron arches straddling the path just inside the hedge; a wooden gate with a brick pier at one end, and a telegraph pole halfway down. The flail cannot swoop closely into any of these, so I would have to cut around them afterwards. But if the sun is at the wrong angle, or the hedge has grown even more than usual, the poor farmer can see none of these, except the pole, as I learnt to my cost one year when the flail bent and snapped the curved tops of the iron arches. So now I prep the patient by cutting around all the obstacles before surgery begins. All in all, I seem to be expending just as much effort on having the hedge cut for me, as when I did it myself. Jane Loudon commented that walls should have 'a good hat and a good pair of shoes'; the same must be said of hedges, with small heads and big feet. This is the outline the batter gives to a well trimmed hedge – allowing light and rain to reach the all-important HQ on the ground floor. It seems the concept of the batter is a difficult one to grasp, or perhaps it is a design failure of the flail, but hedges, around here at least, tend to have small feet and a wide-brimmed hat. The machine cuts the sides straight, and then cuts the top on a diagonal. When both faces of the hedge are cut similarly, it looks like Canary Wharf. Every year I have to ask for mine to have a flat top, and then I narrow the shoulders myself later. Farm hedges need not be thick at the base as they are fenced anyway, nor does it matter that their girth grows wider and more machicolated with time, whereas I need to keep mine as narrow as a cat's forehead, else the snowberry will take over the whole of my world.

The hedges within the garden are a quite different kettle of paint, with soft annual growth that is easy to shave with shears (although the purple plum requires an exercise in Hannahbatics to cut the face that overhangs the stream, where the purple wands curve like spinnakers over the water; if only one could train the squirrels). This ease is due to youth. They were planted by me, so have had my stern eye upon them – since infancy in the case of the aforementioned plum and the two small box hedges, all of which were grown from cuttings, and since conception in the case of the yew hedge, which I grew from seed.

The hedge of *Prunus x cistena*, the dwarf purple plum, was not something I had set my heart on acquiring. It happened by accident within the first few months of moving here. An elderly neighbour, who had a delightful old cottage garden, knocked on my door one morning with an armful of cuttings that she thought I might like. Roses, tamarisk (she gardened on the side of a hill, so had better drainage than me), forsythia, buddleia and a dozen more: masses of stems in a great sheaf. Some of these I still have – including a 'Doctor W.Van Fleet' rose and the pretty little cluster-flowered *Rosa* 'Russelliana'. Thankfully, timely death overtook the seedlings of Japanese knotweed she had included, of which she was inordinately fond and which I, nothing loth, planted on the strength of her nameless description without a second thought. Saint Phocas must have been watching over me.

I had been about to leave for a week in London, so, rushed and heedless, I simply snipped ends off the twiggy cuttings and thrust the stems ruthlessly into the only patch of clean, spare earth. I didn't even stop to water them. Happily it rained that week, which was more than I deserved, as was their perky condition on my return. Some of them survived to be transplanted (although not the buddleia or tamarisk – on seeing the soil they turned up their toeses as well as their noses). So having cleared the decks I realized that the prunus was not only growing apace at the back of the border above the stream wall, but would make a strong bulwark against the north-westerlies if I teamed it up with other shrubs.

At first I planted a mixture there – not as a hedge, but as disparate shrubs – and that's what they looked like. So having moved them out again, I took more cuttings from the original prunus and set them in a row to promote the protection racket. Much better. It makes a semi-transparent jalousie-fretwork through which the water meadows can be glimpsed. The green that twinkles through the interstices lightens the purple magically, as does reflection from the stream below. Not that *Prunus x cistena* is heavy in hand, in the way that purple hazel is a dense black sponge that mops up every atom of light with a greed that is palpable. Its leaves are smaller, for one thing, and the longish petioles inspire them to flutter in the softest breeze, flirting their mossy-bronze underclothes. Planted, as this is, in full sun, the 'purple' takes on a dozen different shades of sienna-crimson and chestnut-madder that change continually throughout the seasons. Its blush-pink spring blossom is an arresting sight, scattered among the dark twigs as the newly hatched leaves appear dressed in cinnamon mixed with murrey.

It will achieve 6 feet or so, left to its own devices, but I prefer mine shorter – for ease of cutting, and to tie in with the contours of the bank beyond the meadows: any higher and it would exclude rather than include this shared landscape. I trim it twice during the summer to keep this line explicit and, so far, there is no sign of leaf curl, silver leaf or any other disease of bots and warbles to which prunus can be such a martyr. It makes a sumptuous backdrop for tawny pinks and maroon, so has become the anchor of my Beetroot Border. Even its bare winter stems keep these colours in mind, being the deepest chocolate brown, buffed with a steely, gun-metal polish, echoing black and crimson forms of *Helleborus* x *hybridus* planted to one side.

Traditionally, box hedges were cut on Derby Day. I have a suspicion this was simply to keep garden boys out of the betting shops, as cutting hedges so early in June would make another trim essential before the winter: box, *Buxus sempervirens*, like yew, can grow faster than is generally supposed. The tradition is a sensible one, though, as the box hedges will then look ship-shape and all-ataunto for the summer, instead of like whiskery chins if you leave them for an annual clip in August. By getting them out of the way in June, ideally on a rainy day, as box cuts better when it is wet, you will have more time to concentrate on the yew hedges in late summer – they'll not put on any growth until the spring, so will look sharp for months. I try to give my box hedges a second cut as early as possible (if they need it – a drought summer will slow them to first gear, so it may not be necessary) or else I just nip off extra long whiskers as I'm passing. I can't afford to give them a short back and sides at this time: if autumn is kind, they would put on new shoots only to be blasted by frost later; if autumn is hard, the lightly clad stems would suffer and die back. Yes, box is hardy, but it likes to be snug, so I allow it a stubble of growth for the winter that can be sacrificed to the ice gods. The Derby Day trim here, will be shearing off these frost-damaged shoots.

Even yew, *Taxus baccata,* can have its fingers pinched in cruel winters, so as my hedge is still a mere babe – yews of a thousand years old being stupendous but not unusual – it seems prudent to cosset it a little by not cutting it to the bone and not cutting it at all either before or after August, so that no new tender growth will be stung and no semi-tender wood will be chilled. It means a somewhat more shaggy effect than is usual with yew, but I don't mind that. If I had objected to a hirsute hedge, I should not have grown it from seed. Inevitably there are differences between plants – colour, habit, stance. It is not enough to warrant terming it a tapestry hedge, but I like its DIY attitude; it fits well with the informality of my garden much more than would a smart hedge from cloned cuttings of sonorous blackened-green, which would make the rest of us feel deeply inferior and self-conscious about trying to live up to it. As Logan Pearsall Smith said, it can be difficult to possess one's own possessions; my garden and I are too rustic to possess an excessively formal hedge.

Both seeds and seedlings were collected from beneath a middle-aged yew tree in my parents' garden over a period of several years. Grown on in increasingly larger pots, some took to the restriction and delay with the most perfect manners. Others did not, so it was necessary to grow more. The eventual planting out had to wait until I had cleared so far, as I wanted my yew hedge as a dividing rampart before the kitchen garden, with a looping arch over the central path. I cleared one side of the path earlier than the other, so that side had the pick of the yews in pots. The other side was planted the following year with the also-rans. It has taken only three years for there to be so little difference in size between the two sides that I need no longer offer any explanation. The yews planted immediately beside the path as fuglemen were the tallest and, I suspected, the most pot-bound. But they have done surprisingly well, given an encouraging trim each year and plenty of muck for pudding. Last year I assembled the cheap metal arch over which they are to be trained and clipped, and tied in the top stems. They have about a foot to go to meet overhead – an impressive achievement in only five years from planting at about 4 feet tall.

The hedges on either side of the arch will be kept much lower, to about 4 feet, (yes, I know they will grow much taller eventually, but that can be someone else's problem – they can cruise along at 4 feet as long as I'm around). Simple to cut at that height, maybe into an inky wave of swags if I'm feeling frivolous, they will give sufficient protection to the kitchen garden beyond and be enough of a vertical to fool the eye. I don't want them to look so much of a barrier as to be a place called Stop. These yews have grown sturdily too; from an odd-job mixture between 8 and 18 inches tall when planted, they have joined up, thickened up and have had their tops trimmed. Last spring a robin had an appointment to view one side of the arch and has used it as a penthouse roost overwinter, so there may be a nest this year.

Meanwhile, I have been noticing that small branches on one of the yews (it is looking suspiciously like an Irish yew in habit – how did that get in?) are turning russet-brown and dying. Worry, worry, worry. Is this the start of some new and dreadful yew blight, I wonder? Probably not. Squirrels, mice and voles, whose numbers are legion here, are partial to ring-barking yew. I understand that the vast, billowing yews on the terraces at Powis Castle have achieved their eccentric shapes by the repeated attentions of squirrels, who must have Japanese souls, so adept are they at cloud-pruning. I shan't mind if my yew hedge turns into a plump feather-bed courtesy of the squirrel pruners in a hundred years or so, particularly as it won't be me climbing scaffolding to trim it. But I may be blaming the squirrels unfairly for the die back: tortrix moth caterpillers hibernate in yew over winter and ring-bark in spring as they emerge. Certainly I noticed the problem first in the spring. Bats are their natural predators and there are plenty of those here too, although with *à la carte* mayfly on the menu at much the same time, they might not bother with a humble *plat du jour* tortrix moth. Perhaps the squirrels would help.

Frog Hollow

HERE IN THIS COLD FROG HOLLOW, I am reminded constantly of the importance of flexibility. The received wisdom with regard to planting positions is less successful, in many instances, than some unorthodox placings. Every gardener has a lucky break now and then with plants or positions that one didn't think would work; still more, where one didn't think at all. Sadly, the obverse is true, too, so one loses more plants than one need, even when care is taken and homework is done – by which I mean that the plant's partialities and proclivities are researched and acted upon.

Received wisdom is, after all, the result of centuries of generality. A useful guide, for first consideration, but always subject to adaptation and experiment by those with an adventurous or questioning spirit. The variations in soil and weather conditions that occur within a hosepipe's length across these small islands create differences from garden to garden that can rebut ropes of pearls of received wisdom. I am not suggesting that every grain should be gone against, merely that your own garden's temperament should call its own tune.

The garden, here, runs east to west in a narrow strip between the ha-ha wall above the stream to the north and the mixed boundary hedge to the south. This means that more sun and better drainage affect the northern side, although its open aspect suffers the full blast of the prevailing winds, whereas the southerly portion of the garden is somewhat shadier, damper and a fraction less gale-ridden. As would be supposed, these conditions alter with the seasons. The shade, inevitably, is less pronounced when the sun is higher, so this area becomes arid in midsummer, when the rays can reach to toast the surface soil and the hedge, by then in full leaf, sucks all moisture available from below. Conversely, the low winter sun never penetrates sufficiently to melt the frost from this part of the garden. It takes until June for the soil to begin to warm. So any plant requiring shade must reconcile itself to both the Scylla of wet, frozen winter and the Charybdis of baking summer. A tall order, but there are plenty of good plants that will flourish here – *Iris sibirica*, Japanese anemones, *Saponaria officinalis*, roses, camassias, astilbes – all contented with their bed-and-breakfast accommodation; many more, however, simply rot.

Unwilling to give up entirely without a couple of fights, I keep trying to find more congenial billets for particular plants, which leads to some surprises: cimicifuga, for example. Every word spoken or written about these enchanting pipe-cleaner plants begins with a caution: do not allow them near sunshine; they need the horticultural equivalent of factor 35 sunblock; damp shade is vital. Here in damp shade, despite being hardy, they die. In full sun, however, they thrive and, so far, have never been scorched in the heat. Hot sun, up here at 800 feet, is invariably tempered by a fresh breeze and, as the stream holds down the temperature, it also adds dampness and movement to the air. Equally, this clay soil never dries out completely down where the roots are feeding; the water table is too high for that. The surface may be dry, although it rarely bakes to cracked cement, as there are so many stones in it. These also aid drainage, and hold moisture – even the dry-bobs, dianthus and sedum revel more luxuriantly where their toes are tucked beneath a sizeable stone.

So after many losses and much experimentation, I have found that several plants that are said to demand shade, or damp soil, or both, will do very nicely, thank you, given more sun, or drier soil, or both. Monardas are a good example: they drown here in damp soil but succeed in well-drained, rather dry conditions. A surprise, as their superficial roots should be chary of such droughty quarters. Again surprisingly, they rarely succumb to mildew, as the buoyant air does not stagnate around their stems. They grow shorter too, which is a boon in a windy garden. Admittedly I now grow only the older cultivars of the colourful monarda, such as 'Croftway Pink' and 'Cambridge Scarlet', plus a nameless lilac one that I grew from seed. I have tried several of the newer hybrids, but none of them lasts very long or bulks up well into buxom clumps.

Erythroniums, the dog-tooth violets, disappear forever in damp shade here, but one canine root of the yellow-flowered hybrid 'Citronella', planted in full sun in dry soil at the foot of a yew hedge, has multiplied into a full set of dentures in a few years and flowers splendidly. This parched patch holds other damp-lovers, including *Narcissus bulbocodium* – the only place in the garden where it will flower; *Arum italicum* subsp. *italicum* 'Marmoratum' – the only place in the garden where its seed heads don't recline, slug-temptingly, upon the ground; and the so-called hardy ginger, *Roscoea cautleyoides* – the only ditto in the ditto where it will grow at all.

An ongoing experiment is with *Saxifraga fortunei*, another plant with a government shade warning. It survives in damp shade here, but early frosts always blitz the flowers to purée. Clearly better drainage could improve its chances of flowering, as would warmer soil, but will it be out of the freezer box into the fire, if the sun destroys it instead of the frost? In the dank soil of the shady border, it shivered, invisibly, under the covers during a long spring lie-in, so migration to sunnier climes could not take place until June. It was unfortunate that a blistering heatwave set in the following week and, not having settled itself into its new home, it was frazzled to extinction while I turned a forgetful back. I must try again, as the autumn flowers, like tattered ribbons, are a joy too wondrous to lose as repeatedly as I do.

Trillium is another genus that I hope to grow more successfully with the benefit of quicker drainage and, as a consequence, more sun. Flowering early in May, when the sun is not yet at full strength, the soil should be a mite warmer, which can only help, but they must not dry out too much, over summer, as the leaf canopy expands around them. I am always suspicious that American plants – especially those native to the East Coast – will be intolerant of my neutral-to-limey soil. Planting them dry will exacerbate the problem. Trilliums are expensive to buy, so the risk is greater. I am biding my time until I have cleared further ground at the bottom of the garden, as there should be shade, keener drainage and a little more protection from the south-westerlies there. I might be able to gull a trillium into thinking it is Massachusetts rather than the Marches.

Solomon's seal and pulmonaria are two more woodlanders that perform and flower more abundantly in full sun in my garden. I grow several species of polygonatum that suffer horribly, some years, from the ravages of the saw-fly grub, a wriggly grey larva that consumes all but the stems and leaf-veins, reducing the poor solomon's seal to a ragged brown skeleton by midsummer. By growing the plants in sun, however, they have, as yet, avoided this attention. Fooling the enemy is always gratifying.

The only pulmonaria that remains in damp shade here is *P. rubra* 'Redstart'. Its light green, unspotted leaves are thinner in texture than the other lungworts, whose tubercular spottles can bear almost any heat, provided their roots are not thirsty, whereas 'Redstart' wilts in the sun like cooked spinach. But neither does it appear entirely seventh-heavened in its present frosty hollow, so I must experiment again.

It is well known that *Iris laevigata* and *I. ensata* must have full sun and plentiful moisture – paddling up to their ankles, even. My best clumps grow on the desiccated edge of a dry-stone wall. My one orthodox planting of *I. laevigata* struggles manfully but is far from happy. I have left it in its dungeon, dark, dank and drear because its gentle pinkish-mauve colouring exactly matches a *Thalictrum aquilegiifolium* near by. But it is pointless torture for the iris, as its few flowers just miss those of the thalictrum, held back, I suspect, by its damp feet. Elsewhere, drier, they flower earlier and more bountifully.

Astilbes too, plume themselves on dry-stone wall edges, and display more pronounced leaf colour – both early and late – in the desert conditions. A nameless one was mistaken for a fox curled up in the autumn sunshine, so rich was its rufous foliage; I have called it *Astilbe* Sleeping Fox ever since. The invasive thugs of the bog garden, such as *Sinacalia tangutica* and *Carex riparia* 'Variegata' will grow tighter and shorter if planted in dust-bowl conditions. Their leaves are deeply indented or needle-thin, so will not lose too much of the sparse moisture available, by heavy transpiration.

As with everything in gardening, in life (which is the same thing to many of us), the noticing eye learns most. It is crucial to be observant of all the little quirks and fancies of your plants. Often it is the fractious, more eccentric ones that give the greatest satisfaction, by repaying any small trouble one takes on behalf of their welfare. 'The farmer's boots are the best muck.' Yes, indeed, and the gardener's eye is the kindest sun.

Euonymus

THE GENUS *EUONYMUS* IS FULL of good things. It is very much an all things to all men sort of group, including standard municipal evergreens of unmitigated dullness, as well as some of the most magical of all deciduous shrubs and small trees. Let's deal with those first, lest I use up all my superlatives on the awfulness of the others.

Euonymus europaeus is an English native that has been prized for its hard, close-grained timber since Anglo-Saxon farmers first began coppicing woodlands 1, 5oo years ago. It was probably their wives who called it the spindle tree – its straight stems were whittled at first and then later turned on primitive lathes into spindles and bobbins for holding their homespun wool and flax. The wood is so smooth and splinter-free that it has never been bettered for this purpose, although later spinning wheels and their attachments would be made from beech. Charcoal burners and artists would prize the spindle too, for its dense, slow-burning qualities and residual strength once burnt.

Gardeners love it for its delicacy of growth; it is light and airy, allowing close planting around its feet, such as a scrambling clematis to grasp its slowly extending arms. Its own token flowers are greenish-cream and small enough to be unnoticed. But everyone admires its dashing autumn colours and eccentric fruits – both leaf and seed capsule are brilliant pink, the latter splitting at a fontanelle to reveal the satsuma-orange seeds within. It is a remarkably exotic performance for an otherwise quiet English hedgerow plant, like a belly dancer in a village hall.

There are spindles of other nationalities too – all a rhapsody on the same theme of brilliance for a blow-out in autumn, following a year of gentle abstinence. Frank Kingdon-Ward saw a euonymus in the jungles of Assam with seeds the size of crab apples. One from the Pacific coast of Siberia and

Kamschatka, *E. planipes* (syn. *sachalinensis*) is known as the dingle-dangle tree because its seeds hang from threads, or funicles, causing them to tremble in the slightest breeze, or the vibrations engendered by a rumbustious performance of *Funiculi, funicula!* perhaps. *E. sachalinensis*, therefore, verges upon saccharinensis, but any other spindle would taste as sweet.

And so to the more prosaic (let's be charitable) species of euonymus. Scarcely a garden exists without a hybrid of *E. fortunei* – 'Silver Queen', 'Emerald Gaiety' or 'Emerald 'n' Gold' (how I loathe that 'n'). My sister inherited 'Silver Queen' with her garden; I took cuttings that finally made roots after eighteen months of sitting, like patience on a monument, quite contentedly, in a pot, doing nothing at all. That's the kind of guy it is, *Euonymus fortunei*, so laid back that nothing fazes or excites it. It grows so slowly that you forget it is there, for all its brilliance of colour. The worst soil, the driest position, the coldest draughts – all are tolerated with equanimity. You cannot help but admire such a sterling plant, nor help being bored by it, particularly in its all-green form, which looks like fake Astroturf.

My yawningly slow cuttings have at last grown sufficiently to be trimmed back – I want them as flattish ground-cover over daffodils – but if one could ever live long enough, one might see 'Silver Queen' ambling up a wall or fence, even strolling through some neighbouring shrubs with the lethargic torpidity of a two-toed sloth on tranquillizers. But, as grudging as I may sound about it, it does begin to look good, with the lightening effect of its pearly cream and pallid grey-green, which, as temperatures cool, become suffused with ripples of raspberry. So much so that I have moved one clump to form a harmonious grouping with *Epimedium* x *versicolor* 'Sulphureum' and *Luzula sylvatica* 'Aurea', with which I am feeling rather smug, as it is on an awkward bone-dry corner, where nothing, previously, would prosper, and which now glows with interest for eleven-twelfths of the year. The epimedium makes a tuffet of shield-shaped leaves, the liverish colour of a springer spaniel; the luzula has arching strap-shaped leaves of talmi-gold; and the small, dappled leaves of 'Silver Queen' are beginning to mingle most persuasively.

On the strength of this success, I have bought 'Emerald Gaiety' for another problem patch. It is not the most descriptive of names, as it is more cream than green, and can gaiety ever be achieved in quite such slow motion? I may know the answer to that in twenty years or so. (A couple of months later: the cream revealed itself to be polytunnel-pallor and the plant itself mislabelled, as its overstimulating football-strip variegation of shiny, acrylic poster-paint yellow and green proves it to be 'Emerald 'n' Gold', which serves me right for being so scathing about the 'n'.)

The Tesco car park evergreens of the Euonymus family must be expounded by someone else, as I neither know them nor grow them. I do feel the deepest pity for them, however: backed into, driven over, choked with exhaust fumes, filled with plastic rubbish and hacked back with flails or chainsaws if they dare to grow one twig that might tear a kiddy's cardi and cause transcendent compensation to be paid out. If I had acres to spare I would plant them, just to see what they could do: well grown and fed, properly spaced and pruned, I have no doubt they would be wonderful plants, quite as bewitching in their way as their colourful cousins the deciduous spindles. But someone ought to do that soon, or, evolution being what it is, in a very few years' time Euonymus tescoensis will actually require its roots to be fed with take-away polystyrene and exhaust fumes, and its arms to be cradled by trolleys.

Ferns

I AM BECOMING STEADILY MORE interested in ferns. Most make a dignified block of quiet green: a Greek chorus that occasionally attracts the limelight but rarely takes centre stage. The native male fern, *Dryopteris filix-mas*, is of that ilk: nothing sensational, but always valuable, particularly when it sows itself into hedge bottoms or among tree roots.

But some are still more enthralling. If evergreen, they will grab your attention from afar, especially when the rest of the garden is passively snoozing and will hold it fast as you approach close enough to detect all the feathers and dimples, crests and curlicues. The polystichum ferns are notable for this evergreen detail – there is not a month of the year when they could be described as dull or past their sell-by date. The fronds stay slick right through the winter and, when finally cut back to base in spring, give way to extraordinary reptilian new growth, curving and arching cobra-like necks as they unfurl. The most effective of all, here, in its new spring apparel, is a fern from the *Polystichum setiferum* Acutilobum Group whose freshly croziered fronds look like the waving tentacles on a fox-fur octopus. It retains a little of that tawny shade throughout the year at the heart of the bright grass-green foliage.

Polystichum munitum is almost black in its shining yew-green. A simple ladder-back shape, it is firmly evergreen and sprightly throughout the coldest winter. It can grow 5 feet tall in damp conditions. Mine is planted in full sun and dryish soil, so is much shorter, which suits me and its position well, particularly when it is seen against the subdued winter browns of its neighbours' uncut top growth.

And that is the point: not all ferns demand shade. Many will relish sharp drainage even when it means they are a little dry, so they are extremely easy to suit. Dryopteris ferns, in particular, cope well with less damp sites. *D. erythrosora* has even more Venetian red in its toffee-coloured shiny new fronds if it is a bit on the dry side. I don't mean dust and ashes, but not having a shady bog does not preclude you from growing contented ferns. If all you have is a sunny wall, there are still good ferns for you: the native hart's tongue fern, *Asplenium scolopendrium*, is blissful spreading through old mortar. It will be smaller and tighter in such desert conditions, which is no bad thing, and gives you an easier view of the furry black dashes, or sori, beneath its strap-shaped, leathery leaves, that gave it the name skolopendra, a millipede. The variety *A.s.* 'Undulatum' is, perhaps, better in moist conditions, so that its fluted, pie-crust edges are seen to their best advantage and true length of 12 inches or so.

Osmunda regalis must be damp at all times to achieve its magnificent 5-foot fronds. In autumn the whole plant is caramel coloured and, unlike other ferns, it flowers: great feathery plumes, 6 feet tall. It is another English native and was named after the Anglo-Saxon king, Osmund, who hid his daughter within a large stand of the fern to escape the Vikings. Ancient clumps can be big enough to conceal a whole village from marauders. I planted a small piece in a new bed beside the stream and looked forward to the display, but, sadly, floods washed it out before it had had the chance to anchor itself securely. I hope someone downstream might have found and replanted it; or, better still, that it has lodged on a silty bank somewhere and gone native.

A chance find on my own stream bank is still a mystery: it grows to 3 feet, has very feathery, finely-cut fronds, which are knocked back by the first frost, and black stems (or stipes, in fern-speak) – most distinguished. This needs perpetual moisture, although being entirely herbaceous, to the point where its vanishing act should have a built-in *aide memoire*, I do wonder if it might prefer less sorbet-like conditions in winter.

The Japanese painted fern was called *Athyrium goeringianum* 'Pictum', formerly, after its collector, the father of Hermann Goering. Would that the son had aspired only to the gentle pursuit of the father. Now known as *A. niponicum* var. *pictum*, it is not entirely hardy, and is said to require both moisture and shade, otherwise its delicate fronds will frizzle in too much sun. As these are a mottled mixture of mulberry, grey and khaki, they are worth considerable trouble. My first one, carefully placed, rotted over winter so I have planted another with rather less of both requirements. So far so good; it has come through its first, admittedly mildish, winter and has coped well with an unusually dry spring. It has also had to deal with the too-close proximity of a viola that I planted in June, thinking that the fern had not survived. Lesson learnt: the Japanese painted fern is a springtime slug-a-bed that hides itself below ground as successfully as Princess Osmunda hid from the Danes, from November till June. A colony of them would be excellent taking the stage from snowdrops or other early bulbs. My single fern looks fetching beneath the *recherché Rosa* x *odorata* 'Viridiflora'; a purplish-grey fern and a green rose are not everyone's cup of tea. I love them.

I have bought the shuttlecock fern twice now and still don't have it. This is not a Mad Hatter's tea party riddle, but a simple and irritating fact: each time I have ordered *Matteucia struthiopteris* (which I find I cannot say without an Australian accent) it has turned out to be something else. This is dispiriting, as it can be years before the imposter is exposed. I have no idea what mine are, but they are not the elegant shuttlecock fern.

Another fern that I lost, and would love to have again, is *Dryopteris sieboldii.* It had halberd-shaped fronds, which, in spring, were lemon-yellow. It comes from Japan, where woods are sheltered and acidic. On looking it up, I can find no mention of the lemon yellow, so perhaps that was just chlorosis rearing its ugly head.

Clearing

THE AUTUMN WEATHER IS STILL open, with neither constant hard frosts nor constant rain – just a useful amount of each . . . so far. (In England one needs always to qualify every sweeping statement about the weather, as it changes even more rapidly and completely than a politician's mind.) So I have been taking advantage of the comparative stillness and firmness underfoot to clear some more ground. There is still plenty to tackle, so I need not yet eke it out for fear of finishing it all too soon and having to weep like Alexander for having no more worlds to conquer. Tears of conclusion are well in the future, but there is endless opportunity for tears of frustration as my fork hits yet another builder's cemetery of buried detritus: coils of wire, enough broken glass to have furnished the Crystal Palace, forgotten bags of petrified cement, sheets of lino – half crumbled, half burned and melted into an imperishable blob. Peter the Great had the right approach to builders, using them, instead of their rubbish, as the foundation for his great city.

Of much more interest are the sites of domestic bonfires and waste disposal. Few, because this was clearly the abode of generations of avid recyclers, although they weren't called that then, merely sensible people who would never waste something that could be mended or used again. I know from the old deeds that this was primarily a house where women lived on their own, spinsters or widows; but even without the deeds, I could make a guess about that from the bits and bobs of rubbish in the garden: corset bones and suspenders, hooks and eyelets, buttons and buckles – these feature again and again. I keep hoping that I shall unearth some Roman glass, left from the encampments all over this area, but so far there have been only Victorian jam jars and sugar basins. Pottery and china shards are everywhere, but again, they are mostly Victorian, and must have been scattered over pathways to add a little blue and white hardcore to the mud.

The area I am clearing now was shaded by an enormous Bramley apple when I arrived and graced by a large Anderson shelter that had been used as a pigsty. This was ringed with gin-traps, some rusted open, others rusted shut. As I am still digging up the staking pins and chains, no doubt I shall find yet more, although hopefully not of the size of a mantrap in the local museum, still in use in 1828. Of more immediate danger to me are the nettles. Archaeologists tell us that sites of human habitation can be recognized from the stands of nettles and elder scrub that continue to thrive upon the minerals and nitrogen that we, and our domesticated animals, leave behind us. As this small area housed not only the pigsty but also the outside privy and the hen house, these nettles are of biblical dimensions and satanic spite – even Job would have been sorely tried by a tussle with these amongst all his boils and botherations.

After an hour's pulling and tugging, digging and hauling, I feel as soaked in acid as the Brides in the Bath. The nettle tops have died back to dry husks this late in the year, but their bite is still worse than their bark. I remember reading that on moving the archive of preserved plants away from imminent bomb damage at the Natural History Musuem during the Blitz, someone was stung by a nettle pressed by Linnaeus himself over two hundred years previously. Nettles, said Culpepper, 'may be found by feeling, in the darkest night'. Pulling them by the roots is safer. But these have fed in undisturbed luxury for decades, so will not be evicted easily. They are thicker than my thumb, and intertwined with ground elder and bindweed – an unholy trinity of weeds. Am I alone in enjoying the task of unravelling this tightly woven rug of roots? No doubt it is a peculiar pleasure, but I confess to it nonetheless. Given ample time, reasonable weather, a light soil and no particularly pressing annoyances upon which I need to vent verbal spleen (these roots must not stand proxy for a current foe, or you will be tearing rather than teasing, and each broken morsel will sprout again, quicker than you can say Lernaean Hydra), given, then, this gentle *mise en scène*, chasing scraps of root can, indeed, be an agreeable way to spend an afternoon.

The nettle roots are gnarled and brilliant chrome yellow, with a surprisingly elastic quality – pulling them from the soft earth has the same tension as a blackbird pulling a worm. Ground elder roots are narrow and slippery, with whiskers every few inches, fastening them like couched embroidery threads. They will snap all too easily when pulled, but are not as brittle as bindweed roots, whose thick, creamy-white fatness reminds me of suet. This patch of soil is merely visited by the bindweed, not infested, so it has not penetrated too deeply, and can be tracked within the top few inches of leafy litter, and eased out with a gentle, but firm pull. I inspect each piece as it comes free. Is the end freshly broken, so that I must hunt again? Is the break old and brown? Or have I traced it to the fresh questing tip (it has a minute curved hook, like a spider's foot)? Can I relax my vigilance?

I have been unpicking the knitting for some time before the sensation strikes me that never before in this garden has soil been quite so meringue-light: this is Baked Alaska, Queen of Puddings and Eton Mess all in one forkful – it is sublime! Decades of undisturbed leaf-mould lying on further decades of sty and hen-house sweepings (not to mention the privy bucket), well turned and aerated by enterprising snouts and exploratory beaks, kept at the peak of fertility by all those nettles, shaded by them too, and held by their roots from gale-erosion – this is perfect soil. Perfect for me, perhaps, but too much of a good thing for the old Bramley, for whom the surfeit of nitrogenous lampreys proved just too indigestible. A goat willow had seeded itself under the Anderson shelter and had swelled like a baobab on the rich living, pushing the corrugated iron against the Bramley's trunk and then squeezing still more until the iron was embedded in both trees. The willow's branches, waving around like the arms on a Hindu god, clashed against those of the apple, causing damage there too. The willow was removed, as was the pigsty, but it was too late for the Bramley, weakened by all the nitrogen, damaged beyond repair. Sadly, by the time it had to be felled, I had lost the other apple trees too – one to a lightning strike and the other to a hurricane in 1990. Naturally, I have planted more.

This soil discovery is most exciting, particularly as the area will be relatively sheltered, even after all the rubbish is cleared, so gives me an opportunity to plant all those enchanting woodland-edge beauties that demand just such conditions, and have, as a consequence, previously been denied me. There is an old damson tree, no doubt bird-sown, but a graceful shape of multi-stems and airy branches. Already my eye is seeing trilliums beneath the damson, interspersed with snowdrops and *Anemone appenina*. Then *Dicentra macrantha*, which flowers in May, with 3-inch-long creamy lockets and delicate glaucous foliage. This plant is not easy either to acquire or to grow, and almost impossible to flower if your garden has one whiff of wind or chilly soil. I have recently acquired *Eranthis pinnatifida*, the delicate white-flowered, Japanese version of the more familiar varnished yellow winter aconite, *E. hyemalis*. Best in an alpine house, which I do not have, it will be worth trying it beneath the damson, with extra grit in its bedclothes and an ash-and-bracken igloo for the winter.

The same recipe would help the so-called hardy fuchsias here too. I dote upon the gentle rose-grey, desert sand colours of *Fuchsia magellanica* 'Versicolor'. Yes, I know it is so hardy it would grow on an iceberg. But the kind of winter that I think of as mild here the fuchsia thinks is bitter. *F.* 'Hawkshead', which has pretty white flowers with green tips to the outer sepals, rather like *Galanthus nivalis* 'Viridapice', is another bone-hardy fuchsia that I am forced to treat like a tender one – kept dry in a shed overwinter. But the damson gin-trap patch might make all the difference.

I have two seedling veratrums gathering speed in yearly larger pots, which should find this rich, well-drained, sheltered billet exactly to their taste. With luck, the ghosts of all those hens will scare off the slugs, otherwise five years' worth of veratrum growth will make one slug's breakfast. *Heloniopsis orientalis* is another woodlander that I could plant there for the special delectation of the guzzling gastropods. No, I still won't use odious slug pellets, nor systemic herbicides to kill off the nettles. Glyphosate is being found in ground water, despite all the promises from the manufacturers, and more enlightened governments than ours are banning its use. I have no wish to poison the water, myself or the nettles, which, as I have said, are a pleasure to dig. Nor do I wish to swell the coffers of the megalomaniac agro-chemical companies, whose activities do not yet convince me that they justify their own continuance. Rachel Carson's *Silent Spring* should be compulsory reading for all young people contemplating a career in any branch of science.

It would be an interesting exercise to record the favourite weed of gardeners around the country. One would need to define favourite: favourite for ease of removal; favourite for its beauty, thereby discouraging removal; or favourite for the satisfaction experienced after a long battle towards removal, preferably without resorting to napalm? Groundsel, *Senecio vulgaris*, would be at the top of the list in the first category, for me, and doubtless most gardeners – it pulls so sweetly. But there is a sting in its innocuous tail, as the seeds will continue to ripen after the plant itself is moribund, so you must massacre the innocents before adolescence as resolutely as Herod. Jack Frost would act as executioner with unfailing precision each winter when I were a lad, but cannot be relied upon now – even here. This makes me think not so much about global warming as about selective genetics: is groundsel becoming more hardy? Of all plants, weeds are surely the most fervent disciples of Thomas Malthus, agreeing that their population shall overwhelm their means of subsistence, and living by the creed of the survival only of the fittest. One has to admire their fortitude, even when one forgets to be grateful to them for their habit of covering spare ground, holding soil and maintaining fertility levels. I have left the as-yet-uncultivated areas of the garden to the weeds for this very reason: they are ground-cover *par excellence*, without the chore of mowing the grass with which others encouraged me to replace them. As grass it would have required weeding as well as mowing, and the resulting soil would not have been so rich in nutrients beneath the monoculture of grass as it is beneath the natural mixture of vetches and tares.

For beauty, few weeds can match the creeping speedwell, *Veronica filiformis*, with its white-winking, lapis-blue eyes. A large patch, glinting in dappled sunlight, can look as much like the sky fallen down as a bluebell wood in full chime. A small sprig becomes a large patch within a moment, so the effect is achievable by all. It is well named, as creeping at high speed is its sworn mission. Within a short time of its introduction as an ornamental plant suitable for border edging, or for fashionable rock gardens, it had emulated William Kent by leaping the fence and seeing that all nature was a garden, especially needful of its decorative insistence. In Shropshire, it was known as everlasting sin, being both prevalent and attractive. It began its mission here by gathering in clumps beneath the boundary hedge, which looked perfect, continuing the blue theme begun by the bluebells, and competing creditably with the native ransoms, *Allium ursinum*. But after a couple of years of cosy adjournment, it began to stretch its legs through the path and into the border beyond. Enough. I haul it out by the bucketful, but still it persists in spreading its cloak of glory beneath my feet. Elizabeth forgave Raleigh again and again, as I do the speedwell, *pour les beaux yeux*, but there may come a time . . .

And the favourite recalcitrant? The one whose removal would give me most satisfaction? I think it must be horseradish, *Armoracia rusticana*. Not generally classed as a weed, perhaps, but then, define weed. I don't go along with all the trite aphorisms about plants in the wrong place, or plants that are not yet appreciated. A weed, to me, is anything that qualifies itself as a damned nuisance. Horseradish fits this criterion effortlessly. Yes, I know it is very good to eat − not only the root but, even better, the young leaves shredded on to roasted beetroot and smoked mackerel. (Young nettle-tips can flavour a worthwhile spring soup too and ground elder leaves are said to make an interesting salad − all imbued with the added seasoning of knowing that one is eating one's enemies.) But although as a gardener you may despair of the vast dock-like leaves and even vaster root to dig out, as a cook you need not worry about the digging − you will never lose your horseradish, however often or completely it is removed. There is a cook in New Zealand who is using the other end of the very same root.

Mushrooms

FINDING MUSHROOMS IN THE GARDEN is always exciting. They have such an inexplicable air of suddenness, as though the earth has been rubbed and the genie-mushroom has materialized in a millisecond. A bizarre shape, a weird smell, some dissolved slime, then – nothing again. Alien and ancient, their lives are largely a mystery. They perform the beneficial service of rubbish disposal in a (mostly) benign way, and yet are villified as man-killers and kicked by little boys, in the charming way that ignorant mankind treats everything it fails to understand. Were I a destroying angel, I should take delight in answering back.

Each year seems to bring forth different varieties in the garden: one autumn it was shaggy ink-caps, then blewits in the compost heap; the prince appeared under the gean and jew's ears on the stream-bank, surviving a drowned night as flood-water flashed over them. Unidentified little tinies thread in and out of damp walls, as transparent and pearly as a baby's finger-nail; others, much bigger, are as greasy as mutton-fat jade or as marbled as agate, with feathery curls like whitey-brown paper. Candle-snuffs litter the hedge-bottom and bracket-fungi ascend alder trunks like spiral staircases. One year a morel appeared beneath an old apple tree, which sounds like the start of a cautionary tale by Louisa M. Alcott. This year's offering was more Restoration Rochester than Miss Alcott – the stinkhorn, *Phallus impudicus*, appeared beside a gate, its stink both visible and audible, with its attendant frenzy of flies. It is said to be edible, but I found no difficulty in denying myself the pleasure.

Occasionally a nearby meadow is generously bestrewn with early-morning spilt pearls and the owner has allowed me to gather them. Field mushrooms, parasols and my favourite, puff-balls, whose velvety texture, in extreme infancy, is like eating the finest kid gloves melted in butter. The following day they will have turned into woolly mittens and then a hand grenade full of weevily flour. Mushrooming is treasure hunting; it could never be equated with anything so prosaic as crop gathering. There will be maggots – there always are – but no matter; as my father always reassured us as children, they are all mushroom, having fed on nothing else.

The pre-war fruit expert Raymond Bush relates how a research scientist once told him that if mushrooms are burnt to ash by intense heat, it is possible to obtain a globule of pure silver. This destroys the theory of the maggot being all mushroom; apparently he is partly sterling. It also starts an interesting idea for toasting mushrooms as well as potatoes in the embers of a bonfire, giving a Christmas-puddingish, find-the-sixpense element to the proceedings.

I have no regrets about being unable to grow pieris or kalmia in my limey soil, but I am sorry that it is unlikely ever to sprout a fly agaric mushroom. They favour birch roots, and I do grow those, so perhaps one day I may be lucky. A well-spent childhood, savouring lavishly illustrated books of fairy tales, promotes this red and white spotted toadstool to a mythical status. I remember feeling vaguely disappointed, at my first sight of one, that it had no front door.

Conversely, I shall not welcome honey fungus when it arrives, as it will. Its habit of parasitizing live wood is not unusual among mushrooms, even though one tends to think of them (wrongly, in fact) consuming only dead material, rotten wood and so on. I am not averse to parasites in the garden, as long as they're not human. Yellow rattle on long grass; toothwort on willow roots. I can do without dodder; it looks weird enough, with its mesh of bilious-pink spaghetti, but I do enough doddering myself.

Names

WHAT'S IN A NAME? For all gardeners, names are unavoidable. Even those who have no interest in either traditional common names or botanical Latin will call a plant by its donor's name. We need to identify, differentiate and categorize, in an atavistic safety-check that all the good guys are within the stockade, so that nameless mayhem remains without. Thus we require an introduction of name, rank and number, from everyone and everything we encounter, not just plants.

Unlike many people, who suffer for eternity from the whim of fashion-conscious parents, plants have names that are not only rhythmically entrancing – *Xanthorhiza simplicissima*, *Sorbaria arborea* – but actively descriptive too, such as the rowan tree, *Sorbus aucuparia*, whose specific name means bird-catcher, with which no one could argue who has watched such a tree stripped of fruit by a winter flock of redwings and fieldfares. Or the butterbur, *Petasites hybridus*, whose vast leaves were used to wrap pats of butter, and whose generic name would be a good label for a milliner, as it comes from the Greek for a broad-brimmed hat.

Many seem to believe that Latin names are a pointless complication; why bother with them when all plants have common names? But there are many plants with no common name, and still more with dozens of contradictory names, such as bluebell and harebell. This confusion would be multiplied by hundreds of diverse common names from each country where the plants are found and could cause interesting developments if plants destined for the drug industry were delivered instead to a food processing factory – flopper dock is a common name for digitalis, rather than for a flaccid form of spinach. Latin names, being universal, make life simpler and safer, and, being largely phonetic, they are also easier in pronunciation than suspicious gardeners realize.

When seed packets have only a name and no description, and you have reached the giddy heights of growing plants not covered by basic reference books, specific names can give helpful clues as to planting positions: palustris, montanum, rivularis, sylvatica; or to eventual shape and size: altissimum, minima, columnaris, prostratum. Just as importantly, the country or area of origin will sound tocsins of warning on acidity and temperature requirements: japonica, dolomiticum, creticus, africanum. I know that a species designated himalaica or sibiricum should be all right here, whereas drakensburgensis or mexicana would be a risk. Australis may mean merely southern, just as indica and orientalis point only generally to the east; botanical geography tends not to be exact by the standards of modern cartography. Professor Stearn suggests that plants sent home from the East in ships known as Indiamen would be specified as indica forthwith, regardless of their true provenance. Much the same happened to the scilla bulbs brought home from the Mediterranean in a ship called the Peru, and, with a slight twist, to the amaryllis bulbs from South Africa that were washed up from a shipwreck in the Channel Islands, and ever after known as the Jersey lily.

But tracing the actual locations of plants can be exhilarating armchair travel. Each of us will have our own plant Shangri-la, whether it be calceolarias from Patagonia, forget-me-nots from the Arctic tundra (where, claimed Eleanour Sinclair Rohde, they are strongly scented), epiphytic orchids from Brazilian rainforests or sky-scraping mountain ash gum-trees from Australia (note the common name shared with our wholly dissimilar rowan). The names that cause a flurried frisson to ripple down my spine are those of the mountainous regions of Central Asia. I have only to read that a plant comes from the Celestial Mountains of the Tien Shan or the Pamir Alai, the Altai and the Western Gobi, Kopet Dag or the black sands of the Kara Kum, Tashkent and Samarkand, and my mental caravan is camel-mounted and tracking the elusive snow leopard. It is classic tulip country, fritillary too – hard, cold and dry in winter; hard, hot and dry in summer. Not in any way comparable to the Shropshire Marches, but a gardener's reach should exceed his grasp, or what's a Hindu Kush for?

Names are useful in the garden to describe different areas and borders for various reasons: in large gardens it may be practical to state that you will be found in the Cloister Garden or by the middle lake. But for those of us whose gardens are only a whisper-hail long, it is still helpful to be able to differentiate between one border and another for the sake of the plants. A visitor/builder/uninitiated husband may ask about a plant after stealing cuttings/dumping a bag of cement on it/digging it up. It may be reassuring to realize that the victim is the crataegus in the Red Border that cost an arm and a leg, rather than the one in the Gold Border you grew from unrepeatable seed from the Novosibirsk Botanical Garden.

Naming borders may sound pretentious, but it is vital for those of us who have reached the age when memory-hold-the-door is overtaken by memory-muddle-the-door. It is not so bad in the early stages of making a garden, when one still feels merely heeled-in to this new plot of soil and plants are few. But confusion will reign as soon as more plants are acquired than the rapidly decreasing number of one's remaining brain-cells. Writing down the what and, more importantly, the where, fixes them in my mind, and saves my garden from the dogs' graveyard litter of labels, particularly when the plant retires below ground for several months of each year: is that blank soil-face a single president, clintonia, or a double president, *Jeffersonia dubia*?

Names will suggest themselves from the predominant colours within the border – thus I have had a Beetroot Border for twenty years. Its prevailing trendiness causes me to colour similarly and apologize; doubtless by the time this is read it will be old hat, and the border and I shall be contentedly *passé* once again. Or topography will lead to a name – a friend calls his modest potting shed Petra, as, with a magnificent vine trellised to the front elevation, it is undeniably all façade and not much behind. My border named Jericho is above a wall that tumbles regularly. It was some time afterwards I discovered that Jericho was an eighteenth-century nickname for the earth closet. Fittingly, the small building that housed this domestic convenience is straitly shut up to one side of the border and none now go in or come out, save a nesting blackbird.

It is certain I shall not be the last, nor was I the first, to name another biblical border: Sennacherib was duly planted in crimson and gold, although, over the years, the gold has been replaced by sulphurous-cream and purple has been added to pep-up the crimson. It is close to the slowly progressing excavation of what will be the pond, which is a work of superfluity, I feel, on equinoctial nights, when a Niagara of surface water from the Welsh hills is thundering past, and occasionally over, the garden. It would be a suitable place for hordes of golden Assyrians in the shape of goldfish but, much as I like the thought (rarely the sight) of glinting sequins suspended in duckweed soup, goldfish eat tadpoles. Frogs are a vital part of the workforce, unlike the entirely decorative fish, so must be top of the list for accommodation. Besides, herons eat goldfish. They eat tadpoles too, but that seems more natural from a nationalistic point of view. The poor tadpoles are eaten either way, so I don't suppose it matters much to them whether the dentures eating them are made in England or Taiwan.

As the soil is removed for the pond, teeth are all too apparent. Those of sheep and pigs predominate; all that remains from decades of brawn and potted-meat preparation by thrifty housewives, followed by the burying of the bones as a slow soil fertilizer. The teeth are fluted like linenfold panelling and have the manilla envelope-colour and soft sheen of Grinling Gibbons' carved lime-wood. There ought to be some means of displaying these surprisingly attractive objects of social history, just as many people arrange the bits of rusty ironwork and potsherds that come to light as soil is turned. I keep a trugful of fossils from the garden, but an ossuary of teeth has a chillingly charnel-house air. Maybe, like Roman mosaic pavements, they should be unearthed, studied, then buried once more, sightless, nameless, until someone else comes along to disinter them again.

Someone, someday, will take over this garden. I try to keep him in mind when I'm updating the garden records, ensuring the picture is clear, the names straight; at least he will know what he is discarding. People who take over faded but once-lovingly-tended gardens are to be applauded, certainly, for their selfless enthusiasm. But I do wonder about preserving gardens in aspic, as it seems unlikely that the fertile imagination that first forged the garden would have kept it forever unchanged; even Miss Jekyll might have tired of bergenias and yuccas by now. To preserve a border by replanting only those plants, or their modern equivalents, that appear on an original plan may be a living tribute to a dead designer, but it is 'theming' the garden like a working museum. We wait with bated breath for the owner, dressed as a reconstructed Miss Jekyll, to be glimpsed through an archway, as a Percy Grainger tape tinkles in the background.

I should not expect my successor to keep it all as I have it; that would be a pointless restraint upon his talents and desires. It was my garden, but I have gone; I no longer have it; it no longer has me. So my choice of border names will be irrelevant; the unofficial names I have given to sports that have turned up, forms grown from seed or begged from other gardens will be immaterial; sentimental additional names of plants given by special people or grown from a bunch of flowers or cuttings from remembered gardens will be meaningless. When I have gone, they will be just a rose or a snowdrop, and will have shed their emotional baggage like falling leaves. It should not matter even if those plants, memorable only to me, become nameless yahoos in the mayhem beyond the stockade. For I have made my garden; it has lived for me.

NURSERIES

The following nurseries grow splendid plants and offer a mail-order service of an excellence that has encouraged me to deal with them again and again. Most of them have developed their skills of packing the plants into a fine art (Old Master experience, that is, rather than Turner Prize juvenilia), with straw, shredded paper, loo-roll tubes and sliced-off plastic pots to protect the precious cargo. Once I received a gentian in full bloom through the post; cloched with an upturned pot, cowled with Kleenex, it emerged the pink of perfection. Heath Robinson would approve the ingenuity, as do I the compostable content of the protection apparatus – my strawberries are under-skirted with mail-order packing straw every year.

I have tried many more mail-order nurseries over the years, which have not performed to the high standard that those listed below have inspired me to expect. Vita Sackville-West claimed that the death rate of mail-order plants equalled infant mortality in the Middle Ages; sadly, this has been my experience too on a few occasions. Good plants may be let down by poor packing or by extortionate delivery charges; excitingly catalogued plants turn out to be wrong and complaints sometimes fall of deaf ears. But, by and large, nurseries do a wonderful job and supply good plants, and we are incredibly lucky in this country that, despite the impossible regulations with which all small businesses are humbugged, there are still dedicated nurserymen who continue to grow such a vast range of plants.

Some of the nurseries listed below are open to the public, with show gardens, national collections and delicious teas. Others are not, so please consult the *Plantfinder* or their individual websites for additional information, such as opening hours (if any), cost of catalogue and alternative ways of techno-contact.

Trees

Paul Jasper Trees
www.jaspertrees.co.uk
For grafted trees, both ornamental and
fruit, including an extensive collection of
historic and Herefordshire-bred apple trees.

Shrubs

Glenville Nurseries
King John Bank
Walpole St Andrew
Wisbech
Cambridgeshire PE14 7LD
www.glenvillenurseries.co.uk
For small, well-rooted cuttings, at a
reasonable price, for growing on.

Roses

Acton Beauchamp Roses
Acton Beauchamp
Worcester WR6 5AE
www.actonbeaurose.co.uk
For a wide range of species, old and
modern roses, grown in tough, cold,
Midland clay.

Peter Beales Roses
London Road
Attleborough
Norwich
Norfolk NR17 1AY
www.classicroses.co.uk
Again, a huge range of roses of all types.

Herbaceous

Cally Gardens
Gatehouse of Fleet
Castle Douglas
Kirkcudbrightshire DG7 2DJ
www.callygardens.co.uk
For unusual plants, including many
introduced by the nurseryman, Michael
Wickenden, from his expeditions.

Elizabeth MacGregor
Ellenbank
Tongland Road
Kirkcudbright
Dumfries and Galloway DG6 4UU
Who has a special interest in violas and
violets, as well as a good range of cottage
garden perennials.

Perhill Nurseries
Worcester Road
Great Witley
Worcestershire WR6 6JT
www.perhillplants.co.uk
For an extensive range of alpines and
perennials, grown hard on an exposed site,
so good doers from birth.

Alpines
Christie's Nursery
Downfield
Westmuir
Kirriemuir
Angus DD8 5LP
www.christiealpines.co.uk
For perfectly packed gentians and unusual,
as well as classic alpines.

White Cottage Alpines
Sunnyside Nurseries
Hornsea Road
Sigglesthorne
East Yorkshire HU11 5QL
www.whitecottagealpines.co.uk
For a wide range of rock plants, small
bulbs and dwarf shrubs, beautifully grown
and presented.

Bulbs
Avon Bulbs
Burnt House Farm
Mid- Lambrook
South Petherton
Somerset TA13 5HE
www.avonbulbs.co.uk
For woodland plants, as well as bulbs.

Broadleigh Gardens
Bishops Hull
Taunton
Somerset TA4 1AE
www.broadleighbulbs.co.uk
For small bulbs particularly, both in-the-
green and bare-rooted; a wide selection of
Californian Hybrid irises and woodland
plants.

Seeds
Plant World
St Marychurch Road
Newton Abbot
Devon TQ12 4SE
www.plantworld-devon.co.uk
For a wide range of seeds of perennials,
annuals and bulbs, mostly grown at the
nursery, and newly introduced seeds from
the nurseryman, Ray Brown's, expeditions.

INDEX